# SEARCHING

## *in*
## *California*

A REFERENCE
GUIDE TO
PUBLIC AND
PRIVATE RECORDS

by

**Patricia Sanders**

PRINTED IN THE UNITED STATES OF AMERICA


Cover design by Marcia McCulloch


Library of Congress Catalog Card Number: 82-80341

ISBN: 0-942916-00-X

ACKNOWLEDGEMENTS

A very special thank you goes to Patrice Kaska for
all the time and energy she gave to make this book
a reality.  Thanks also to my other California
friends who have shared ideas, material and time--
Fran Kurrle, Mary Jo Rillera, Vikki Schummer, Marge
Hough, Patty Gaede, Jayne Askin, Barbara Specht,
and Pat Morris.

ISC PUBLICATIONS
P. O. Box 10857
Costa Mesa, CA 92627

# TABLE OF CONTENTS

INTRODUCTION

SECTION I--State-wide Information

SECTION II--County Information

SECTION III--People Who Help

INDEX

## INTRODUCTION

A search of any kind requires time and persistence.
There are a multitude of records, some obvious,
some obscure, but each with the potential of be-
coming the solution to the problem, the missing
puzzle piece.  This book is offered as a means of
locating and utilizing both public and private
records.  Hopefully, it will serve as a valuable
resource tool and handbook for all searchers.

# SECTION I
## State-wide Information

California Counties

| CITY | COUNTY | CITY | COUNTY |
|------|--------|------|--------|
| ACAMPO | SAN JOAQUIN | AUBERRY | FRESNO |
| ACTON | LOS ANGELES | AUBURN | PLACER |
| ADELANTO | SAN BERNARDINO | AVALON | LOS ANGELES |
| ADIN | MODOC | AVENAL | KINGS |
| AGNEW | SANTA CLARA | AVERY | CALAVERAS |
| AGOURA | LOS ANGELES | AVILA BEACH | SAN LUIS OBISPO |
| AGUANGA | RIVERSIDE | AZUSA | LOS ANGELES |
| AHWAHNEE | MADERA | BADGER | FRESNO |
| ALAMEDA | ALAMEDA | BAILEY | LOS ANGELES |
| ALAMO | CONTRA COSTA | BAKER | SAN BERNARDINO |
| ALBANY | ALAMEDA | BAKERSFIELD | KERN |
| ALBION | MENDOCINO | BALBOA | ORANGE |
| ALDERPOINT | HUMBOLDT | BALDWIN PARK | LOS ANGELES |
| ALHAMBRA | LOS ANGELES | BALLICO | MERCED |
| ALISAL | MONTEREY | BANGOR | BUTTE |
| ALLEGHANY | SIERRA | BANNING | RIVERSIDE |
| ALMADEN VALLEY | SANTA CLARA | BANTA | SAN JOAQUIN |
| ALONDRA | LOS ANGELES | BARD | IMPERIAL |
| ALPAUGH | TULARE | BARRINGTON | LOS ANGELES |
| ALPINE | SAN DIEGO | BARSTOW | SAN BERNARDINO |
| ALTO | PLACER | BARTON | FRESNO |
| ALTADENA | LOS ANGELES | BASE LINE | SAN BERNARDINO |
| AL TAHOE | EL DORADO | BASSETT | LOS ANGELES |
| ALTA LOMA | SAN BERNARDINO | BASS LAKE | MADERA |
| ALTURAS | MODOC | BAXTER | PLACER |
| ALVARADO | ALAMEDA | BAY | SAN BERNARDINO |
| ALVISA | SANTA CLARA | BAYSIDE | HUMBOLDT |
| AMADOR CITY | AMADOR | BAY VIEW | SAN FRANCISCO |
| AMBASSADOR | LOS ANGELES | BEAR VALLEY | CALAVERAS |
| AMBOY | SAN BERNARDINO | BEAUMONT | RIVERSIDE |
| AMERICAN CANYON | SOLANO | BECKWOURTH | PLUMAS |
| ANAHEIM | ORANGE | BELDEN | BUTTE |
| ANDERSON | SHASTA | BELL | LOS ANGELES |
| ANDREW JACKSON | SAN DIEGO | BELLA VISTA | SHASTA |
| ANGELS CAMP | CALAVERAS | BELLFLOWER | LOS ANGELES |
| ANGELUS OAKS | SAN BERNARDINO | BELL GARDENS | LOS ANGELES |
| ANGWIN | NAPA | BELMONT | SAN MATEO |
| ANNAPOLIS | SONOMA | BENICIA | SOLANO |
| ANTELOPE ACRES | LOS ANGELES | BEN LOMOND | SANTA CRUZ |
| ANTIOCH | CONTRA COSTA | BENTON | INYO |
| ANZA | RIVERSIDE | BERKELEY | ALAMEDA |
| APPLEGATE | PLACER | BERNAL | SAN FRANCISCO |
| APPLE VALLEY | SAN BERNARDINO | BERRY CREEK | BUTTE |
| APTOS | SANTA CRUZ | BERRYESSA | SANTA CLARA |
| ARBUCKLE | COLUSA | BETHEL ISLAND | CONTRA COSTA |
| ARCADE | LOS ANGELES | BEVERLY HILLS | LOS ANGELES |
| ARCADIA | LOS ANGELES | BICENTENNIAL | LOS ANGELES |
| ARCATA | HUMBOLDT | BIEBER | LASSEN |
| ARDEN | SACRAMENTO | BIG BAR | TRINITY |
| ARGUS | SAN BERNARDINO | BIG BEAR | SAN BERNARDINO |
| ARLETA | LOS ANGELES | BIG BEND | SHASTA |
| ARLINGTON | RIVERSIDE | BIG CREEK | FRESNO |
| ARMONA | KINGS | BIGGS | BUTTE |
| ARNOLD | CALAVERAS | BIG OAK FLAT | TUOLUMNE |
| AROMAS | MONTEREY | BIG PINE | INYO |
| ARROYO GRANDE | SAN LUIS OBISPO | BIG RIVER | SAN BERNARDINO |
| ARTESIA | LOS ANGELES | BIG SUR | MONTEREY |
| ARTOIS | GLENN | BIOLA | FRESNO |
| ARVIN | KERN | BIRDS LANDING | SOLANO |
| ASTI | SONOMA | BISHOP | INYO |
| ATASCADERO | SAN LUIS OBISPO | BIXBY | LOS ANGELES |
| ATHERTON | LOS ANGELES | BLAIRSDEN | PLUMAS |
| ATWATER | MERCED | BLOCKSBURG | HUMBOLDT |
| ATWOOD | ORANGE | BLOOMINGTON | SAN BERNARDINO |

| CITY | COUNTY | CITY | COUNTY |
|------|--------|------|--------|
| BLOSSOM HILL | SANTA CLARA | CAMBRIAN PARK | SANTA CLARA |
| BLOSSOM VALLEY | SANTA CLARA | CAMINO | EL DORADO |
| BLUE JAY | SAN BERNARDINO | CAMPBELL | SANTA CLARA |
| BLUE LAKE | HUMBOLDT | CAMPO | SAN DIEGO |
| BLYTHE | RIVERSIDE | CAMPTONVILLE | YUBA |
| BODEGA | SONOMA | CANBY | MODOC |
| BODFISH | KERN | CANOGA PARK | LOS ANGELES |
| BOLINAS | MARIN | CANTIL | KERN |
| BONITA | SAN DIEGO | CANTUA CREEK | FRESNO |
| BONSALL | SAN DIEGO | CANYON | CONTRA COSTA |
| BOONVILLE | MENDOCINO | CANYON COUNTRY | LOS ANGELES |
| BORON | KERN | CANYONDAM | PLUMAS |
| BORREGO SPRINGS | SAN DIEGO | CANYON LAKE | RIVERSIDE |
| BOSTONIA | SAN DIEGO | CAPAY | YOLO |
| BOULDER CREEK | SANTA CRUZ | CAPISTRANO BEACH | ORANGE |
| BOULEVARD | SAN DIEGO | CAPITOLA | SANTA CRUZ |
| BOWMAN | PLACER | CARDIFF BY THE SEA | SAN DIEGO |
| BOYES HOT SPRINGS | SONOMA | CARDWELL | FRESNO |
| BOYLE | LOS ANGELES | CARLOTTA | HUMBOLDT |
| BRADBURY | LOS ANGELES | CARLSBAD | SAN DIEGO |
| BRADFORD | ALAMEDA | CARMEL | MONTEREY |
| BRADLEY | MONTEREY | CARMICHAEL | SACRAMENTO |
| BRANDEIS | VENTURA | CARNELIAN BAY | PLACER |
| BRANSCOMB | MENDOCINO | CARPINTERIA | SANTA BARBARA |
| BRAWLEY | IMPERIAL | CARSON | LOS ANGELES |
| BREA | ORANGE | CARTAGO | INYO |
| BRENTWOOD | CONTRA COSTA | CARUTHERS | FRESNO |
| BRIDGEPORT | MONO | CASMALIA | SANTA BARBARA |
| BRIDGEVILLE | HUMBOLDT | CASSEL | SHASTA |
| BRISBANE | SAN MATEO | CASTAIC | LOS ANGELES |
| BRISTOL | ORANGE | CASTELLA | SHASTA |
| BROADWAY | SACRAMENTO | CASTROVILLE | MONTEREY |
| BRODERICK | YOLO | CATHEDRAL CITY | RIVERSIDE |
| BROOKDALE | SANTA CRUZ | CATHEYS VALLEY | MARIPOSA |
| BROOKS | YOLO | CAYUCOS | SAN LUIS OBISPO |
| BROWNS VALLEY | YUBA | CAZADERA | SONOMA |
| BROWNSVILLE | YUBA | CEDAR GLEN | SAN BERNARDINO |
| BRUNDAGE | KERN | CEDAR RIDGE | NEVADA |
| BRYANT | LOS ANGELES | CEDARVILLE | MODOC |
| BRYN MAWR | SAN BERNARDINO | CENTERVILLE | ALAMEDA |
| BUELLTON | SANTA BARBARA | CENTRAL VALLEY | SHASTA |
| BUENA PARK | ORANGE | CENTRE | SACRAMENTO |
| BURBANK | LOS ANGELES | CENTURY CITY | LOS ANGELES |
| BURLINGAME | SAN MATEO | CERES | STANISLAUS |
| BURNEY | SHASTA | CHALLENGE | YUBA |
| BURNT RANCH | TRINITY | CHANNEL ISLANDS | BUTTE |
| BURREL | FRESNO | CHATSWORTH | LOS ANGELES |
| BURSON | CALAVERAS | CHERRY VALLEY | RIVERSIDE |
| BUTTE CITY | GLENN | CHESTER | PLUMAS |
| BUTTONWILLOW | KERN | CHICAGO PARK | NEVADA |
| BYRON | CONTRA COSTA | CHICO | BUTTE |
| CABAZON | RIVERSIDE | CHILCOOT | PLUMAS |
| CABRILLO | LOS ANGELES | CHINESE CAMP | TUOLUMNE |
| CADIZ | SAN BERNARDINO | CHINO | SAN BERNARDINO |
| CALAVERAS | SAN JOAQUIN | CHOLAME | SAN LUIS OBISPO |
| CALEXICO | IMPERIAL | CHOWCHILLA | MADERA |
| CALIENTE | KERN | CHUALAR | MONTEREY |
| CALIFORNIA CITY | MOJAVE | CHULA VISTA | SAN DIEGO |
| CALIMESA | RIVERSIDE | CIMA | SAN BERNARDINO |
| CALIPATRIA | IMPERIAL | CITRUS HEIGHTS | SACRAMENTO |
| CALISTOGA | NAPA | CITY OF COMMERCE | LOS ANGELES |
| CALLAHAN | SISKIYOU | CITY OF INDUSTRY | LOS ANGELES |
| CALPELLA | MENDOCINO | CLAREMONT | LOS ANGELES |
| CALPINE | SIERRA | CLARKSBURG | YOLO |
| CALWA | FRESNO | CLAYTON | CONTRA COSTA |
| CAMARILLO | VENTURA | CLEARLAKE HIGHLANDS | LAKE |
| CAMBRIA | SAN LUIS OBISPO | CLEARLAKE OAKS | LAKE |

| CITY | COUNTY | CITY | COUNTY |
|---|---|---|---|
| CLEARLAKE PARK | LAKE | DARDANELLE | TUOLUMNE |
| CLEMENTS | SAN JOAQUIN | DARWIN | INYO |
| CLINTER | FRESNO | DAVENPORT | SANTA CRUZ |
| CLIO | PLUMAS | DAVIS | YOLO |
| CLIPPER MILLS | BUTTE | DAVIS CREEK | MODOC |
| CLOVERDALE | SONOMA | DEATH VALLEY | INYO |
| CLOVIS | FRESNO | DEER PARK | NAPA |
| COACHELLA | RIVERSIDE | DELANO | KERN |
| COALINGA | FRESNO | DELEVAN | GLENN |
| COARSEGOLD | MADERA | DELHI | MERCED |
| COBB | LAKE | DELKERN | KERN |
| CODDINGTOWN | SANTA ROSA | DEL MAR | SAN DIEGO |
| COLE | LOS ANGELES | DEL PASO HEIGHTS | SACRAMENTO |
| COLEVILLE | MONO | DEL REY | FRESNO |
| COLFAX | PLACER | DEL REY OAKS | MONTEREY |
| COLLEGE CITY | COLUSA | DEL ROSA | SAN BERNARDINO |
| COLLEGE GROVE CENTER | SAN DIEGO | DELTA | SAN JOAQUIN |
| COLLIER | LOS ANGELES | DENAIR | STANISLAUS |
| COLMA | SAN MATEO | DESCANSO | SAN DIEGO |
| COLOMA | EL DORADO | DESERT CENTER | RIVERSIDE |
| COLONIAL | SACRAMENTO | DESERT HOT SPRINGS | RIVERSIDE |
| COLTON | SAN BERNARDINO | DIABLO | CONTRA COSTA |
| COLUMBIA | TUOLUMNE | DIAMOND BAR | LOS ANGELES |
| COLUSA | COLUSA | DIAMOND HEIGHTS | SAN FRANCISCO |
| COMPTCHE | MENDOCINO | DIAMOND SPRINGS | EL DORADO |
| COMPTON | LOS ANGELES | DI GIORGIO | KERN |
| CONCORD | CONTRA COSTA | DILLON BEACH | MARIN |
| CONEJO VALLEY | VENTURA | DIMOND | ALAMEDA |
| COOL | EL DORADO | DINUBA | TULARE |
| COPPEROPOLIS | CALAVERAS | DIXON | SOLANO |
| CORCORAN | KINGS | DOBBINS | YUBA |
| CORNING | TEHAMA | DOLLAR RANCH | CONTRA COSTA |
| CORONA | RIVERSIDE | DORRIS | SISKIYOU |
| CORONA DEL MAR | ORANGE | DOS PALOS | MERCED |
| CORONADO | SAN DIEGO | DOUGLAS CITY | TRINITY |
| CORTE MADERA | MARIN | DOWNEY | LOS ANGELES |
| COSTA MESA | ORANGE | DOWNIEVILLE | SIERRA |
| COTATI | SONOMA | DOYLE | LASSEN |
| COTTONWOOD | SHASTA | DRYTOWN | AMADOR |
| COULTERVILLE | MARIPOSA | DUARTE | LOS ANGELES |
| COURTLAND | SACRAMENTO | DUBLIN | ALAMEDA |
| COVELO | MENDOCINO | DUCOR | TULARE |
| COVINA | LOS ANGELES | DULZURA | SAN DIEGO |
| COYOTE | SAN JOSE | DUNCANS MILLS | SONOMA |
| CRENSHAW | LOS ANGELES | DUNLAP | FRESNO |
| CRESCENT CITY | DEL NORTE | DUNNIGAN | YOLO |
| CRESCENT MILLS | PLUMAS | DUNSMUIR | SISKIYOU |
| CRESSEY | MERCED | DURHAM | BUTTE |
| CRESTLINE | SAN BERNARDINO | DUTCH FLAT | PLACER |
| CRESTON | SAN LUIS OBISPO | EAGLE MOUNTAIN | RIVERSIDE |
| CREST PARK | SAN BERNARDINO | EAGLE ROCK | LOS ANGELES |
| CROCKETT | CONTRA COSTA | EAGLEVILLE | MODOC |
| CROMBERG | PLUMAS | EARLIMART | TULARE |
| CROWLEY LAKE | MONO | EARP | SAN BERNARDINO |
| CROWS LANDING | STANISLAUS | EASTGATE | LOS ANGELES |
| CUCAMONGA | SAN BERNARDINO | EASTMONT | ALAMEDA |
| CUDAHY | LOS ANGELES | EAST NICOLAUS | SUTTER |
| CULVER CITY | LOS ANGELES | EASTON | FRESNO |
| CUPERTINO | SANTA CLARA | ECHO LAKE | EL DORADO |
| CUTLER | TULARE | EDENDALE | LOS ANGELES |
| CUTTEN | HUMBOLDT | EDGEWOOD | SISKIYOU |
| CUYAMA | SANTA BARBARA | EDISON | KERN |
| CYPRESS | ORANGE | EDWARDS | KERN |
| DAGGETT | SAN BERNARDINO | EL CAJON | SAN DIEGO |
| DALY CITY | SAN MATEO | EL CENTRO | IMPERIAL |
| DANA POINT | ORANGE | EL CERRITO | CONTRA COSTA |
| DANVILLE | CONTRA COSTA | EL DORADO | EL DORADO |

| CITY | COUNTY | CITY | COUNTY |
|---|---|---|---|
| ELDRIDGE | SONOMA | FORTUNA | HUMBOLDT |
| EL GRANADA | SAN MATEO | FOSTER CITY | SAN MATEO |
| ELK | MENDOCINO | FOUNTAIN VALLEY | ORANGE |
| ELK CREEK | GLENN | FOWLER | FRESNO |
| ELK GROVE | SACRAMENTO | FRANKLIN | NAPA |
| ELLWOOD | SANTA BARBARA | FRAZIER PARK | KERN |
| ELMHURST | ALAMEDA | FREEDOM | SANTA CRUZ |
| ELMIRA | SOLANO | FREMONT | ALAMEDA |
| EL MONTE | LOS ANGELES | FRENCH CAMP | SAN JOAQUIN |
| EL NIDO | MERCED | FRENCH GULCH | SHASTA |
| EL PORTAL | MARIPOSA | FRESNO | FRESNO |
| EL SEGUNDO | LOS ANGELES | FRIANT | FRESNO |
| EL SOBRANTE | CONTRA COSTA | FRUITVALE | ALAMEDA |
| EL TORO | ORANGE | FULLERTON | ORANGE |
| EL VERANO | SONOMA | FULTON | SONOMA |
| ELVERTA | SACRAMENTO | GALT | SACRAMENTO |
| EL VIEJO | STANISLAUS | GARBERVILLE | HUMBOLDT |
| EMERYVILLE | ALAMEDA | GARDENA | LOS ANGELES |
| EMIGRANT GAP | PLACER | GARDEN GROVE | ORANGE |
| EMPIRE | STANISLAUS | GARDEN VALLEY | EL DORADO |
| ENCANTO | SAN DIEGO | GASQUET | DEL NORTE |
| ENCINITAS | SAN DIEGO | GAZELLE | SISKIYOU |
| ENCINO | LOS ANGELES | GEORGETOWN | EL DORADO |
| ENTERPRISE | SHASTA | GERBER | TEHAMA |
| ESCALON | SAN JOAQUIN | GEYSERVILLE | SONOMA |
| ESCONDIDO | SAN DIEGO | GILROY | SANTA CLARA |
| ESPARTO | YOLO | GLENCOE | CALAVERAS |
| ESSEX | SAN BERNARDINO | GLENDALE | LOS ANGELES |
| ETIWANDA | SAN BERNARDINO | GLENDORA | LOS ANGELES |
| ETNA | SISKIYOU | GLEN ELLEN | SONOMA |
| EUREKA | HUMBOLDT | GLENHAVEN | LAKE |
| EXETER | TULARE | GLENN | GLENN |
| FAIRFAX | MARIN | GLENNVILLE | KERN |
| FAIRFIELD | SOLANO | GOLD RUN | PLACER |
| FAIR OAKS | SACRAMENTO | GOLETA | SANTA BARBARA |
| FALLBROOK | SAN DIEGO | GONZALES | MONTEREY |
| FALL RIVER MILLS | SHASTA | GOODYEARS BAR | SIERRA |
| FARMERSVILLE | TULARE | GOSHEN | TULARE |
| FARMINGTON | SAN JOAQUIN | GRAND LAKE | ALAMEDA |
| FAWNSKIN | SAN BERNARDINO | GRANTVILLE | SAN DIEGO |
| FELLOWS | KERN | GRASS VALLEY | NEVADA |
| FELTON | SANTA CRUZ | GRATON | SONOMA |
| FERNDALE | HUMBOLDT | GREENACRES | KERN |
| FIDDLETOWN | AMADOR | GREENFIELD | MONTEREY |
| FIELDS LANDING | HUMBOLDT | GREENVIEW | SISKIYOU |
| FILLMORE | VENTURA | GREENVILLE | PLUMAS |
| FINLEY | LAKE | GREENWOOD | EL DORADO |
| FIREBAUGH | FRESNO | GRENADA | SISKIYOU |
| FISH CAMP | MARIPOSA | GRIDLEY | BUTTE |
| FISK | SAN FRANCISCO | GRIMES | COLUSA |
| FITCHBURG | ALAMEDA | GRIZZLY FLATS | EL DORADO |
| FIVE POINTS | FRESNO | GROVELAND | TUOLOMNE |
| FLORIN | SACRAMENTO | GROVER CITY | SAN LUIS OBISPO |
| FLORISTON | NEVADA | GUADALUPE | SANTA BARBARA |
| FOLSOM | SACRAMENTO | GUALALA | MENDOCINO |
| FONTANA | SAN BERNARDINO | GUASTI | SAN BERNARDINO |
| FORBESTOWN | BUTTE | GUATAY | SAN DIEGO |
| FOREST FALLS | SAN BERNARDINO | GUERNEVILLE | SONOMA |
| FORESTHILL | PLACER | GUINDA | YOLO |
| FOREST KNOLLS | MARIN | GUSTINE | MERCED |
| FOREST RANCH | BUTTE | HACIENDA HEIGHTS | LOS ANGELES |
| FORESTVILLE | SONOMA | HALCYON | SAN LUIS OBISPO |
| FORKS OF SALMON | SISKIYOU | HALF MOON BAY | SAN MATEO |
| FORT BRAGG | MENDOCINO | HAMILTON | SANTA CLARA |
| FORT JONES | SISKIYOU | HAMILTON CITY | GLENN |
| FORT ORD | MONTEREY | HANFORD | KINGS |
| FORT SUTTER | SACRAMENTO | HAPPY CAMP | SISKIYOU |

| CITY | COUNTY | CITY | COUNTY |
|------|--------|------|--------|
| HARBOR CITY | LOS ANGELES | JANESVILLE | LASSEN |
| HARMONY | SAN LUIS OBISPO | JENNER | SONOMA |
| HAT CREEK | SHASTA | JOHANNESBURG | KERN |
| HATHAWAY PINES | CALAVERAS | JOHNSONDALE | KERN |
| HAVASU LAKE | SAN BERNARDINO | JOLON | MONTEREY |
| HAWAIIAN GARDENS | LOS ANGELES | JOSHUA TREE | SAN BERNARDINO |
| HAWTHORNE | LOS ANGELES | JULIAN | SAN DIEGO |
| HAYFORK | TRINITY | JUNCTION CITY | TRINITY |
| HAYWARD | ALAMEDA | JUNE LAKE | MONO |
| HEALDSBURG | SONOMA | KEELER | INYO |
| HEBER | IMPERIAL | KEENE | KERN |
| HELENA | TRINITY | KELSEY | EL DORADO |
| HELENDALE | SAN BERNARDINO | KELSEYVILLE | LAKE |
| HELM | FRESNO | KELSO | SAN BERNARDINO |
| HEMET | RIVERSIDE | KENWOOD | SONOMA |
| HENDERSON | HUMBOLDT | KERMAN | FRESNO |
| HERALD | SACRAMENTO | KERNVILLE | KERN |
| HERLONG | LASSEN | KETTLEMAN CITY | KINGS |
| HERMOSA BEACH | LOS ANGELES | KEYES | STANISLAUS |
| HESPERIA | SAN BERNARDINO | KING CITY | MONTEREY |
| HICKMAN | STANISLAUS | KINGS BEACH | PLACER |
| HIGHLAND | SAN BERNARDINO | KINGSBURG | FRESNO |
| HILLSDALE | SAN MATEO | KLAMATH | DEL NORTE |
| HILLVIEW | SAN JOSE | KNEELAND | HUMBOLDT |
| HILMAR | MERCED | KNIGHTSEN | CONTRA COSTA |
| HINKLEY | SAN BERNARDINO | KNIGHTS LANDING | YOLO |
| HOLLISTER | SAN BENITO | KORBEL | HUMBOLDT |
| HOLLYWOOD | LOS ANGELES | KYBURZ | EL DORADO |
| HOLT | SAN JOAQUIN | LA CANADA | LOS ANGELES |
| HOLTVILLE | IMPERIAL | LA CRESCENTA | LOS ANGELES |
| HOLY CITY | SANTA CLARA | LAFAYETTE | CONTRA COSTA |
| HOMELAND | RIVERSIDE | LA GRANGE | STANISLAUS |
| HOMEWOOD | PLACER | LAGUNA BEACH | ORANGE |
| HONEYDEW | HUMBOLDT | LAGUNITAS | MARIN |
| HOOD | SACRAMENTO | LA HABRA | ORANGE |
| HOOPA | HUMBOLDT | LA HONDA | SAN MATEO |
| HOPLAND | MENDOCINO | LA JOLLA | SAN DIEGO |
| HORNBROOK | SISKIYOU | LAKE ARROWHEAD | SAN BERNARDINO |
| HORNITOS | MARIPOSA | LAKE CITY | MODOC |
| HORSE CREEK | SISKIYOU | LAKE ELSINORE | RIVERSIDE |
| HUDSON | MODESTO | LAKEHEAD | SHASTA |
| HUGHSON | STANISLAUS | LAKE ISABELLA | KERN |
| HUNTINGTON BEACH | ORANGE | LAKEPORT | LAKE |
| HUNTINGTON PARK | LOS ANGELES | LAKESHORE | FRESNO |
| HURON | FRESNO | LAKESIDE | SAN DIEGO |
| HYAMPOM | TRINITY | LAKEVIEW | RIVERSIDE |
| HYDESVILLE | HUMBOLDT | LAKEWOOD | LOS ANGELES |
| IDYLLWILD | RIVERSIDE | LA MESA | SAN DIEGO |
| IGO | SHASTA | LA MIRADA | LOS ANGELES |
| IMOLA | NAPA | LAMONT | KERN |
| IMPERIAL | IMPERIAL | LANCASTER | LOS ANGELES |
| IMPERIAL BEACH | SAN DIEGO | LA PUENTE | LOS ANGELES |
| INDEPENDENCE | INYO | LA QUINTA | RIVERSIDE |
| INDIO | RIVERSIDE | LARKSPUR | MARIN |
| INGLEWOOD | LOS ANGELES | LA SIERRA | RIVERSIDE |
| INVERNESS | MARIN | LATHROP | SAN JOAQUIN |
| INYOKERN | KERN | LATON | FRESNO |
| IONE | AMADOR | LA VERNE | LOS ANGELES |
| IRVINE | ORANGE | LAYTONVILLE | MENDOCINO |
| IRWINDALE | LOS ANGELES | LEBEC | KERN |
| ISLA VISTA | SANTA BARBARA | LEE VINING | MONO |
| ISLETON | SACRAMENTO | LEGGETT | MENDOCINO |
| IVANHOE | TUALRE | LE GRAND | MERCED |
| JACKSON | AMADOR | LEMONCOVE | TULARE |
| JACUMBA | SAN DIEGO | LEMON GROVE | SAN DIEGO |
| JAMESTOWN | TUOLUMNE | LEMOORE | KINGS |
| JAMUL | SAN DIEGO | LETTERMAN | SAN FRANCISCO |

| CITY | COUNTY | CITY | COUNTY |
|------|--------|------|--------|
| LEWISTON | TRINITY | MC CLOUD | SISKIYOU |
| LIBERTY FARMS | SOLANO | MC FARLAND | KERN |
| LIKELY | MODOC | MC KITTRICK | KERN |
| LINCOLN | PLACER | MEADOW VALLEY | PLUMAS |
| LINDA VISTA | SAN DIEGO | MEADOW VISTA | PLACER |
| LINDEN | SAN JOAQUIN | MECCA | RIVERSIDE |
| LINDSAY | TULARE | MEINERS OAKS | VENTURA |
| LITCHFIELD | LASSEN | MENDOCINO | MENDOCINO |
| LITTLE LAKE · | INYO | MENDOTA | FRESNO |
| LITTLE NORWAY | EL DORADO | MENLO PARK | SAN MATEO |
| LITTLERIVER | MENDOCINO | MENTONE | SAN BERNARDINO |
| LITTLEROCK | LOS ANGELES | MERCED | MERCED |
| LIVE OAK | SUTTER | MERIDIAN | SUTTER |
| LIVERMORE | ALAMEDA | MIDDLETOWN | LAKE |
| LIVINGSTON | MERCED | MIDPINES | MARIPOSA |
| LLANO | LOS ANGELES | MILFORD | LASSEN |
| LOCKEFORD | SAN JOAQUIN | MILLBRAE | SAN MATEO |
| LOCKWOOD | MONTEREY | MILL VALLEY | MARIN |
| LODI | SAN JOAQUIN | MILLVILLE | SHASTA |
| LOLETA | HUMBOLDT | MILPAS | SANTA BARBARA |
| LOMA LINDA | SAN BERNARDINO | MILPITAS | SANTA CLARA |
| LOMA MAR | SAN MATEO | MINERAL | TEHAMA |
| LOMITA | LOS ANGELES | MIRA LOMA | RIVERSIDE |
| LOMPOC | SANTA BARBARA | MIRAMONTE | FRESNO |
| LONE PINE | INYO | MIRANDA | HUMBOLDT |
| LONG BARN | TUOLUMNE | MISSION VIEJO | ORANGE |
| LONG BEACH | LOS ANGELES | MI-WUK VILLAGE | TUOLUMNE |
| LOOKOUT | MODOC | MOCCASIN | TUOLUMNE |
| LOOMIS | PLACER | MODESTO | STANISLAUS |
| LOS ALAMITOS | ORANGE | MOJAVE | KERN |
| LOS ALAMOS | SANTA BARBARA | MOKELUMNE HILL | CALAVERAS |
| LOS ALTOS | SANTA CLARA | MONROVIA | LOS ANGELES |
| LOS ANGELES | LOS ANGELES | MONTAGUE | SISKIYOU |
| LOS BANOS | MERCED | MONTALVO | VENTURA |
| LOS GATOS | SANTA CLARA | MONTARA | SAN MATEO |
| LOS MOLINOS | TEHAMA | MONTCLAIR | SAN BERNARDINO |
| LOS OLIVOS | SANTA BARBARA | MONTEBELLO | LOS ANGELES |
| LOS OSOS | SAN LUIS OBISPO | MONTECITO | SANTA BARBARA |
| LOST HILLS | KERN | MONTEREY | MONTEREY |
| LOTUS | EL DORADO | MONTEREY PARK | LOS ANGELES |
| LOWER LAKE | LAKE | MONTE RIO | SONOMA |
| LOYALTON | SIERRA | MONTGOMERY CREEK | SHASTA |
| LUCERNE | LAKE | MONTROSE | LOS ANGELES |
| LUCERNE VALLEY | SAN BERNARDINO | MOORPARK | VENTURA |
| LUTHER BURBANK | SONOMA | MORAGA | CONTRA COSTA |
| LYNWOOD | LOS ANGELES | MORENO | RIVERSIDE |
| MACDOEL | SISKIYOU | MORGAN HILL | SANTA CLARA |
| MADELINE | LASSEN | MORONGO VALLEY | SAN BERNARDINO |
| MADERA | MADERA | MORRO BAY | SAN LUIS OBISPO |
| MADISON | YOLO | MOSS BEACH | SAN MATEO |
| MAD RIVER | TRINITY | MOSS LANDING | MONTEREY |
| MAGALIA | BUTTE | MOUNTAIN CENTER | RIVERSIDE |
| MALIBU | LOS ANGELES | MOUNTAIN RANCH | CALAVERAS |
| MAMMOTH LAKES | MONO | MOUNTAIN VIEW | SANTA CLARA |
| MANCHESTER | MENDOCINO | MOUNT HERMON | SANTA CRUZ |
| MANHATTAN BEACH | LOS ANGELES | MOUNT SHASTA | SISKIYOU |
| MANTECA | SAN JOAQUIN | MT. AUKUM | EL DORADO |
| MANTON | TEHAMA | MT. BALDY | SAN BERNARDINO |
| MARICOPA | KERN | MURPHYS | CALAVERAS |
| MARINA | MONTEREY | MURRIETA | RIVERSIDE |
| MARIPOSA | MARIPOSA | MYERS FLAT | HUMBOLDT |
| MARKLEEVILLE | ALPINE | NAPA | NAPA |
| MARSHALL | MARIN | NATIONAL CITY | SAN DIEGO |
| MARTINEZ | CONTRA COSTA | NEEDLES | SAN BERNARDINO |
| MARYSVILLE | YUBA | NESTOR | SAN DIEGO |
| MAXWELL | COLUSA | NEVADA CITY | NEVADA |
| MC ARTHUR | SHASTA | | |

| CITY | COUNTY | CITY | COUNTY |
|------|--------|------|--------|
| NEW ALMADEN | SANTA CLARA | PALMDALE | LOS ANGELES |
| NEWARK | ALAMEDA | PALM DESERT | RIVERSIDE |
| NEWBURY PARK | VENTURA | PALM SPRINGS | RIVERSIDE |
| NEWCASTLE | PLACER | PALO ALTO | SANTA CLARA |
| NEW CUYAMA | SANTA BARBARA | PALO CEDRO | SHASTA |
| NEWHALL | LOS ANGELES | PALOS VERDES ESTATES | LOS ANGELES |
| NEWMAN | STANISLAUS | PALO VERDE | IMPERIAL |
| NEWPORT BEACH | ORANGE | PANORAMA CITY | LOS ANGELES |
| NICASIO | MARIN | PARADISE | BUTTE |
| NICE | LAKE | PARKER DAM | SAN BERNARDINO |
| NICOLAS | SUTTER | PARKMOOR | SANTA CLARA |
| NILAND | IMPERIAL | PARLIER | FRESNO |
| NILES | ALAMEDA | PASADENA | LOS ANGELES |
| NIPOMO | SAN LUIS OBISPO | PASKENTA | TEHAMA |
| NIPTON | SAN BERNARDINO | PASO ROBLES | SAN LUIS OBISPO |
| NORCO | RIVERSIDE | PATTERSON | STANISLAUS |
| NORDEN | NEVADA | PATTON | SAN BERNARDINO |
| NORTH FORK | MADERA | PAUMA VALLEY | SAN DIEGO |
| NORTH HIGHLANDS | SACRAMENTO | PEBBLE BEACH | MONTEREY |
| NORTH HOLLYWOOD | LOS ANGELES | PENNGROVE | SONOMA |
| NORTHRIDGE | LOS ANGELES | PENRYN | PLACER |
| NORTH SAN JUAN | NEVADA | PERRIS | RIVERSIDE |
| NORWALK | LOS ANGELES | PESCADERO | SAN MATEO |
| NOVATO | MARIN | PETALUMA | SONOMA |
| NUBIEBER | LASSEN | PETROLIA | HUMBOLDT |
| NUEVO | RIVERSIDE | PHELAN | SAN BERNARDINO |
| OAKDALE | STANISLAUS | PHILLIPSVILLE | HUMBOLDT |
| OAKHURST | MADERA | PHILO | MENDOCINO |
| OAKLAND | ALAMEDA | PICO RIVERA | LOS ANGELES |
| OAKLEY | CONTRA COSTA | PIEDMONT | ALAMEDA |
| OAK RUN | SHASTA | PIEDRA | FRESNO |
| OAK VIEW | VENTURA | PIERCY | MENDOCINO |
| OAKVILLE | NAPA | PILOT HILL | EL DORADO |
| OCCIDENTAL | SONOMA | PINECREST | TUOLUMNE |
| OCEANO | SAN LUIS OBISPO | PINEDALE | FRESNO |
| OCEANSIDE | SAN DIEGO | PINE GROVE | AMADOR |
| OCOTILLO | IMPERIAL | PINE VALLEY | SAN DIEGO |
| OILDALE | KERN | PINOLE | CONTRA COSTA |
| OJAI | VENTURA | PINON HILLS | SAN BERNARDINO |
| OLANCHA | INYO | PIONEER | AMADOR |
| OLD STATION | SHASTA | PIRU | VENTURA |
| OLEMA | MARIN | PISMO BEACH | SAN LUIS OBISPO |
| OLIVEHURST | YUBA | PITTSBURG | CONTRA COSTA |
| O'NEALS | MADERA | PIXLEY | TULARE |
| ONTARIO | SAN BERNARDINO | PLACENTIA | ORANGE |
| ONYX | KERN | PLACERVILLE | EL DORADO |
| ORANGE | ORANGE | PLANADA | MERCED |
| ORANGE COVE | FRESNO | PLATINA | SHASTA |
| ORANGEVALE | SACRAMENTO | PLAYA DEL REY | LOS ANGELES |
| ORDBEND | GLENN | PLEASANT GROVE | SUTTER |
| OREGON HOUSE | YUBA | PLEASANTON | ALAMEDA |
| ORICK | HUMBOLDT | PLYMOUTH | AMADOR |
| ORINDA | CONTRA COSTA | POINT ARENA | MENDOCINO |
| ORLAND | GLENN | POLLICK PINES | EL DORADO |
| ORLEANS | HUMBOLDT | POMONA | LOS ANGELES |
| ORO GRANDE | SAN BERNARDINO | PONDOSA | SISKIYOU |
| OROSE | TULARE | POPE VALLEY | NAPA |
| OROVILLE | BUTTE | PORT COSTA | CONTRA COSTA |
| OXNARD | VENTURA | PORTERVILLE | TULARE |
| PACIFICA | SAN MATEO | PORT HUENEME | VENTURA |
| PACIFIC GROVE | MONTEREY | PORTOLA | PLUMAS |
| PACIFIC HOUSE | EL DORADO | POSEY | TULARE |
| PACIFIC PALISADES | LOS ANGELES | POTRERO | SAN DIEGO |
| PACOIMA | LOS ANGELES | POTTER VALLEY | MENDOCINO |
| PAICINES | SAN BENITO | POWAY | SAN DIEGO |
| PALA | SAN DIEGO | PRATHER | FRESNO |
| PALERMO | BUTTE | PRINCETON | COLUSA |

14

| CITY | COUNTY | CITY | COUNTY |
|---|---|---|---|
| PROBERTA | TEHAMA | SAN CLEMENTE | ORANGE |
| PRUNEDALE | MONTEREY | SAN DIEGO | SAN DIEGO |
| QUINCY | PLUMAS | SAN DIMAS | LOS ANGELES |
| RACKERBY | YUBA | SAN FERNANDO | LOS ANGELES |
| RAIL ROAD FLAT | CALAVERAS | SAN FRANCISCO | SAN FRANCISCO |
| RAISIN | FRESNO | SAN GABRIEL | LOS ANGELES |
| RAMONA | SAN DIEGO | SANGER | FRESNO |
| RANCHITA | SAN DIEGO | SAN GERONIMO | MARIN |
| RAVENDALE | LASSEN | SAN GREGORIO | SAN MATEO |
| RAYMOND | MADERA | SAN JACINTO | RIVERSIDE |
| RED BLUFF | TEHAMA | SAN JOAQUIN | FRESNO |
| REDCREST | HUMBOLDT | SAN JOSE | SANTA CLARA |
| REDDING | SHASTA | SAN JUAN BAUTISTA | SAN BENITO |
| REDLANDS | SAN BERNARDINO | SAN JUAN CAPISTRANO | ORANGE |
| REDONDO BEACH | LOS ANGELES | SAN LEANDRO | ALAMEDA |
| RED TOP | MERCED | SAN LORENZO | ALAMEDA |
| REDWAY | HUMBOLDT | SAN LUCAS | MONTEREY |
| REDWOOD CITY | SAN MATEO | SAN LUIS OBISPO | SAN LUIS OBISPO |
| REDWOOD ESTATES | SANTA CLARA | SAN LUIS REY | SAN DIEGO |
| REDWOOD VALLEY | MENDOCINO | SAN MARCOS | SAN DIEGO |
| REEDLEY | FRESNO | SAN MARINO | LOS ANGELES |
| RESCUE | EL DORADO | SAN MARTIN | SANTA CLARA |
| RESEDA | LOS ANGELES | SAN MATEO | SAN MATEO |
| RIALTO | SAN BERNARDINO | SAN MIGUEL | SAN LUIS OBISPO |
| RICHGROVE | TULARE | SAN PEDRO | LOS ANGELES |
| RICHMOND | CONTRA COSTA | SAN RAFAEL | MARIN |
| RICHVALE | BUTTE | SAN RAMON | CONTRA COSTA |
| RIDGECREST | KERN | SAN ROQUE | SANTA BARBARA |
| RIMFOREST | SAN BERNARDINO | SAN SIMEON | SAN LUIS OBISPO |
| RIO DELL | HUMBOLDT | SANTA ANA | ORANGE |
| RIO LINDA | SACRAMENTO | SANTA BARBARA | SANTA BARBARA |
| RIO OSO | SUTTER | SANTA CLARA | SANTA CLARA |
| RIO VISTA | SOLANO | SANTA CRUZ | SANTA CRUZ |
| RIPLEY | RIVERSIDE | SANTA FE SPRINGS | LOS ANGELES |
| RIPON | SAN JOAQUIN | SANTA MARGARITA | SAN LUIS OBISPO |
| RIVERBANK | STANISLAUS | SANTA MARIA | SANTA BARBARA |
| RIVERDALE | FRESNO | SANTA MONICA | LOS ANGELES |
| RIVER PINES | AMADOR | SANTA PAULA | VENTURA |
| RIVERSIDE | RIVERSIDE | SANTA RITA PARK | MERCED |
| ROBBINS | SUTTER | SANTA ROSE | SONOMA |
| ROCKLIN | PLACER | SANTA SUSANA | VENTURA |
| RODEO | CONTRA COSTA | SANTA YNEZ | SANTA BARBARA |
| ROSAMOND | KERN | SANTA YSABEL | SAN DIEGO |
| ROSELAND | SANTA ROSA | SANTEE | SAN DIEGO |
| ROSEMEAD | LOS ANGELES | SAN YSIDRO | SAN DIEGO |
| ROSEVILLE | PLACER | SARATOGA | SANTA CLARA |
| ROSS | MARIN | SATICOY | VENTURA |
| ROUGH AND READY | NEVADA | SATTLEY | SIERRA |
| ROUND MOUNTAIN | SHASTA | SAUGUS | LOS ANGELES |
| RUBIDOUX | RIVERSIDE | SAUSALITO | MARIN |
| RUMSEY | YOLO | SCOTIA | HUMBOLDT |
| RUNNING SPRINGS | SAN BERNARDINO | SCOTT BAR | SISKIYOU |
| RUTHERFORD | NAPA | SCOTTS VALLEY | SANTA CRUZ |
| RYDE | SACRAMENTO | SEAL BEACH | ORANGE |
| SACRAMENTO | SACRAMENTO | SEASIDE | MONTEREY |
| SAINT HELENA | NAPA | SEBASTOPOL | SONOMA |
| SAINT MATTHEW | SAN MATEO | SEELEY | IMPERIAL |
| SALIDA | STANISLAUS | SEIAD VALLEY | SISKIYOU |
| SALINAS | MONTEREY | SELMA | FRESNO |
| SALYER | TRINITY | SEPULVEDA | LOS ANGELES |
| SAMOA | HUMBOLDT | SHAFTER | KERN |
| SAN ANDREAS | CALAVERAS | SHANDON | SAN LUIS OBISPO |
| SAN ANSELMO | MARIN | SHASTA | SHASTA |
| SAN ARDO | MONTEREY | SHAVER LAKE | FRESNO |
| SAN BERNARDINO | SAN BERNARDINO | SHERIDAN | PLACER |
| SAN BRUNO | SAN MATEO | SHERMAN OAKS | LOS ANGELES |
| SAN CARLOS | SAN MATEO | SHINGLE SPRINGS | EL DORADO |

15

| CITY | COUNTY | CITY | COUNTY |
|------|--------|------|--------|
| SHINGLETOWN | SHASTA | TUSTIN | ORANGE |
| SHOSHONE | INYO | TWAIN | PLUMAS |
| SIERRA CITY | SIERRA | TWAIN HARTE | TUOLUMNE |
| SIERRAVILLE | SIERRA | TWENTYNINE PALMS | SAN BERNARDINO |
| SILVERADO | ORANGE | TWIN BRIDGES | EL DORADO |
| SIMI VALLEY | VENTURA | TWIN PEAKS | SAN BERNARDINO |
| SKYFOREST | SAN BERNARDINO | UKIAH | MENDOCINO |
| SMARTVILLE | YUBA | UNION CITY | ALAMEDA |
| SMITHFLAT | EL DORADO | UNIVERSAL CITY | LOS ANGELES |
| SMITH RIVER | DEL NORTE | UPLAND | SAN BERNARDINO |
| SNELLING | MERCED | UPPERLAKE | LAKE |
| SODA SPRINGS | NEVADA | VACAVILLE | SOLANO |
| SOLANA BEACH | SAN DIEGO | VALENCIA | LOS ANGELES |
| SOLEDAD | MONTEREY | VALLECITO | CALAVERAS |
| SOLVANG | SANTA BARBARA | VALLEJO | SOLANO |
| SOMERSET | EL DORADO | VALLEY FORD | SONOMA |
| SOMIS | VENTURA | VALLEY HOME | STANISLAUS |
| SONOMA | SONOMA | VALYERMO | LOS ANGELES |
| SONORA | TUOLUMNE | VAN NUYS | LOS ANGELES |
| SOQUEL | SANTA CRUZ | VENICE | LOS ANGELES |
| SOULSBYVILLE | TUOLUMNE | VENTURA | VENTURA |
| SOUTH DOS PALOS | MERCED | VERNALIS | SAN JOAQUIN |
| SOUTH LAKE TAHOE | EL DORADO | VICTOR | SAN JOAQUIN |
| SOUTH SAN FRANCISCO | SAN MATEO | VICTORVILLE | SAN BERNARDINO |
| TAFT | KERN | VIDAL | SAN BERNARDINO |
| TAHOE CITY | PLACER | VILLA GRANDE | SONOMA |
| TAHOE VISTA | PLACER | VINA | TEHAMA |
| TAHOMA | PLACER | VINEBURG | SONOMA |
| TALMAGE | MENDOCINO | VINTON | PLUMAS |
| TARZANA | LOS ANGELES | VISALIA | TULARE |
| TAYLORSVILLE | PLUMAS | VISTA DEL MAR | SAN DIEGO |
| TECATE | SAN DIEGO | VOLCANO | AMADOR |
| TECOPA | INYO | WALLACE | CALAVERAS |
| TEHACHAPI | KERN | WALNUT CREEK | CONTRA COSTA |
| TEHAMA | TEHAMA | WALNUT GROVE | SACRAMENTO |
| TEMECULA | RIVERSIDE | WARNER SPRINGS | SAN DIEGO |
| TEMPLE CITY | LOS ANGELES | WASCO | KERN |
| TEMPLETON | SAN LUIS OBISPO | WASHINGTON | NEVADA |
| TERMO | LASSEN | WATERFORD | STANISLAUS |
| TERRA BELLA | TULARE | WATSONVILLE | SANTA CRUZ |
| THORNTON | SAN JOAQUIN | WATTS | LOS ANGELES |
| THOUSAND OAKS | VENTURA | WEAVERVILLE | TRINITY |
| THOUSAND PALMS | RIVERSIDE | WEED | SISKIYOU |
| THREE RIVERS | TULARE | WEIMAR | PLACER |
| TIBURON | MARIN | WELDON | KERN |
| TIPTON | TULARE | WEOTT | HUMBOLDT |
| TOLLHOUSE | FRESNO | WESTLEY | STANISLAUS |
| TOMALES | MARIN | WESTMINSTER | ORANGE |
| TOPANGA | LOS ANGELES | WESTMORLAND | IMPERIAL |
| TOPAZ | MONO | WEST POINT | CALAVERAS |
| TORRANCE | LOS ANGELES | WESTWOOD | LASSEN |
| TRACY | SAN JOAQUIN | WHEATLAND | YUBA |
| TRANQUILLITY | FRESNO | WHISKEYTOWN | SHASTA |
| TRAVER | TULARE | WHITETHORN | HUMBOLDT |
| TRES PINOS | SAN BENITO | WHITE WATER | RIVERSIDE |
| TRINIDAD | HUMBOLDT | WHITMORE | SHASTA |
| TRINITY CENTER | TRINITY | WHITTIER | LOS ANGELES |
| TRONA | SAN BERNARDINO | WILDOMAR | RIVERSIDE |
| TROPICO | LOS ANGELES | WILLIAMS | COLUSA |
| TROWBRIDGE | SUTTER | WILLITS | MENDOCINO |
| TRUCKEE | NEVADA | WILLOW CREEK | HUMBOLDT |
| TUJUNGA | LOS ANGELES | WILLOWS | GLENN |
| TULARE | TULARE | WILMINGTON | LOS ANGELES |
| TULELAKE | SISKIYOU | WILSEYVILLE | CALAVERAS |
| TUOLUMNE | TUOLUMNE | WILTON | SACRAMENTO |
| TUPMAN | KERN | WINCHESTER | RIVERSIDE |
| TURLOCK | STANISLAUS | WINDSOR | SONOMA |

| CITY | COUNTY |
|------|--------|
| WINTERHAVEN | IMPERIAL |
| WINTERS | YOLO |
| WINTON | MERCED |
| WISHON | MADERA |
| WOFFORD HEIGHTS | KERN |
| WOODACRE | MARIN |
| WOODBRIDGE | SAN JOAQUIN |
| WOOKLAKE | TULARE |
| WOODLAND | YOLO |
| WOODLAND HILLS | LOS ANGELES |
| WOODY | KERN |
| WRIGHTWOOD | SAN BERNARDINO |
| YALE | SAN BERNARDINO |
| YERMO | SAN BERNARDINO |
| YETTEM | TULARE |
| YOLO | YOLO |
| YORBA LINDA | ORANGE |
| YORKVILLE | MENDOCINO |
| YOSEMITE | MARIPOSA |
| YOUNTVILLE | NAPA |
| YREKA | SISKIYOU |
| YUBA CITY | SUTTER |
| YUCAIPA | SAN BERNARDINO |
| ZAMORA | YOLO |
| ZENIA | TRINITY |

# CALIFORNIA LAWS PERTAINING TO ADOPTION

Adoptees' California birth certificates have been amended since before 1933. There is no access to original birth certificates or other pertinent documents without a specific court order. According to the California Health & Safety Code, Section 10439:

> "All records and information . . . shall be available only upon the order of the superior court of the county of residence of the adopted child or the superior court of the county granting the order of adoption. No such order shall be granted . . . unless a verified petition setting forth facts showing the necessity of such an order has been presented to the court and good and compelling cause is shown for the granting of the order . . The name and address of the natural parents shall be given to the petitioner only if he can demonstrate that such name and address, or either of them, are necessary to assist him in establishing a legal right."

The laws pertaining to the issuance of an amended certificate of birth spell out, in great detail, the contents and deletions allowable on the amended certificate:

> " . . . no reference shall be made in the new birth certificate to the adoption of the child. When requested by the adopting parents, the new birth certificate shall not include the specific name and address of the hospital or other facility where the birth occurred."

In addition, by filing yet another amended certificate, the adopting parents may ask that the city and county of birth and race of parents be omitted.

When the new, amended birth certificate is established, the local registrar and the county recorder
forward the original certificate to the State
Registrar, so the two certificates can be filed
together. If it is impractical for the original
to be forwarded, the local registrar is ordered to
seal a cover over the copy of the original and send
Sacramento a statement to that effect.

Birthparents of any age, including very young minors,
have the right to relinquish a child for adoption to
a licensed adoption agency or attorney and that relinquishment is not subject to revocation because
of age.

If a birthparent has relinquished his or her child
for adoption, or has signed a consent for adoption,
he or she will not be notified at the time of the
finalization of the adoption. This usually takes
place six months to a year after relinquishment.
However, if one parent is not aware that the adoption of the child is imminent, the petitioners are
obliged to publish a notice in a "newspaper to be
named and designated as most likely to give notice
to the father or mother." This notice is to be
published once a week for four successive weeks.
The last of these usually appears one week to one
month before the hearing for adoption finalization.

# CALIFORNIA ADOPTION PRACTICES

Four adoption programs are available in the state
of California.

> Relinquishment/Agency Adoptions
> Independent Adoptions
> Step-Parent Adoptions
> Intercountry Adoptions

A relinquishment adoption is one in which children
are placed through a licensed adoption agency to
which the child has been relinquished by its birth
parent(s). The term "relinquishment" refers to a
legal document signed by a parent and the adoption
agency which has agreed to accept the child for
adoptive placement. The relinquishment terminates
all parental responsibility for the care and custody
of the child and transfers this responsibility to
the agency. Persons who wish to adopt a child may
then contact one of the public or private agencies
to investigate that possibility. When an application
is accepted, the agency makes a study of the suitability of the adopting home. This study is required
by law.

In California public adoption agencies include those
operated by the following 28 counties:

| | | |
|---|---|---|
| Alameda | Orange | Santa Barbara |
| Contra Costa | Placer | Santa Clara |
| El Dorado | Riverside | Santa Cruz |
| Fresno | Sacramento | Shasta |
| Imperial | San Bernardino | Solano |
| Kern | San Diego | Stanislaus |
| Los Angeles | San Francisco | Tulare |
| Marin | San Joaquin | Ventura |
| Merced | San Luis Obispo | |
| Monterey | San Mateo | |

Private adoption agencies include:

Catholic Social Services of San Francisco
Children's Bureau of Los Angeles
Children's Home Society of California
Church of Jesus Christ of Latter Day Saints
Family Ministries
Holy Family Adoption Services
Infant of Prague Adoption Service
Vista Del Mar Adoption Service

An independent adoption refers to an adoption which is not handled through a licensed adoption agency, but one in which the child is placed directly by the birthmother or father with an adopting family. The birthparents sign a "consent" in this type of adoption. A public agency conducts a study of the prospective adopting home to determine if it is suitable and of the child to determine if he or she is a proper subject for adoption. In independent adoptions there is usually a "middle man" who may be an attorney, a doctor, or a minister. These are often called "gray market" adoptions.

In both step-parent and intercountry adoptions the procedures are similar, except that in a step-parent adoption the suitability of the home is more or less taken for granted. Whatever the form of the adoption, state laws, regulations, and other requirements must be met, by both the natural as well as the adopting parents.

IMMIGRATION AND NATURALIZATION SERVICE (INS)

These records are not commonly used, but may hold
valuable clues for searchers.  Immigration and
naturalization files are reportedly kept from
public view for 75 years; however, proceedings are
recorded in a U. S. District Court.  These are
public, but cannot be photocopied.  Contact may be
made with the Immigration and Naturalization Service
at the following addresses:

INS                        INS
P. O. Box 1780             880 Front Street
Calexico, CA 92231         San Diego, CA 92188
714/357-1143               714/293-6250


INS                        INS
U. S. Courthouse           630 Sansome Street
1130 "O" Street            San Francisco, CA 94111
Fresno, CA 93721           415/556-2070
209/487-5091


INS                        INS
300 N. Los Angeles         Terminal Island
Los Angeles, CA 90012      San Pedro, CA 90731
213/688-2780               213/831-9281


NATIONAL (FEDERAL) ARCHIVES

The Archives contain census records, 1790 through
1910 which are open to public inspection.  The 1910
census has just become available as of April 1982.
Census records must be viewed at the Archives and
are no longer available through interlibrary loan.
The 1900 and 1910 census records, especially, may
be helpful to those tracing someone presumed still

living or a descendant of that person.  Information
included in the 1900 census is:

        Names of all in household
        Month and year of birth of all in household
        Place of birth of all in household
        Place of birth of parents of each in household
        Number of years married
        Number of children born to the marriage
        When immigrated
        When naturalized
        Occupation

The National Archives house other types of records,
including immigration and passport information,
military records, Indian tribal records and some
land dealings.

There are two branches of the National Archives
located in the State of California:

        1000 Commodore Drive    24000 Avila Road
        San Bruno, CA 94066     Laguna Niguel, CA 92677
        415/876-9009            714/831-4242


SOCIAL SECURITY

The social security offices will not give out names
and addresses to anyone.  They will, however, forward a letter if they consider it to be important
and non-threatening.  A searcher should contact the
following office to get details on the exact pro-
cedure to be used:

        Region 9
        Social Security Administration
        100 Van Ness Avenue
        San Francisco, CA 94102

It is possible to elicit some information from the social security numbers themselves. By looking at a person's social security number you can learn approximately where he lived when it was issued, how long ago it was assigned, and if he ever worked for the railroad. All California issued numbers begin with the numbers 545 through 573. Contact a local social security office for help in breaking down the code.

VETERANS' ADMINISTRATION

Some veteran's data is required by law to be released to any requester. Section 1.502 of the Veteran Administration's Freedom of Information Act reads:

> "The monthly rate of pension, compensation, dependency and indemnity compensation, retirement pay, subsistence allowance, or educational allowance to any beneficiary shall be made known to any person who applies for such information."

In California, the Veterans' Administration may be contacted at these offices:

Veterans' Administration
11000 Wilshire Blvd.
Los Angeles, CA 90024

Veterans' Administration
2022 Camino Del Rio North
San Diego, CA 92108

Veterans' Administration
211 Main Street
San Francisco, CA 94105

BUREAU OF VITAL STATISTICS

Vital Statistics Section
State Department of Health
410 "N" Street
Sacramento, CA 95814

This office has birth, marriage, and death records
since July 1, 1905, and divorce records since January 1, 1962. The present cost of a certified copy
of any certificate is $3.00. Earlier records may
be found on a county level, at the county clerk's
or recorder's office. *Note to adoptees and birth
parents--Registration numbers on amended and original birth certificates for the same person are said
to be identical.

CALIFORNIA STATE ARCHIVES

The California State Archives has an extensive
collection of records from the agencies of California state government. Information on individual
citizens may be found in these records. There are
land grants and property records which may be of
specific help to genealogists. For a full list of
what is available, write to:

California State Archives
Room 200
1020 "O" Street
Sacramento, CA 95814

CALIFORNIA STATE LIBRARY

The California Section of the California State
Library has a variety of materials that may prove
helpful. The Library staff can do little by mail
or phone, but will make material available on
interlibrary loan. Among the more helpful kinds
of records are:

1. California State Census--1852 (the only
   California census taken of the state as
   as a whole).

2. California Cemetery Records--Various
   counties and sites.

3. Cemetery Records--Los Angeles County to
   1940 and veterans' grave registrations.

4. Courthouse Records--Alameda and Stanislaus
   Counties.

5. Great Registers of Voters--Lists of registered voters, 1866-1944.

6. City and County Directories.

7. Telephone Directories--1897 to date.

8. County Histories--one or more for each
   county, with biographical sections.

9. Newspapers--California newspapers from 1846
   to the present.

COLLEGES, UNIVERSITIES AND SCHOOLS

Colleges and universities are sometimes of help to
searchers. It is wise to check with both the offices of past student records and the alumni associations. Things you may ask for are:

Full name of student
Address at entrance
Age at entrance or birthdate
Date of entrance
Next of kin
Major field of study
Date graduated
High School last attended
Colleges requesting transcripts

Some searchers have been able to obtain lists of
all graduating seniors in particular fields. A
school library usually houses yearbooks from many
years, complete with pictures.

## DEPARTMENT OF MOTOR VEHICLES

The Department of Motor Vehicles maintains two basic
sets of records. The first pertains to car registration and the second to drivers' records. In
California, state law requires that auto registration
information be considered public. Anyone can fill
out a request form, pay the fee, and learn the name
and address of the registered owner of a vehicle.
The DMV states it will notify the person named so
that he or she will know someone is looking for him
or her.

Driver's license information is not considered generally available to the public, but is readily
obtained by a variety of businesses and individuals.
Form #75000 is in current use. A requester need
only obtain this form from a local DMV office, fill
in sections 2, 4 and 6 and print his name and address in section 7. This is then sent with a check
for $2.00 directly to the Department of Motor
Vehicles, P. O. Box 11231, Sacramento, CA 95813.

Booth Memorial Hospital/Home
2670 Griffin Avenue
Los Angeles, CA 90031
213/225-1586
Established in 1899 by the Salvation Army.
Babies were delivered at this facility until
1972. They are now delivered at White Memorial Hospital in Los Angeles.

Booth Memorial Hospital/Home
2794 Garden St.
Oakland, CA 94601
415/532-3345
Established in 1926 by the Salvation Army.
Babies were delivered at this facility until
approximately 1970.

Door of Hope Home
2799 Health Center Drive
San Diego, CA 92123
714/279-1100
Another Salvation Army facility, established
in 1949. Births took place here until 1975.
Babies are now delivered at Mercy Hospital
in San Diego.

Florence Crittendon Services
600 N. Harbor Blvd.
Fullerton, CA 92632
714/870-5522
Established in 1966. No deliveries took
place here. Most mothers-to-be are referred
to St. Jude or Martin Luther Hospitals in
Orange County.

Florence Crittendon Services
234 E. Avenue 33
Los Angeles, CA 90031
213/225-4211

This Crittendon Home was begun in 1892. It served as a home for unwed mothers, and their babies were delivered on the premises until 1956. Present day deliveries take place at Hollywood Presbyterian Hospital.

St. Anne's Maternity Hospital/Home
155 N. Occidental Blvd.
Los Angeles, CA 90026
213/381-2931
St. Anne's began in 1908 in downtown Los Angeles. It then moved to Hollywood, and is now located back in Los Angeles. St. Anne's delivered babies until as recently as 1978. They are now born at Queen of Angels Hospital in Los Angeles, where St. Anne's has a special unit.

Florence Crittendon Services
840 Broderick Street
San Francisco, CA 94115
415/567-2357

Big Sister League (now Children's Institute)
711 S. New Hampshire
Los Angeles, CA 90005
213/385-5104
Big Sister League was established in 1918 and babies were born there until very recently. Big Sister League closed its doors at the end of September, 1981.

# SOCIAL SERVICE AGENCIES

The office which oversees all adoptions within the State of California is the following:

> Department of Social Services
> 744 "P" Street
> Sacramento, CA 95814

If the individual placing agency or attorney is unknown, a notarized request to this state office will produce that information. In addition, they maintain files from defunct agencies, including Native Sons and Daughters of the Golden West. *Important note: If the adoption was private (handled through an attorney rather than a social service agency), the birthparent(s) and adoptive parents who signed the papers of transfer now have the right to request and obtain copies of those documents. Both parties signed the same paper.

Local social service or adoption agencies hold many keys for a searcher. Their policies differ from office to office, depending a great deal on the director at any given time. California agencies generally are excellent in providing non-identifying information to the adoptee and to the birth and adoptive parents upon request. This includes:

> Ages of parents
> Educational background
> Occupations (not always specific)
> Reasons for relinquishment (birthparents)
> Reasons for adoption (adoptive parents)
> Background of family
> Health history
> Nationality
> Hobbies

An adoptee or adoptive parent may request the above
pertaining to the birthparents' families. A birthparent may request the information which pertains
to the adoptive family.

State controlled adoption agencies and private
adoption agency headquarters are listed here. For
county branches of agencies, consult the specific
county in Section II of this book.

STATE ADOPTION AGENCY

State Department of Social Services
California Adoption Service
500 Cohasset Rd., Suite 34
Chico, CA 95926
916/891-1986
Serves Butte, Colusa, Glenn, Lassen, Modoc,
Nevada, Plumas, Sierra, Siskiyou, Sutter,
Tehama, Trinity, and Yuba Counties with relin-
quishment services upon request of the county.

California Adoption Service
2400 Glendale Lane, Suite B
Sacramento, CA 95825
916/920-6897
Serves Amador, Calaveras, Kings, Madera, Mariposa, Mono, San Benito, Tuolumne and Yolo
Counties with relinquishment services upon
request of the county.

California Adoption Service
2350 Professional Dr.
Santa Rosa, CA 95406
707/545-2921
Serves Del Norte, Humboldt, Lake, Mendocino,
Napa, and Sonoma Counties with relinquishment
services upon request of the county.

PRIVATE ADOPTION AGENCIES

AASK (Aid to Adoption of Special Kids)
3530 Grand Avenue
Oakland, CA 94610
415/451-1748

Catholic Social Service of San Francisco
2045 Lawton Street
San Francisco, CA 94122
415/665-5100

Children's Home Society
5429 McConnell Avenue
Los Angeles, CA 90066
213/306-4654
Children's Home Society maintains the records
of the now defunct Adoption Institute.

LDS Social Services
333 North Glenoaks Blvd., Suite 650
Burbank, CA 91502
213/841-2640

STATE HEADQUARTERS FOR PROFESSIONAL ASSOCIATIONS

When a person's occupation is known, oftentimes a
professional association may be of great help. In
many cases extensive files are kept by these organizations which may help track a person both back
and forward. Many professions require annual or
periodic licensing and these applications and re-
newals will be included in that individual's file.


Board of Chiropractic Examiners
921 11th Street, Suite 601
Sacramento, CA 95814
916/445-3244

Board of Dental Examiners
1021 "O" Street, Room A-102
Sacramento, CA 95814
916/445-6407

Board of Funeral Directors & Embalmers
1021 "O" Street
Sacramento, CA 95814
916/445-2413

Board of Medical Quality Assurance
1430 Howe Avenue
Sacramento, CA 95825
916/920-6343

Board of Registered Nursing
1020 "N" Street, Room 448
Sacramento, CA 95814
916/322-3350

California Medical Association
731 Market Street
San Francisco, CA 94103

California State Bar
555 Franklin Street
San Francisco, CA 94102
800/622-0585 (membership records)

California State Chamber of Commerce
1027 10th Street
Sacramento, CA 95808
916/444-6670

Cemetery Board
1434 Howe Avenue, Suite 88
Sacramento, CA 95825
916/920-6078

Commission for Teacher Preparation & Licensing
1020 "O" Street, Room 222
Sacramento, CA 95814
916/445-7254

Contractors' State License Board
1020 "N" Street, Room 579
Sacramento, CA 95814
916/366-5253

Health Facilities Commission
555 Capitol Mall
Sacramento, CA 95814
916/322-2810

Teachers' Retirement System
1010 Hurley Way
Sacramento, CA 95825
916/920-7011

## COUNTY ASSESSOR

Each county has an assessor's office. There are no
fees involved in using their records, except a nominal fee for photocopies. Basically, the assessor's
office contains property records. Some materials
are on the public side of the clerk's counter and
may be used by anyone. There are usually a number
of folios and display maps. Other information may
require a clerk's assistance and will be found on
microfilm or microfiche. To use the assessor's
records, a researcher can take the addresses he has
and cross reference them to ascertain the block or
tract number, then the lot number. Once these numbers are obtained, he can consult the sales ledgers
and find the names of the property owners, as well
as those of neighbors. In many county assessors'
offices there is a master index where a researcher
may look up any individual's name and obtain a list
of all real property owned by that person in the
county.

## COUNTY CLERK

In California, sometimes the County Clerk and the
County Recorder are one and the same. Birth,
death, marriage and other vital records are housed
with the Clerk-Recorder, or, if the offices are
separate, may be located at either. This division
is usually determined by the size of the county,
the smaller counties combining functions of both
offices.

The County Clerk usually maintains marriage records,
including the marriage license application--a gold

35

mine of information. Some of the information to
be found on a marriage license application is:

| | |
|---|---|
| full names | previous marriages |
| names of parents | place of employment |
| ages/birthdates | highest grade in |
| addresses | school |
| occupations | person performing |
| birthplaces | ceremony |
| maiden names of mothers | signatures of couple |
| social security numbers | driver's license #s |

Marriage records are alphabetical, usually by both
bride's and groom's names, and are sometimes grouped
by month as well as by year. Keep in mind that the
State of California does allow confidential marriages. In a confidential marriage no blood test
or license are required. These marriages are not
a matter of public record and may be viewed only
with a court order. A specific law allowing the
confidential marriage was passed in 1972. During
that first year there were little more than 100
such marriages recorded. Since then the rate of
confidential marriages has grown enormously. In
1980 Orange County alone reported 4332 confidential
marriages had been filed with the county clerk.

The county clerk is the custodian of superior court
records in each county, including civil and crimi-
nal, as well as juvenile matters. Probate records
are to be found in the clerk's office also, and
include wills, adoption and confidential parentage,
paternity, mental, and such legal proceedings.

The probate index is usually organized alphabetically for a 15-20 year span. The entries are not
entirely alphabetical, but all surnames beginning
with the same initial should be grouped together.
Once the case number is determined from the index,
the probate clerk can locate the file. Old records

will no doubt be stored in a separate location and it sometimes is a matter of days before the information becomes available.

## COUNTY COURTS

Juvenile Court--Juvenile court records usually do not come into play, except occasionally in adoption related searches. It is possible, in these cases, for juvenile records to supply additional data to the adoptee. Only the person on whom the records are kept may have access to them, and then only by petitioning the juvenile court. If anything unusual occurred, such as abandonment, abuse, or paternity suits which may have affected the original adoption, juvenile records may help. Possibly a social worker's report, filed with the juvenile records will offer clues to the adoptee's background.

Superior Court--The superior court of each county is the court of jurisdiction in all 58 counties for adoption matters. The sealed file in the superior court may contain the following:

> Petition to adopt
> Interlocutory decree of adoption
> Case worker's report
> Final decree of adoption
> Original (unamended) certificate of birth
> Relinquishment papers or termination order
> Amended birth certificate

California law states that access may be granted to this file only by parties directly involved, upon "good and compelling cause", and only if necessary to assist in "establishing a legal right." Judges rarely open records, but have been known to do so for legal and medical reasons. It is reported that more than one superior court judge has honored an out-of-state court order and has granted access.

Divorce records will also usually be found in the custody of the Clerk of the Superior Court in the county where the proceedings took place. These are generally available to the public, unless the Court has ordered them sealed.

Naturalization records are kept in the Superior Court and also in the United States Circuit Courts in Los Angeles and San Francisco.

COUNTY RECORDER

Each county recorder's office is structured to be a storehouse for vital record information. Births, deaths, marriages and some land records are housed at the recorder's. In California, each county possesses sets of state-wide indices for births, deaths and marriages. These are alphabetical and by year. Some are in books, others are on microfiche. All marriage indices are divided into separate sections, one for grooms and another for brides. Each county also maintains an index for births, deaths, and marriages pertaining only to that county. Access to county or state indices varies greatly from county to county. In some, a searcher pays the $2.00 per hour fee and may use any records there. In other counties he may use them only under the strict supervision of a state employee. In yet others, he must submit a particular name which a clerk will attempt to locate, eliminating the chance to do a thorough search. Always check very carefully to see which records may be available in a particular county.

It should be noted here that the majority of birth, death, and marriage records, whether in books or on microfiche, are number coded. A complete coding breakdown is included at the beginning of the county section of this book.

## VOTER REGISTRATION

An affidavit of registration is stored by the registrar of voters in the county of a person's residence. This is public information and may be viewed in person or may be requested by mail at the appropriate county office, usually listed as the Registrar of Voters. Information found on the affidavit is:

> Full name
> Address
> Occupation
> Birthdate (may delete year)
> Birthplace
> Party affiliation
> Social Security (optional)
> Telephone number (optional)
> Physical description (limited)

All of these may not be found on any one record. Currently, there is no charge for obtaining voter information, other than nominal photocopy costs. If you go to the registrar of voters in person, consult the index of current affidavits. The index contains surnames, listed alphabetically, with the registrant's precinct number. This number will correspond to files usually kept in trays, again alphabetically by surname. Unfortunately, in the state of California, cancelled affidavits must be kept only four years. Many counties do keep them for longer periods of time, some since county records have been maintained.

CEMETERIES

Every genealogist knows how very valuable the records kept by a funeral home can be.  Cemeteries,
as well, have vital records which are often separate
and complete.  These are to be found at the main
office, in a nearby church, or in a building on the
cemetery grounds.  Often complete obituaries are
in the files, listing survivors, addresses, and mis-
cellaneous genealogical data.  Many generations of
a particular family may be buried in a family plot
and their records can tie up many loose ends for the
searcher.

CHAMBERS OF COMMERCE

The majority of cities and towns have Chambers of
Commerce.  Their biggest attraction to searchers
is that they keep close tabs on businesses and on
prominent members of the community.  They usually
have local city or criss-cross directories and will
be as helpful as possible.  In a small community it
is not uncommon for the staff of a local Chamber of
Commerce to know who is related to whom, as well as
other interesting data.

CHURCH RECORDS

If the parents' (adoptive or birth) religion and or
denomination is known, it is reasonable to investigate church records.  Catholic, Lutheran, Methodist
and Episcopal baptisms and christenings should be
recorded.  Less structured denominations, such as
the Baptists, do not christen or baptize infants,
but may have infant dedications and cradle rolls
which list children.  Remember also that most

churches keep records of deaths and marriages and usually are amenable to letting genealogical researchers make use of files. Many Protestant denominations use letters of membership transfer, which may help trace a family from one community or state to another. Because of space, specific churches are not listed in this book. The yellow pages of local telephone books are an excellent source for names and addresses of most churches and synagogues.

CITY HALLS

City halls of large, incorporated cities may contain vital records of births, deaths, marriages, and even divorces. Sometimes what cannot be gained from contacting state or county offices can be found on a city level at city hall.


HOSPITALS

California law requires hospitals to keep patient records for a minimum of seven years, or with minors, until one year after the patient reaches legal age. After that the file may be destroyed, but is nearly always retained indefinitely in some murky basement, often on microfilm.

AB610, signed into law in early 1982, gives all Californians the right to view their medical records held by doctors, hospitals and other health providers. They may inspect the records in person within five days, or may obtain copies of the records within 15 days after submitting a written request. AB610 will go into effect January 1, 1983.

Remember that newborn children are patients and records will be kept on them. There may be several kinds of records on each newborn baby. In addition to the attending physician's notes there are test results, a birth ledger, a birth index card, and

the obstetrician's logbook, each kept separately.
If the birth index card can be located (usually on
microfilm) there should be a number listed on it
which corresponds directly to the birthmother's
files.

LIBRARIES

A wealth of information is sitting on shelves in
both public and private libraries. Some specialize
in particular books, such as city directories, genealogical materials, or newspapers. If the library
a researcher consults does not have what is needed,
interlibrary loan may solve the problem. Books
and microfilm can usually be borrowed through this
department from most libraries in the United States.
The Church of Jesus Christ of Latter Day Saints
(Mormon) maintains genealogy libraries in most areas
of the state. While the official Church stand on
adoption-related searches varies in interpretation,
all of their libraries are more than anxious to
help anyone conduct a search for family members.
These libraries are listed in the county section,
and are earmarked with asterisks. Other libraries
with special collections of interest to searchers are
also starred.

NEWSPAPER NOTICES

Obituaries are the most complete source of data
about a person's background and family usually
available in one place. They may list date and
place of birth, occupation and place of employ-
ment, parents' names, spouses' names, funeral
home, and names and addresses of all survivors.
Remember that it is possible to borrow microfilmed
newspapers through interlibrary loan. A twenty-
fifth or fiftieth wedding anniversary, engagement
and wedding announcement may provide a lot of
information. Don't overlook the society section.

# SECTION II
## County Information

CODING BREAKDOWN

In order to use some county records listed in this section of the book, it will be
necessary to understand the California system of number coding. Each county (CN) is
assigned a code, beginning with #01 Alameda, and continuing alphabetically through
#58 Yuba. Four large counties have been assigned a second number, so either code
represents that particular county.

The 58 California counties and their codes are:

| | | | |
|---|---|---|---|
| #01 and #60 Alameda | #21 | Marin | #41 | San Mateo |
| #02 Alpine | #22 | Mariposa | #42 | Santa Barbara |
| #03 Amador | #23 | Mendocino | #43 | Santa Clara |
| #04 Butte | #24 | Merced | #44 | Santa Cruz |
| #05 Calaveras | #25 | Modoc | #45 | Shasta |
| #06 Colusa | #26 | Mono | #46 | Sierra |
| #07 Contra Costa | #27 | Monterey | #47 | Siskiyou |
| #08 Del Norte | #28 | Napa | #48 | Solano |
| #09 El Dorado | #29 | Nevada | #49 | Sonoma |
| #10 Fresno | #30 | Orange | #50 | Stanislaus |
| #11 Glenn | #31 | Placer | #51 | Sutter |
| #12 Humboldt | #32 | Plumas | #52 | Tehama |
| #13 Imperial | #33 | Riverside | #53 | Trinity |
| #14 Inyo | #34 | Sacramento | #54 | Tulare |
| #15 Kern | #35 | San Benito | #55 | Tuolumne |
| #16 Kings | #36 | San Bernardino | #56 | Ventura |
| #17 Lake | #37 and #80 San Diego | #57 | Yolo |
| #18 Lassen | #38 and #90 San Francisco | #58 | Yuba |
| #19 and #70 Los Angeles | #39 | San Joaquin | | |
| #20 Madera | #40 | San Luis Obispo | | |

Each large city (CT) also is coded and smaller cities are grouped into coded areas.
City codes are listed in the individual counties.


Other State Index Codes:

| Units of Age | Race | Sex |
|---|---|---|
| 1  Years | 1  White/Mexican | 1  Male |
| 2  Months | 2  Black | 2  Female |
| 3  Days | 3  Indian | 9  Not stated or unknown |
| 4  Hours | 4  Chinese | |
| 9  Not stated or unknown | 5  Japanese | |
| | 9  Other or unknown | |

A sample entry in the county records might read as follows:

    Johnson   John   32   Brown   Margaret   31   03 15 69   70 53   1543   19837

This would indicate that John Johnson, age 32, married Margaret Brown, age 31, on
March 15, 1969 in Los Angeles County, city of Los Angeles. The Registrar's file
number is #1543 and the state file number is #19837.


The following abbreviations will be used in this book to designate kinds of records.

| | | | |
|---|---|---|---|
| b | birth records | min | mining claims |
| d | death records | nat | naturalization records |
| m | marriage records | pro | probate records |
| div | divorce records | crm | criminal records |
| civ | civil records | ins | insanity records |
| bur | burial records | ine | inebriate records |
| lnd | land records | grd | guardianship records |

45

County Seat:  Oakland

| | | | |
|---|---|---|---|
| 6001 | Alameda | 6012 | Livermore |
| 6002 | Albany | 6015 | Oakland |
| 6005 | Berkeley | 6016 | Piedmont |
| 6008 | Fremont | 6018 | San Leandro |
| 6009 | Emeryville | 6097 | Rest of County |
| 6010 | Hayward | | |

## ALAMEDA COUNTY OFFICES

| COUNTY OFFICE | ADDRESS | PHONE |
|---|---|---|
| Assessor | 1221 Oak Street<br>Oakland  94612 | 415/874-5205 |
| Clerk-Recorder<br>　b　 from 1919<br>　m　 from 1853<br>　div from 1853<br>　civ from 1853 | 1225 Fallon Street<br>Room 105<br>Oakland  94612 | 415/874-6545 |
| Courts<br>　Juvenile<br><br><br>　Superior | 2200 Fairmont Drive<br>San Leandro  94578<br><br>Courthouse<br>12th & Fallon<br>Oakland  94612 | |
| Health Department<br>　b & d records<br><br>Voter Registration | 2180 Milvia<br>Berkeley  94703<br><br>1225 Fallon Street<br>Oakland  94612 | 415/644-6489<br><br>415/874-6361 |

## ADOPTION AGENCIES

Alameda Social Services Agency
Adoption Services
401 Broadway
Oakland, CA 94607
415/874-6722

Children's Home Society
Golden Gate District
3200 Telegraph Avenue
Oakland, CA 94609
415/655-7406

LDS Social Services
4510 Peralta Blvd.
Fremont, CA 94536
415/792-3721

## CEMETERIES

| | | | | |
|---|---|---|---|---|
| Cedar Lawn Memorial Park | 48800 Warm Springs Blvd. | Fremont | 94538 | 415/656-5565 |
| Chapel of the Chimes | 32992 Mission Blvd. | Hayward | 94544 | 471-3363 |
| Evergreen Cemetery | 6450 Camden St. | Oakland | 94536 | 632-1602 |
| Holy Ghost | Central Avenue | Fremont | 94538 | |
| Holy Sepulchre Cemetery | 26320 Mission Blvd. | Hayward | 94544 | 581-2488 |
| Irvington Memorial Cem. | 41001 Chapel Way | Fremont | 94538 | 656-5800 |
| Jewish Cemetery | End of Piedmont | Oakland | 94611 | |
| Lone Tree Cemetery | 24591 Fairview Avenue | Hayward | 94542 | 582-1274 |
| Memory Gardens | 3873 East Avenue | Livermore | 94550 | 447-8417 |
| Mountain View Cemetery | 5000 Piedmont Avenue | Oakland | 94611 | 658-2588 |
| Mt. Eden Cemetery | Depot Road | Mt. Eden | 94557 | 782-3266 |
| Roselawn Cemetery | 1240 N. Livermore Ave. | Livermore | 94550 | 581-1206 |
| St. Joseph's Cemetery | Mission Boulevard | Fremont | 94538 | |
| St. Mary's Cemetery | 4529  Howe Street | Oakland | 94611 | 654-0936 |
| St. Michael's Cemetery | East Avenue | Livermore | 94550 | |

## CHAMBERS OF COMMERCE

| | | | |
|---|---|---|---|
| Alameda | 2437 Santa Clara Ave. | Alameda | 94501 |
| Albany | 1108 Solano Avenue | Albany | 94706 |
| Berkeley | P. O. Box 210 | Berkeley | 94701 |
| Castro Valley | 21096 Redwood Road | Castro Vly | 94546 |
| Dublin | 7996 Amador Valley Blvd. | Dublin | 94566 |
| Fremont | 39737 Paseo Padre Pkwy. | Fremont | 94538 |
| Hayward | 22300 Foothill Blvd. | Hayward | 94541 |
| Livermore | 1510 Holmes | Livermore | 94550 |
| Newark | 59208 Thornton Ave. | Newark | 94560 |
| Oakland | 1939 Harrison | Oakland | 94612 |
| Pleasanton | 10 W. Neal Street | Pleasanton | 94566 |
| San Leandro | 262 Davis Street | San Leandro | 94577 |
| Union City | 33367 Alvarado-Niles | Union City | 94587 |

## COLLEGES & UNIVERSITIES

| | | | |
|---|---|---|---|
| American Baptist Seminary | 2508 Hillegass Ave. | Berkeley | 94704 |
| Armstrong College | 2222 Harold Way | Berkeley | 94704 |
| Calif. College of Arts & Crafts | Broadway at College | Oakland | 94618 |
| Calif. School of Psychology | 1900 Addison St. | Berkeley | 94110 |
| California State University | | Hayward | 94542 |
| Chabot College | 25555 Hesperian Blvd. | Hayward | 94545 |
| College of Alameda | 555 Atlantic Ave. | Alameda | 94501 |
| Holy Name College | 3500 Mountain Blvd. | Oakland | 94619 |
| Laney College | 900 Fallon St. | Oakland | 94612 |
| Merritt College | 12500 Campus Dr. | Oakland | 94619 |
| Mills College | MacArthur & Sem | Oakland | 94613 |
| Ohlone College | P.O. Box 909 | Fremont | 94537 |
| Patten Bible College | 2433 Coolidge Ave. | Oakland | 94601 |
| Saint Albert's College | 5890 Birch Court | Oakland | 94618 |
| Starr King School for Ministry | 2441 Le Conte Ave. | Berkeley | 94709 |
| University of California | 2200 University Ave. | Berkeley | 94720 |
| Wright Institute | 2728 Durant Ave. | Berkeley | 94704 |

## HOSPITALS

| | | | |
|---|---|---|---|
| Alameda Hospital | 2070 Clinton | Alameda | 94501 |
| Albany Hospital | 1247 Marin Ave. | Albany | 94706 |
| Alta Bates Hospital | 1 Colby Plaza | Berkeley | 94705 |
| Calif. Surgical | 390 40th St. | Oakland | 94611 |
| Children's Hospital | 51st & Grove | Oakland | 94609 |
| Cowell Memorial | U.C. Campus | Berkeley | 94708 |
| Doctors' Hospital | 4600 Fairfax Ave. | Oakland | 94601 |
| Doctors' Hospital | 13855 E. 14th St. | San Leandro | 94578 |
| Eden Hospital | 20103 Lake Chabot | Castro Valley | 94546 |
| Fairmont Hospital | 15400 Foothill Blvd. | San Leandro | 94578 |
| Herrick Memorial | 2001 Dwight Way | Berkeley | 94704 |
| Highland General | 1411 E. 31st St. | Oakland | 94608 |
| Kaiser Foundation | 280 W. MacArthur | Oakland | 94610 |
| Kaiser Foundation | 27400 Hesperian | Hayward | 94545 |
| Laurel Grove Hosp. | 19933 Lake Chabot | Castro Valley | 94546 |
| Levine General | 22455 Maple Court | Hayward | 94541 |
| Merritt Hospital | Hawthorne & Webster | Oakland | 94609 |
| Oakland Hospital | 2648 E. 14th St. | Oakland | 94601 |
| Peralta Hospital | 450 30th St. | Oakland | 94609 |
| Providence Hosp. | 30th & Summit | Oakland | 94609 |
| St. Rose Hospital | 27200 Calaroga Ave. | Hayward | 94545 |
| U.S. Naval Hospital | 8750 Mountain Blvd. | Oakland | 94605 |
| Valley Memorial | 1111 E. Stanley | Livermore | 94550 |
| Vesper Memorial | 2800 Benedict Dr. | San Leandro | 94577 |
| Veterans Admin. | Arroyo Road | Livermore | 94550 |
| Washington Hospital | 2000 Mowry Ave. | Fremont | 94538 |
| Women's Hospital | 390 40th St. | Oakland | 94609 |

| | | | | |
|---|---|---|---|---|
| Alameda Branch | 8th & Santa Clara | Alameda | 94501 | 415/522-4959 |
| Alameda Law Library | 1225 Fallon St. | Oakland | 94612 | 832-8667 |
| Alameda Main | 2264 Santa Clara | Alameda | 94501 | 522-5413 |
| Albany | 1216 Solano Ave. | Albany | 94706 | 526-3720 |
| *Bancroft Library | U. of California | Berkeley | 94720 | 642-3781 |
| Baymont Branch | 10617 MacArthur | Oakland | 94605 | 568-1579 |
| Berkeley Main | Shattuck & Kittredge | Berkeley | 94704 | 644-6100 |
| Berkeley Branch N. | 1170 The Alameda | Berkeley | 94707 | 644-6850 |
| Berkeley Branch So. | 1901 Russell St. | Berkeley | 94703 | 644-6860 |
| Berkeley Branch W. | 1125 University Ave. | Berkeley | 94702 | 644-6870 |
| Broadmoor Branch | 629 Dutton Ave. | San Leandro | 94577 | 638-9050 |
| Brookfield | 9600 Edes Ave. | Oakland | 94603 | 569-2061 |
| Business/Gov't | 22505 Montgomery | Hayward | 94541 | 881-6328 |
| Castro Valley | 20055 Redwood Rd. | Castro Valley | 94546 | 881-6036 |
| Centerville | 3801 Nicolet | Fremont | 94536 | 791-4789 |
| Claremont Branch | 2940 Benvenue | Berkeley | 94705 | 644-6880 |
| Dimond Branch | 3483 Champion St. | Oakland | 94605 | 530-3881 |
| Dublin | 7606 Amador Valley | Dublin | 94566 | 828-1315 |
| Eastmont Branch | 7900 MacArthur Blvd. | Oakland | 94605 | 568-0503 |
| Eastshore Branch | 1277 Davis St. | San Leandro | 94577 | 632-3703 |
| Elmhurst Branch | 1427 88th Ave. | Oakland | 94621 | 632-1500 |
| Fremont Main | 39770 Paseo Padre | Fremont | 94538 | 791-4794 |
| Glenview Branch | 4231 Park Blvd. | Oakland | 94602 | 530-5770 |
| Golden Gate Branch | 5606 San Pablo Ave. | Oakland | 94608 | 652-3584 |
| Hayward | 22737 Mission Blvd. | Hayward | 94541 | 581-5464 |
| Irvington | 41825 Blacow Rd. | Fremont | 94538 | 791-4785 |
| Lakeview Branch | 550 El Embarcadero | Oakland | 94606 | 451-1610 |
| Latin-American | 1900 Fruitvale Ave. | Oakland | 94601 | 532-7882 |
| Laurel Branch | 3625 MacArthur Blvd. | Oakland | 94619 | 530-1021 |
| Law Library | 224 W. Winton Ave. | Hayward | 94544 | 881-6380 |
| Livermore | 1000 S. Livermore | Livermore | 94550 | 447-2376 |
| Manor Branch | 1307 Manor Blvd. | San Leandro | 94579 | 357-6252 |
| Martin Luther King | 6833 E. 14th | Oakland | 94621 | 632-4861 |
| Marina-Mulford | 13699 Aurora Dr. | San Leandro | 94577 | 357-3850 |
| Melrose Branch | 4905 Foothill Blvd. | Oakland | 94601 | 532-6800 |
| Montclair Branch | 1687 Mountain Blvd. | Oakland | 94611 | 339-9505 |
| Newark | 37101 Newark Blvd. | Newark | 94560 | 791-4792 |
| Niles Branch | 150 1st | Fremont | 94536 | 791-4791 |
| North Oakland | 3132 San Pablo Ave. | Oakland | 94608 | 654-0307 |
| *Oakland LDS | 4780 Lincoln Ave. | Oakland | 94602 | 531-3905 |
| *Oakland Main | 125 14th St. | Oakland | 94612 | 273-3134 |
| Piedmont Avenue | 160 41st St. | Oakland | 94611 | 658-3160 |
| Pleasanton | 4333 Black Ave. | Pleasanton | 94566 | 462-3535 |
| Rockridge Branch | 5701 College Ave. | Oakland | 94618 | 652-1065 |
| San Leandro | 300 Estudillo Ave. | San Leandro | 94577 | 483-1511 |
| San Lorenzo | 395 Paseo Grande | San Lorenzo | 94580 | 881-6034 |
| South Branch | 14799 E. 14th St. | San Leandro | 94578 | 357-5464 |
| Temescal Branch | 5205 Telegraph Ave. | Oakland | 94609 | 652-2504 |
| Union City Branch | 34007 Alvarado-Nils | Union City | 94587 | 471-6771 |
| George Weekes | 27300 Patrick Ave. | Hayward | 94544 | 782-2155 |
| West Oakland Branch | 1801 Adeline St. | Oakland | 94607 | 832-3519 |

## PROFESSIONAL ASSOCIATIONS

Alameda County Bar Association
405 14th Street, Suite 208
Oakland, CA 94612

Alameda/Contra Costa Medical Association
6230 Claremont Avenue
Oakland, CA 94618

ALPINE COUNTY #2

County Seat:  Markleeville
0297  County Code

ALPINE COUNTY OFFICES

| COUNTY OFFICE | ADDRESS | PHONE |
|---|---|---|
| Assessor | P. O. Box 155<br>Markleeville, CA 96120 | 916/694-2283 |
| Clerk<br>  b    from 1900<br>  m    from 1900<br>  d    from 1900<br>  div from 1900<br>  lnd from 1900<br>  pro from 1900 | P. O. Box 158<br>Markleeville, CA 96120 | 916/694-2281 |
| Courts<br>  Juvenile<br><br>  Superior | Courthouse<br>Markleeville, CA 96120<br><br>Courthouse<br>Markleeville, CA 96120 | |
| Recorder | P. O. Box 266<br>Markleeville, CA 96120 | 916/694-2284 |

ADOPTION AGENCIES

Children's Home Society
121 E. Orangeburg Ave., Suite 11
Modesto, CA 95350
209/521-5237

El Dorado County Social Welfare Dept.
Adoption Services
2929 Grandview Street
P.O. Box 1637
Placerville, CA 95667
916/626-2351

AMADOR COUNTY #3

County Seat:  Jackson
0397  Code for entire county

AMADOR COUNTY OFFICES

| COUNTY OFFICE | ADDRESS | PHONE |
|---|---|---|
| Assessor | 108 Court Street<br>Jackson, CA 95642 | 209/223-0732 |
| Clerk<br>  b   from 1872<br>  d   from 1872<br>  m   from 1854<br>  div from 1854<br>  pro from 1854<br>  civ from 1854<br>  lnd from 1854 | 108 Court Street<br>Jackson, CA 95642 | 209/223-0840 |
| Courts<br>  Juvenile<br><br>  Superior | Courthouse<br>Jackson, CA 95642<br><br>108 Court Street<br>Jackson, CA 95642 | |
| Health Department | 810 Court Street<br>Jackson, CA 95642 | 209/223-1696 |
| Recorder | 108 Court Street<br>Jackson, CA 95642 | 209/223-0911 |

ADOPTION AGENCIES

Children's Home Society
Central Valley District
121 E. Orangeburg Ave., Suite 11
Modesto, CA 95350
209/521-5237

State Dept. of Social Services
California Adoption Service
2400 Glendale Lane, Suite B
Sacramento, CA  95825
916/920-6897

CHAMBERS OF COMMERCE

Amador County Chamber of Commerce
P. O. Box 596
Jackson, CA 95642
209/223-0350

HOSPITALS

Amador Hospital
810 Court St.
Jackson, CA 95642

LIBRARIES

| | | | | |
|---|---|---|---|---|
| Amador County | Main Street | Plymouth | 95669 | 209/245-6476 |
| Amador County | 72 Main | Sutter Creek | 95685 | 267-5489 |
| Amador County | East Main | Ione | 95640 | 274-2560 |

50

BUTTE COUNTY #4

County Seat:  Oroville
    0402  Chico
    0405  Gridley
    0407  Oroville
    0498  Rest of County

## BUTTE COUNTY OFFICES

| COUNTY OFFICE | ADDRESS | PHONE |
|---|---|---|
| Assessor | 1855 Bird Street<br>Oroville, CA 95965 | 916/534-4721 |
| Clerk<br>  div from 1850<br>  pro from 1850<br>  civ from 1850 | 25 Country Center Drive<br>Oroville, CA 95965 | 916/534-4296 |
| Courts<br>  Juvenile<br><br>  Superior | Courthouse<br>Oroville, CA 95965<br><br>Courthouse<br>Oroville, CA 95965 | |
| Recorder<br>  b<br>  d<br>  m<br>  lnd | P. O. Box 70<br>Oroville, CA 95965 | 916/534-4691 |
| Vital Statistics | 25 Country Center Drive<br>Oroville, CA 95965 | 916/534-4635 |
| Voter Registration | P. O. Drawer 269<br>Oroville, CA 95965 | 916/534-4296 |

## ADOPTION AGENCIES

Children's Home Society
1216 Sheridon Avenue
Chico, CA 95926
916/342-2464

State Dept. of Social Services
California Adoption Service
500 Cohasset Rd., Suite 34
Chico, CA 95926
916/891-1986

## CEMETERIES

| | | | | |
|---|---|---|---|---|
| Chico Cemetery | 700 Camellia Way | Chico | 95926 | 916/345-7243 |
| Glen Oaks Memorial Pk. | Midway | Chico | 95926 | 343-3002 |
| Gridley-Biggs Cem. Dist. | Highway 99 | Gridley | 95948 | 846-2537 |
| Oroville Cem. Dist. | 5646 Lincoln Blvd. | Oroville | 95965 | 533-2920 |
| Paradise Cem. Dist. | 980 Elliott Rd. | Paradise | 95969 | 877-4493 |

## COLLEGES & UNIVERSITIES

Butte College      Route 1, Box 183A   Oroville 95965
California State U.                    Chico    95929

## HOSPITALS

| | | | |
|---|---|---|---|
| Chico Community Memorial | 560 Cohasset Rd. | Chico | 95926 |
| N. T. Enloe Memorial | 5th Ave & Esplanade | Chico | 95926 |
| Biggs Gridley Memorial | 240 Spruce St. | Gridley | 95948 |
| Medical Center Hospital | 2767 Olive Hwy | Oroville | 95965 |
| Feather River | 5974 Pentz Rd. | Paradise | 95969 |

## LIBRARIES

| | | | | |
|---|---|---|---|---|
| Biggs Branch | 464 A St. | Biggs | 95917 | 916/868-5724 |
| Chico Downtown | West 2nd & Salem | Chico | 95926 | 891-2761 |
| Chico Memorial | 196 Memorial Way | Chico | 95926 | 891-2757 |
| Durham | Dayton Durham Hwy | Durham | 95938 | 343-4094 |
| Gridley | 519 Kentucky | Gridley | 95948 | 846-3323 |
| Paradise | 747 Elliott Rd. | Paradise | 95969 | 872-2961 |
| *Gridley LDS | 348 Spruce St. | Gridley | 95948 | 846-3921 |

## PROFESSIONAL ASSOCIATIONS

Butte-Glenn Medical Society
811 E. Fifth Avenue
Chico, CA 95926

CALAVERAS COUNTY #5

County Seat:  San Andreas
0597  County Code

CALAVERAS COUNTY OFFICES

| COUNTY OFFICE | ADDRESS | PHONE |
|---|---|---|
| Assessor | Government Center<br>San Andreas, CA 95249 | 209/754-4205 |
| Clerk-Recorder<br>b    from 1860<br>m    from 1882<br>d    from 1882<br>div from 1882<br>civ from 1866<br>pro from 1866<br>lnd from 1852<br>min from 1850 | Government Center<br>San Andreas, CA 95249 | 209/754-4285 |
| Courts<br>  Juvenile | Government Center<br>San Andreas, CA 95249 | |
| Superior | Government Center<br>San Andreas, CA 95249 | |
| Elections Clerk | Government Center<br>San Andreas, CA 95249 | 209/754-4252 |

ADOPTION AGENCIES

Children's Home Society
121 E. Orangeburg Ave., Suite 11
Modesto, CA 95350
209/521-5237

State Dept. of Social Services
California Adoption Service
2400 Glendale Lane, Suite B
Sacramento, CA 95825
916/920-6897

CHAMBERS OF COMMERCE

Calaveras County Chamber of Commerce
30 S. Main
San Andreas, CA 95249

HOSPITALS

Mark Twain Hospital District
768 Mountain Ranch Road
San Andreas, CA 95249
209/754-3521

LIBRARIES

| | | | | |
|---|---|---|---|---|
| Angels Camp | 1183 S. Main | Angels Camp | 95222 | 209/736-2198 |
| Arnold Branch | Cedar Center | Arnold | 95223 | 795-1009 |
| Calaveras | 46 N. Main | San Andreas | 95249 | 754-4266 |
| Mokelumne Hill | North Center | Mokelumne | 95245 | 286-1449 |
| Murphys Branch | 384 Main | Murphys | 95247 | 728-3036 |
| Valley Springs | 240 Pine | Valley Spr. | 95252 | 772-1318 |

53

COLUSA COUNTY #6

County Seat:  Colusa
0602  Colusa
0697  Rest of County

COLUSA COUNTY OFFICES

| COUNTY OFFICE | ADDRESS | PHONE |
|---|---|---|
| Assessor | 547 Market Street<br>Colusa, CA 95932 | 916/458-2444 |
| Clerk-Recorder<br>b    from 1873<br>m    from 1853<br>d    from 1889<br>pro from 1851<br>civ from 1851<br>lnd from 1851 | 546 Jay Street<br>Colusa, CA 95932 | 916/458-4660 |
| Courts<br>  Juvenile<br><br>  Superior | Courthouse<br>Colusa, CA 95932<br><br>Courthouse<br>Colusa, CA 95932 | |

ADOPTION AGENCIES

Children's Home Society
Northern District
1216 Sheridon Avenue
Chico, CA 95926
916/342-2464

State Dept. of Social Services
California Adoption Service
500 Cohasset Road., Suite 34
Chico, CA 95926
916/891-1986

CEMETERIES

| | | | |
|---|---|---|---|
| Arbuckle | | Arbuckle | 95912 | 916/476-2534 |
| Catholic | 1741 Wescott Road | Colusa | 95932 | 458-4690 |
| Colusa | 1976 Wilson Ave. | Colusa | 95932 | 458-2650 |
| Williams | Zumwalt Road | Williams | 95987 | 473-5444 |

CHAMBERS OF COMMERCE

Colusa County Chamber of Commerce
506 Market
Colusa, CA 95932
916/458-2541

LIBRARIES

| | | | | |
|---|---|---|---|---|
| Arbuckle | 7th and King | Arbuckle | 95912 | 916/476-2526 |
| Colusa | 738 Market | Colusa | 95932 | 458-7671 |
| Grimes | | Grimes | 95950 | 437-2428 |
| Maxwell | | Maxwell | 95955 | 438-2250 |
| Princeton | | Princeton | 95970 | 439-2235 |
| Williams | | Williams | 95987 | 473-5955 |

County Seat:  Martinez

| | | | |
|---|---|---|---|
| 0701 | Antioch | 0715 | Pittsburg |
| 0704 | Concord | 0718 | Richmond |
| 0707 | El Cerrito | 0720 | San Pablo |
| 0711 | Martinez | 0797 | Rest of County |

## CONTRA COSTA COUNTY OFFICES

| COUNTY OFFICE | ADDRESS | PHONE |
|---|---|---|
| Assessor | 834 Court Street<br>Martinez, CA 94553 | 415/372-2257 |
| Clerk<br>b   from 1850<br>m   from 1850<br>d   from 1850<br>div from 1850<br>pro from 1850<br>civ from 1850<br>lnd from 1850 | 725 Court Street<br>Martinez, CA 94553 | 415/372-2950<br>372-2956 |
| Courts<br>Juvenile<br><br>Superior | 202 Glacier Drive<br>Martinez, CA 94553<br><br>Courthouse<br>Martinez, CA 94553 | |
| Health Department | 1111 Ward<br>Martinez, CA 94553 | 415/372-2516 |
| Recorder | P. O. Box 350<br>822 Main Street<br>Martinez, CA 94553 | 415/372-2366<br>372-2360 |
| Voter Registration | P. O. Box 271<br>524 Main Street<br>Martinez, CA 94553 | 415/372-4166 |

## ADOPTION AGENCIES

Children's Home Society
Golden Gate District
3200 Telegraph Avenue
Oakland, CA 94609
415/655-7406

Contra Costa County Social Services
45 Cleveland Road
Pleasant Hill, CA 94523
415/944-3210

## CEMETERIES

| | | | | |
|---|---|---|---|---|
| Alhambra Cemetery | Carquinez Scenic Dr. | Martinez | 94553 | 415/ |
| Byron B. Knight Cemetery | Highway 4 | Brentwood | 94513 | 634-4748 |
| Catholic Cemetery | Carquinez Scenic Dr. | Martinez | 94553 | |
| Hidden Valley | 4795 Blum Rd. | Pacheco | 94333 | 229-4050 |
| Holy Cross Cemetery | Victory Highway | Antioch | 94509 | 757-0658 |
| Lafayette Cemetery | Mt. Diablo Blvd. | Lafayette | 94549 | 284-1353 |
| Live Oak Cemetery | Academy Road | Concord | 94521 | |
| Memory Gardens | 2011 Arnold Industrial | Concord | 94520 | 685-3464 |
| Oakmont Memorial Park | 2099 Reliez Valley Road | Lafayette | 94549 | 935-3311 |
| Oakview Memorial Park | Hilltop Drive | Antioch | 94509 | 757-4500 |
| Queen of Heaven | 1965 Reliez Valley Road | Lafayette | 94549 | 932-0900 |
| Rolling Hills | Hilltop Drive | Richmond | 94806 | 223-6161 |
| St Joseph Cemetery | 2560 Church Lane | San Pablo | 94806 | 223-1265 |
| St Stephen Cemetery | Monument Boulevard | Concord | 94523 | |
| Sunset Cemetery | 101 Colusa Avenue | El Cerrito | 94530 | 525-5111 |

## CHAMBERS OF COMMERCE

| | | | | |
|---|---|---|---|---|
| Antioch | 414 W. 2nd Street | Antioch | 94509 | 415/757-1800 |
| Bethel Island | P.O. Box 263 | Bethel Island | 94511 | 684-3220 |
| Brentwood | 708 3rd St. | Brentwood | 94513 | 634-3505 |
| Concord | 1331 Concord Ave. | Concord | 94520 | 685-1181 |
| El Cerrito | 10506 San Pablo Ave. | El Cerrito | 94530 | 527-5333 |
| El Sobrante | 3730 San Pablo Dam Rd. | El Sobrante | 94802 | 223-0757 |
| Lafayette | 1003 Oak Hill Road | Lafayette | 94549 | 284-7404 |
| Martinez | 609 Main Street | Martinez | 94553 | 228-2345 |
| Orinda | 61 Moraga Way | Orinda | 94563 | 254-3909 |
| Pinole | P.O. Box 1 | Pinole | 94564 | 758-4484 |
| Pittsburg | 2010 Railroad Ave. | Pittsburg | 94565 | 432-7301 |
| Pleasant Hill | 1881 Contra Costa | Pleasant Hill | 94528 | 687-0700 |
| Richmond | 3925 MacDonald Ave. | Richmond | 94805 | 234-3512 |
| San Pablo | 13858 San Pablo Ave. | San Pablo | 94806 | 234-2067 |
| San Ramon Valley | 375 Diablo Road | Danville | 94526 | 837-4400 |
| Walnut Creek | 1359 Locust Street | Walnut Creek | 94596 | 934-2000 |

## COLLEGES & UNIVERSITIES

| | | | |
|---|---|---|---|
| Contra Costa College | 2600 Mission Bell Dr. | San Pablo | 94806 |
| Diablo Valley College | 321 Golf Club Road | Pleasant Hill | 94523 |
| John F. Kennedy Univ. | 12 Altarinda Road | Orinda | 94563 |
| Los Medanos College | 2700 E. Leland Road | Pittsburg | 94565 |
| St. Mary's College | St. Mary's Road | Moraga | 94556 |

## HOSPITALS

| | | | |
|---|---|---|---|
| Brookside | Vale Road | San Pablo | 94806 |
| Contra Costa County | 2500 Alhambra | Martinez | 94553 |
| Delta Memorial | 3901 Lone Tree | Antioch | 94509 |
| Doctors | 2151 Appian Way | Pinole | 94564 |
| John Muir | 1601 Ygnacio Valley | Walnut Creek | 94598 |
| Kaiser Permanente | 200 Muir Road | Martinez | 94553 |
| Kaiser Permanente | 14th & Cutting Blvd. | Richmond | 94804 |
| Kaiser Permanente | 1425 S. Main | Walnut Creek | 94596 |
| Los Medanos | 550 School Street | Pittsburg | 94565 |
| Mt. Diablo | 2540 East Street | Concord | 94520 |
| Richmond | 23rd & Gaynor | Richmond | 94804 |

## LIBRARIES

| | | | | |
|---|---|---|---|---|
| Antioch | 501 W. 18th Street | Antioch | 94509 | 415/757-2100 |
| Bayview | 5100 Harnett | Richmond | 94804 | 237-3166 |
| Brentwood | 751 3rd St. | Brentwood | 94513 | 634-4101 |
| Central | 1750 Oak Park Blvd. | Pleasant Hill | 94523 | 944-3434 |
| Concord | 2900 Salvio Street | Concord | 94519 | 671-4455 |
| Crockett | 991 Loring Avenue | Crockett | 94525 | 787-2345 |
| El Cerrito | 6510 Stockton | El Cerrito | 94530 | 526-7512 |
| El Sobrante | 4191 Appian Way | El Sobrante | 94803 | 223-1491 |
| Kensington | 61 Arlington | Kensington | 94707 | 524-3-43 |
| LaFayette | 952 Morage Road | LaFayette | 94549 | 283-3872 |
| Martinez | 740 Court Street | Martinez | 94553 | 372-2898 |
| Moraga | 1500 St. Mary's | Moraga | 94556 | 376-6852 |
| Oakley | 210 O'Hara | Oakley | 94561 | 675-2400 |
| Orinda | 2 Irwin Way | Orinda | 94563 | 254-2184 |
| Pacheco | 110 Center Avenue | Pacheco | 94553 | 689-7226 |
| Pinole | 2935 Pinole Valley | Pinole | 94564 | 758-2741 |
| Pittsburg | 80 Power Ave. | Pittsburg | 94565 | 439-4390 |
| Richmond Main | Civic Center Plaza | Richmond | 94804 | 231-2122 |
| Richmond West | 135 Washington Ave. | Richmond | 94801 | 232-7169 |
| Rodeo | 220 Pacific Ave. | Rodeo | 94572 | 799-2606 |
| San Pablo | 2101 Market Avenue | Danville | 94806 | 234-0698 |
| San Ramon Valley | 555 S. Hartz Ave. | Walnut Creek | 94526 | 837-4889 |
| Walnut Creek | 1644 N. Broadway | Walnut Creek | 94596 | 934-5373 |

## PROFESSIONAL ASSOCIATIONS

Alameda-Contra Costa Medical Association
6230 Claremont Avenue
Oakland, CA 94618

Mt. Diablo Bar Association
1910 Olympic Blvd., Suite 325
Walnut Creek, CA 94596

County Seat:  Crescent City
0897  County Code

## DEL NORTE COUNTY OFFICES

| COUNTY OFFICES | ADDRESS | PHONE |
|---|---|---|
| Assessor | 450 "H" Street<br>Crescent City, CA 95531 | 707/464-3115 |
| Clerk<br>  div from 1848<br>  pro from 1848<br>  civ from 1848 | Courthouse, Room 15<br>Crescent City, CA 95531 | 707/464-2167 |
| Courts<br>  Juvenile<br><br>  Superior | Courthouse<br>Crescent City, CA 95531<br><br>Courthouse<br>Crescent City, CA 95531 | |
| Elections Division | Courthouse, Room 15<br>Crescent City, CA 95531 | 707/464-1223 |
| Recorder<br>  b<br>  m<br>  d<br>  lnd | Courthouse, Room 15<br>Crescent City, CA 95531 | 707/464-6911 |

## ADOPTION AGENCIES

Children's Home Society
3200 Telegraph Avenue
Oakland, CA 94609
415/655-7406

State Dept. of Social Services
California Adoption Service
2350 Professional Drive
Santa Rosa, CA 95406
707/545-2921

## HOSPITALS

Seaside Hospital and Medical Clinic
100 A Street
Crescent City, CA 95531

## PROFESSIONAL ASSOCIATIONS

Humboldt-Del Norte County Medical Society
732 Fifth Street
P. O. Box 1395
Eureka, CA 95501

# EL DORADO COUNTY #9

County Seat: Placerville
0902 Placerville
0997 Rest of County

## EL DORADO COUNTY OFFICES

| COUNTY OFFICE | ADDRESS | PHONE |
|---|---|---|
| Assessor | 360 Fair Lane<br>Placerville, CA 95667 | 916/626-2317 |
| Clerk<br>  civ from 1850<br>  pro<br>  min from 1850<br>  lnd from 1850 | 495 Main<br>Placerville, CA 95667 | 916/626-2371 |
| Courts<br>  Juvenile<br><br>  Superior | 295 Fair Lane<br>Placerville, CA 95667<br><br>2850 Cold Springs Road<br>Placerville, CA 95667 | |
| Elections Department<br><br>Health Department | 495 Main<br>Placerville, CA 95667<br><br>931 Spring<br>Placerville, CA 95667 | 916/626-2266<br><br>916/626-2302 |
| Recorder<br>  b   from 1905<br>  d   from 1905<br>  m   from 1905 | 360 Fair Lane<br>Placerville, CA 95667 | 916/626-2461 |

## ADOPTION AGENCIES

Children's Home Society
121 E. Orangeburg, Suite 11
Modesto, CA 95350
209/521-5237

El Dorado County Social Services
2929 Grandview Street
Placerville, CA 95667
916/626-2351

## CEMETERIES

| | | | | |
|---|---|---|---|---|
| Happy Homestead Cemetery | 1261 Johnson Blvd. | S. Lake Tahoe | 95731 | 916/541-7070 |
| Placerville Union | 2855 Cold Springs Rd. | Placerville | 95667 | 622-3813 |
| Westwood Hills | 2720 Cold Springs Rd. | Placerville | 95667 | 622-2223 |

## CHAMBERS OF COMMERCE

El Dorado County Chamber of Commerce
542 Main
Placerville, CA 95667
916/626-2344

COLLEGES AND UNIVERSITIES

Lake Tahoe Community College
2559 Lake Tahoe Blvd.
South Lake Tahoe, CA 95702


HOSPITALS

Barton Memorial Hospital          Marshall Hospital
Fourth and South Streets          Marshall Way
South Lake Tahoe, CA 95731        Placerville, CA 95667


LIBRARIES

| | | | | |
|---|---|---|---|---|
| El Dorado County | 3058 Highway 50 | S. Lake Tahoe | 95731 | 916/544-4416 |
| Georgetown Main | | Georgetown | 95634 | 333-4724 |
| Shingle Springs | French Creek Rd. | Shingle Springs | 95682 | 677-2463 |

FRESNO COUNTY #10

County Seat: Fresno
1003 Clovis      1017 Sanger
1004 Coalinga    1019 Selma
1008 Fresno      1097 Rest of County
1016 Reedley

## FRESNO COUNTY OFFICES

| COUNTY OFFICE | ADDRESS | PHONE |
|---|---|---|
| Assessor | 201 Hall of Records<br>Tulare & "M" Streets<br>Fresno, CA 93715 | 209/488-3514 |
| Clerk<br>  b  from 1855<br>  d  from 1855<br>  m  from 1855<br>  div from 1860<br>  civ from 1860<br>  pro from 1860<br>  bur from 1900 | 1100 Van Ness Avenue<br>Fresno, CA 93715 | 209/488-3003<br>488-3617 |
| Courts<br>  Juvenile | Room 100, Courthouse<br>P. O. Box 1628<br>Fresno, CA 93717 | |
|   Superior | Courthouse<br>P. O. Box 1628<br>Fresno, CA 93717 | |
| Recorder | 2281 Tulare, Room 303<br>P. O. Box 1628<br>Fresno, CA 93728 | 209/488-3476 |
| Voter Registration | 1234 "L" Street<br>Fresno, CA 93721 | 209/488-3246 |

## ADOPTION AGENCIES

Children's Home Society
703 North Fulton
Fresno, CA 93728
209/486-0355

Infant of Prague Adoption Service
1510 N. Fresno Street
Fresno, CA 93703
209/237-0851

Department of Social Services
4455 Kings Canyon Road
Fresno, CA 93702
209/255-9711

## CEMETERIES

| | | | | |
|---|---|---|---|---|
| Ararat Cemetery Asso. | W. Belmont Avenue | Fresno | 93728 | 209/237-8115 |
| Belmont Memorial | 201 N. Teilman | Fresno | 93706 | 237-6185 |
| Clovis Cemetery Dist. | 305 N. Villa | Clovis | 93612 | 299-6057 |
| Fresno Catholic | 264 N. Blythe | Fresno | 93706 | 485-6422 |
| Fresno Memorial | 175 S. Cornelia | Fresno | 93706 | 268-7823 |
| Kingsburg | S. Academy Avenue | Kingsburg | 93631 | 897-2426 |
| Mountain View | 1411 W. Belmont | Fresno | 93728 | 233-3327 |
| Selma Cemetery | E. Floral Avenue | Selma | 93662 | 896-2412 |
| Washington Colony | 7318 S. Elm Avenue | Fresno | 93706 | 264-7577 |

## CHAMBERS OF COMMERCE

| | | | | |
|---|---|---|---|---|
| Firebaugh | 1501 16th | Firebaugh | 93622 | 209/659-3701 |
| Fresno | P.O. Box 1460 | Fresno | 93716 | |
| Kingsburg | 1401 California | Kingsburg | 93631 | 897-2925 |

## COLLEGES & UNIVERSITIES

| | | | |
|---|---|---|---|
| California Christian | 4881 E. University | Fresno | 93703 |
| California State U. | | Fresno | 93740 |
| Fresno City College | 1101 University | Fresno | 93741 |
| Mennonite Brethren | 4824 E. Butler | Fresno | 93727 |
| Pacific College | 1717 S. Chestnut | Fresno | 93702 |
| Reedley College | 995 N. Reed | Reedley | 93654 |
| West Coast Bible | 6901 N. Maple | Fresno | 93710 |
| West Hills College | 300 Cherry Lane | Coalinga | 93210 |

## HOSPITALS

| | | | |
|---|---|---|---|
| Clovis Memorial | 88 N. Dewitt | Clovis | 93612 |
| Coalinga District | Sunset & Washington | Coalinga | 93210 |
| Fowler Memorial | 420 E. Merced | Fowler | 93625 |
| Fresno Community | Fresno & R Streets | Fresno | 93715 |
| Kings View | 42675 Road 44 | Reedley | 93654 |
| Sanger | 2558 Jensen Ave. | Sanger | 93657 |
| Selma District | 1141 Rose Avenue | Selma | 93662 |
| Sierra | 2025 E. Dakota | Fresno | 93726 |
| Sierra Kings | 372 W. Cypress | Reedley | 93654 |
| St. Agnes | 1303 E. Herndon | Fresno | 93710 |
| Valley Medical | 445 S. Cedar Ave. | Fresno | 93702 |

## LIBRARIES

| | | | | |
|---|---|---|---|---|
| Cedar-Clinton | 4150 E. Clinton | Fresno | 93703 | 209/442-1770 |
| Clovis | 1155 5th | Clovis | 93612 | 299-9531 |
| Coalinga | N. 4th & Durian | Coalinga | 93210 | 935-1676 |
| Easton | 24 W. Willamette | Easton | 93706 | 237-3929 |
| Fig Garden | 5041 N. Palm Ave. | Fresno | 93704 | 222-7445 |
| Fresno County | 13357 S. Henderson | Caruthers | 93609 | 864-8766 |
| Fresno County | 1310 Draper | Kingsburg | 93631 | 897-3710 |
| Fresno County | 667 Quince | Mendota | 93640 | 655-3391 |
| Fresno County | 523 Park Blvd. | Orange Cove | 93646 | 626-7942 |
| Fresno County | 2200 Selma | Selma | 93662 | 896-3393 |
| Gillis | 629 W. Dakota | Fresno | 93705 | 225-0140 |
| Huron | 36050 Huron | Huron | 93234 | 945-2284 |
| Ivy Center | E. Annadale | Fresno | 93706 | 264-6119 |
| *LDS | 1838 Echo | Fresno | 93704 | 485-9522 |
| Mosqueda | 4670 E. Butter | Fresno | 93702 | 488-3212 |
| Pinedale | 7170 N. San Pablo | Pinedale | 93650 | 439-0486 |
| Politi | 5771 N. 1st | Fresno | 93710 | 431-6450 |
| Sunnyside | 5574 E. Kings Canyon | Fresno | 93727 | 255-6594 |

## PROFESSIONAL ASSOCIATIONS

Fresno County Bar Association
409 T W Patterson Building
Fresno, CA 93721

GLENN COUNTY #11

County Seat: Willows
1102   Willows
1197   Rest of County

GLENN COUNTY OFFICES

| COUNTY OFFICE | ADDRESS | PHONE |
|---|---|---|
| Assessor | 526 W. Sycamore Street<br>Willows, CA 95988 | 916/934-4789 |
| Clerk-Recorder<br>m     from 1891<br>div from 1891<br>pro<br>civ | 526 W. Sycamore Street<br>Willows, CA 95988 | 916/934-3367 |
| Courts<br>  Juvenile<br><br>  Superior | Courthouse<br>Willows, CA 95988<br><br>Courthouse<br>Willows, CA 95988 | |
| Elections Clerk | Courthouse<br>Willows, CA 95988 | 916/934-3364 |

ADOPTION AGENCIES

Children's Home Society
1216 Sheridan Avenue
Chico, CA 95926
916/342-2464

State Dept. of Social Services
California Adoption Service
500 Cohasset Road, Suite 34
Chico, CA 95926
916/891-1986

CHAMBERS OF COMMERCE

Glenn County Chamber of Commerce
920 W. Wood
Willows, CA 95988

Willows Chamber of Commerce
920 W. Wood
Willows, CA 95988

HOSPITALS

Glenn General Hospital
1133 W. Sycamore
Willows, CA 95988
916/934-3351

LIBRARIES

North State Library System
135 S. Tehama
Willows, CA 95988
916/934-7841

Orland City Library
333 Mill
Orland, CA 95963
916/865-3465

Willows City Library
201 N. Lassen
Willows, CA 95988
916/934-5156

PROFESSIONAL ASSOCIATIONS

Butte-Glenn Medical Society
811 E. Fifth Avenue
Chico, CA 95926

# HUMBOLDT COUNTY #12

### County Seat: Eureka
1201 Arcata
1205 Eureka
1297 Rest of County

## HUMBOLDT COUNTY OFFICES

| COUNTY OFFICE | ADDRESS | PHONE |
|---|---|---|
| Assessor | 825 5th Street<br>Eureka, CA 95501 | 707/445-7276 |
| Clerk<br>  m<br>  div from 1886<br>  pro from 1886<br>  civ from 1886<br>  nat from 1886 | 825 5th Street<br>Eureka, CA 95501 | 707/445-7503 |
| Courts<br>  Juvenile<br><br>  Superior | 2002 Harrison Ave.<br>Eureka, CA 95501<br><br>825 5th Street<br>Eureka, CA 95501 | |
| Recorder<br>  b<br>  d<br>  lnd | 825 5th Street<br>Eureka, CA 95501 | 707/445-7593 |
| Voter Registration | 3033 "H" Street<br>Eureka, CA 95501 | 707/445-7678 |

## ADOPTION AGENCIES

Children's Home Society
2575 Harris, Apt. 1
Eureka, CA 95501
707/442-8912

State Dept. of Social Services
California Adoption Service
2350 Professional Drive
Santa Rosa, CA 95406
707/545-2921

## CEMETERIES

Greenwood Cemetery Association
1757 J Street
Arcata, CA 95521
707/822-1664

Ocean View Cemetery
P. O. Box 998
Eureka, CA 95501
707/442-4173

## CHAMBERS OF COMMERCE

| | | | | |
|---|---|---|---|---|
| Arcata | Avenue of the Giants | Arcata | 95521 | 707/822-3619 |
| Eureka | 2112 Broadway | Eureka | 95501 | 442-3738 |
| Fortuna | 734 14th | Fortuna | 95540 | 725-3959 |
| Rio Dell | 715 Wildwood | Rio Dell | 95562 | 764-3436 |
| Trinidad | Scenic Drive & Main | Trinidad | 95570 | 677-3874 |

## COLLEGES & UNIVERSITIES

College of the Redwoods
Eureka, CA 95501
707/443-8411

Humboldt State University
Arcata, CA 95521
707/826-3011

## HOSPITALS

| | | | |
|---|---|---|---|
| General Hospital | Harris & H Streets | Eureka | 95501 |
| Humboldt Medical | Box 1328 | Hoopa | 95546 |
| Mad River | 3800 James Road | Arcata | 95521 |
| Redwood Memorial | 3300 Renner Drive | Fortuna | 95540 |
| St. Joseph | 2700 Dolbeer St. | Eureka | 95501 |

## LIBRARIES

| | | | | |
|---|---|---|---|---|
| Fortuna Public | 14th and N. | Fortuna | 95540 | 707/725-3460 |
| *LDS | 2734 Dolbeer | Eureka | 95501 | 443-7411 |
| Rio Dell | 714 Wildwood | Rio Dell | 95562 | 764-3436 |
| Trinidad | 410 Trinity | Trinidad | 95570 | 677-0227 |

## PROFESSIONAL ASSOCIATIONS

Humboldt-Del Norte County Medical Society
732 Fifth Street
P. O. Box 1395
Eureka, CA 95501

# IMPERIAL COUNTY #13

County Seat: El Centro
1301 Brawley
1302 Calexico
1304 El Centro
1397 Rest of County

## IMPERIAL COUNTY OFFICES

| COUNTY OFFICE | ADDRESS | PHONE |
|---|---|---|
| Assessor | 939 Main Street<br>El Centro, CA 92243 | 714/339-4375 |
| Clerk<br>  m   from 1907<br>  div from 1907<br>  pro from 1907<br>  civ from 1907 | 939 Main Street<br>P. O. Box 1560<br>El Centro, CA 92243 | 714/339-4375 |
| Courts<br>  Juvenile<br><br><br>  Superior | Courthouse<br>939 Main Street<br>El Centro, CA 92243<br><br>Courthouse<br>939 Main Street<br>El Centro, CA 92243 | |
| Recorder<br>  b from 1907<br>  m from 1907<br>  d from 1907 | 939 Main Street<br>El Centro, CA 92243 | 714/339-4375 |
| Voter Registration | 939 Main Street<br>El Centro, CA 92243 | 714/339-4375 |

## ADOPTION AGENCIES

Children's Home Society
7695 Cardinal Court
San Diego, CA 92123
714/278-7800

Imperial County Welfare Dept.
1070 N. Imperial Avenue
El Centro, CA 92243
714/353-1400

## CEMETERIES

Evergreen Cemetery
201 E. Gillette Road
El Centro, CA 92243
714/352-1468

Riverview Cemetery
4700 Hovley Drive
Brawley, CA 92227
714/344-4921

## COLLEGES & UNIVERSITIES

Imperial Valley College
111 & Ira Aten Road
Imperial, CA 92251

## HOSPITALS

Calexico Hospital
450 Birch Street
Calexico, CA 92231

Pioneers Memorial Hospital
207 W. Legion Road
Brawley, CA 92227

## LIBRARIES

| Brawley | 400 Main | Brawley | 92227 | 714/344-1891 |
| Calexico | 420 Heber | Calexico | 92231 | 357-2605 |
| El Centro | 539 State | El Centro | 92243 | 352-0751 |
| Imperial | 200 W. 9th | Imperial | 92251 | 355-1332 |

## PROFESSIONAL ASSOCIATIONS

Imperial County Medical Society
Imperial, CA 92251

INYO COUNTY #14

County Seat: Independence
1401 Bishop
1497 Rest of County

INYO COUNTY OFFICES

| COUNTY OFFICE | ADDRESS | PHONE |
|---|---|---|
| Assessor | Courthouse, N. Edwards<br>Independence, CA 93526 | 714/878-2411 |
| Clerk<br>  b   from 1904<br>  d   from 1904<br>  m   from 1866<br>  div from 1866<br>  pro from 1866<br>  civ from 1866<br>  lnd from 1866<br>  min from 1872 | Courthouse, Drawer F<br>Independence, CA 93526 | 714/878-2411 |
| Courts<br>  Juvenile<br><br>  Superior | P. O. Box 306<br>Independence, CA 93526<br><br>Courthouse<br>Independence, CA 93526 | |
| Voter Registration | P. O. Drawer F<br>Independence, CA 93526 | 714/878-2411 |

ADOPTION AGENCIES

Children's Home Society
703 Truxtun Avenue
Bakersfield, CA 93301
805/324-4091

Kern County Welfare Dept.
Adoption Services
1800 19th St.
Bakersfield, CA 93301
805/861-3558

CEMETERIES

Pioneer Cemetery District
Bishop, CA 93514
714/873-6260

CHAMBERS OF COMMERCE

Bishop Chamber of Commerce
690 N. Main
Center City Park
Bishop, CA 93514
714/872-4731

HOSPITALS

Northern Inyo Hospital
150 Pioneer Lane
Bishop, CA 93514

Southern Inyo Hospital
501 E. Locust Street
Lone Pine, CA 93545

## KERN COUNTY #15

County Seat: Bakersfield

| | | | |
|---|---|---|---|
| 1502 | Bakersfield | 1528 | Wasco |
| 1518 | Delano | 1597 | Rest of County |
| 1520 | Taft | | |

## KERN COUNTY OFFICES

| COUNTY OFFICE | ADDRESS | PHONE |
|---|---|---|
| Assessor | 1415 Truxtun Avenue<br>Bakersfield, CA 93301 | 805/861-2311 |
| Clerk<br>  div from 1866<br>  pro from 1866<br>  civ from 1866 | 1415 Truxtun Avenue<br>Bakersfield, CA 93301 | 805/861-2621 |
| Courts<br>  Juvenile<br><br><br><br>  Superior | P. O. Box 3309, Station A<br>1830 Ridge Road<br>Bakersfield, CA 93305<br><br>1415 Truxtun Avenue<br>Bakersfield, CA 93301 | |
| Recorder<br>  b<br>  d<br>  m | 1415 Truxtun Avenue<br>Bakersfield, CA 93301 | 805/861-2181 |
| Voter Records | Kern County Civic Center<br>1415 Truxtun Avenue<br>Bakersfield, CA 93301 | 805/861-2625 |

## ADOPTION AGENCIES

Children's Home Society
703 Truxtun Avenue
Bakersfield, CA 93301
805/324-4091

Kern County Welfare Dept.
Adoption Services
1800 19th St.
Bakersfield, CA 93302
805/861-2558

## CEMETERIES

| | | | |
|---|---|---|---|
| California City | 22000 Mojave-Randsberg | California City | 93505 |
| Desert Memorial | San Bernardino Road | Ridgecrest | 93555 |
| East Kern | 2040 Belshaw Street | County | |
| Greenlawn | 3700 River Blvd. | Bakersfield | 93305 |
| Hillcrest | 9101 Kern Canyon | Bakersfield | 93306 |
| Johannesburg | Fremont & Mountain | County | 93528 |
| Kern River Valley | Burlando Road | County | |
| North Kern | 35 Garces Highway | Delano | 93215 |
| Shafter | 18662 Central Valley | County | 93263 |
| Tehachapi | 208 S. Green Street | Tehachapi | 93561 |
| Union | King & Potomac | Bakersfield | 93307 |
| Wasco | Highway 46 & Leonard | County | 93280 |

## CHAMBERS OF COMMERCE

| | | | |
|---|---|---|---|
| Arvin | 419 N. Hill Street | Arvin | 93203 |
| Bakersfield | 1807 19th Street | Bakersfield | 93301 |
| California City | 9501 Calif. City Blvd. | Calif City | 93505 |
| Delano | 9th and High | Delano | 93215 |
| Frazier Park | 3537 Mt. Pinos Road | County | 93225 |
| McFarland | 401 W. Kern Avenue | McFarland | 93250 |
| Mojave | 15954 Sierra Hwy | County | 93501 |
| Ridgecrest | 303 S. China Lake | Ridgecrest | 93555 |
| Rosamond | 2875 Sierra Hwy | Rosamond | 93560 |
| Shafter | 109 Pacific Ave. | Shafter | 93263 |
| Taft | 314 4th Street | Taft | 93268 |
| Tehachapi | P. O. Box 410 | Tehachapi | 93561 |
| Wasco | 628 'E' Street | Wasco | 93280 |

## COLLEGES & UNIVERSITIES

| | | | |
|---|---|---|---|
| Bakersfield College | 1801 Panorama | Bakersfield | 93305 |
| California State | 4001 Stockdale | Bakersfield | 93309 |
| Cerro Coso Community | College Heights | Ridgecrest | 93555 |
| Taft College | 29 Emmons Park | Taft | 93268 |

## HOSPITALS

| | | | |
|---|---|---|---|
| Bakersfield Community | 901 Olive Drive | Bakersfield | 93308 |
| Boron Citizens | 12500 Boron Ave. | Boron | 93516 |
| Delano Community | Oxford & Garces | Delano | 93215 |
| Greater Bakersfield | 420 34th St. | Bakersfield | 93302 |
| Kern Medical Center | 1830 Flower | Bakersfield | 93305 |
| Mercy | 2215 Truxtun | Bakersfield | 93301 |
| North Kern | Palm & 7th | Wasco | 93280 |
| Ridgecrest Community | 1081 N. China Lake | Ridgecrest | 93555 |
| San Joaquin | 2615 Eye Street | Bakersfield | 93301 |
| Tehachapi | 115 W. 'E' Street | Tehachapi | 93561 |
| West Side | 110 E. North St. | Taft | 93268 |

## LIBRARIES

| | | | |
|---|---|---|---|
| Arvin | 123 'A' Street | Arvin | 93203 |
| Baker | 1400 Baker St. | Bakersfield | 93305 |
| Beale | 1315 Truxtun Ave. | Bakersfield | 93301 |
| Boron | 27070 Twenty Mule Team | Boron | 93516 |
| Buttonwillow | 116 S. Buttonwillow | Buttonwillow | 93206 |
| California City | 8146 Aspen Mall | Calif City | 93505 |
| Delano | 925 10th Avenue | Delano | 93215 |
| Edwards | Popson Avenue | Edwards AFB | 93523 |
| Holloway-Gonzales | 506 E. Brundage Lane | Bakersfield | 93307 |
| Kernville | 48 Tobias Street | Kernville | 93238 |
| Lamont | 10517 Main Street | Lamont | 93241 |
| *LDS | 316 'A' Street | Bakersfield | 93304 |
| *LDS | 501 Norma Street | Ridgecrest | 93555 |
| McFarland | 200 2nd Street | McFarland | 93250 |
| Mojave | 2320 Belshaw Street | Mojave | 93501 |
| Oildale | 1119 N. Chester Ave. | Oildale | 93308 |
| Ridgecrest | 250 W. Ridgecrest | Ridgecrest | 93555 |
| Rosamond | 2645 Diamond Street | Rosamond | 93560 |
| Shafter | 236 James Street | Shafter | 93263 |
| Taft | 27 Emmons Park Drive | Taft | 93268 |
| Tehachapi | 310 S. Green Street | Tehachapi | 93561 |
| Wasco | 1102 7th Street | Wasco | 93280 |

## PROFESSIONAL ASSOCIATIONS

Kern County Medical Society
2012 18th Street
Bakersfield, CA 93301

KINGS COUNTY #16

County Seat:  Hanford
             1603  Corcoran
             1604  Hanford
             1697  Rest of County

## KINGS COUNTY OFFICES

| COUNTY OFFICE | ADDRESS | PHONE |
|---|---|---|
| Assessor | Box C, Courthouse<br>Hanford, CA 93230 | 209/582-3211 |
| Clerk<br>  b    from 1893<br>  d    from 1893<br>  m    from 1893<br>  div from 1893<br>  pro from 1893<br>  civ from 1893<br>  nat from 1893 | 1400 W. Lacey Boulevard<br>Hanford, CA 93230 | 209/582-3211 |
| Courts<br>  Juvenile<br><br><br><br>  Superior | Courthouse<br>P. O. Box C<br>Hanford, CA 93230<br><br>Courthouse<br>P. O. Box C<br>Hanford, CA 93230 | |
| Recorder | 1400 W. Lacey Boulevard<br>Hanford, CA 93230 | 209/582-3211<br>EX2470 |
| Voter Registration | 1400 W. Lacey Boulevard<br>Hanford, CA 93230 | 209/582-3211<br>EX2433 |

## ADOPTION AGENCIES

Children's Home Society
703 Truxtun Avenue
Bakersfield, CA 93301
805/324-4091

State Dept. of Social Services
California Adoption Service
2400 Glendale Lane, Suite B
Sacramento, CA 95825
916/920-6897

## CEMETERIES

Hanford Cemetery District
10500 10th Avenue
Hanford, CA 93230
209/584-3937

Lemoore Cemetery District
1441 18th Avenue
Lemoore, CA 93245
209/924-2185

## HOSPITALS

| | | | |
|---|---|---|---|
| Avenal District | 3rd and Alpine | Avenal | 93204 |
| Corcoran | 1310 Hanna Ave. | Corcoran | 93212 |
| Hanford Community | 450 Greenfield | Hanford | 93230 |
| Sacred Heart | 1025 N. Douty | Hanford | 93230 |

## LIBRARIES

| | | | | |
|---|---|---|---|---|
| Armona | 10953 14th Avenue | Armona | 93202 | 209/584-6293 |
| Avenal | 236 Fresno | Avenal | 93204 | · 386-5741 |
| Grangeville | 14020 School | Grangeville | 93203 | 584-4805 |
| Hanford | 401 N. Douty | Hanford | 93230 | 582-0261 |
| Lemoore | 457 C. | Lemoore | 93245 | 924-2188 |
| Stratford | 20300 Main | Stratford | 93244 | 947-3003 |

## PROFESSIONAL ASSOCIATIONS

Kings County Medical Society
P. O. Box 1003
Hanford, CA 93230

LAKE COUNTY #17

County Seat: Lakeport
1979 County

LAKE COUNTY OFFICES

| COUNTY OFFICE | ADDRESS | PHONE |
|---|---|---|
| Assessor | Courthouse, Main Street<br>Lakeport, CA 95453 | 707/263-2302 |
| Clerk<br>  b    from 1867<br>  d    from 1867<br>  m    from 1867<br>  div from 1867<br>  lnd from 1867<br>  map indices | 255 N. Forbes Street<br>Lakeport, CA 95453 | 707/263-2371 |
| Courts<br>  Juvenile<br><br><br>  Superior<br>  div from 1867<br>  pro from 1867<br>  civ from 1867 | Courthouse<br>Lakeport, CA 95453<br><br>Courthouse<br>Lakeport, CA 95453 | |
| Recorder | 255 N. Forbes Street<br>Lakeport, CA 95453 | 707/263-2293 |
| Voter Registration | 225 N. Forbes Street<br>Lakeport, CA 95453 | 707/263-2372 |

ADOPTION AGENCIES

Children's Home Society
3200 Telegraph Avenue
Oakland, CA 94609
415/655-7406

State Dept. of Social Services
California Adoption Service
2350 Professional Drive
Santa Rosa, CA 95406
707/545-2921

CEMETERIES

Hartley Cemetery District
2552 Hill Road
Lakeport, CA 95453
707/263-0910

CHAMBERS OF COMMERCE

Clear Lake   Lakeshore Drive     Clear Lake Park   95424
Lake City    875 Lakeport Blvd.  Lake City         95453
Lakeport     364 Main            Lakeport          95453

HOSPITALS

Lakeside Community Hospital     Redbud Community Hospital
5176 Hill Road East             15630 18th Avenue
Lakeport, CA 95453              Clearlake Highlands, CA 95422

LIBRARIES

Lakeport     200 Park                Lakeport              95453   707/263-2291
Middletown   Calistoga & Callayomi   Middletown            95461         987-3674
Redbud       Golf Avenue             Clear Lake Highlands  95422         994-5115
Upper Lake   310 2nd                 Upper Lake            95485         275-2049

County Seat:  Susanville
1801  Susanville
1897  Rest of County

LASSEN COUNTY OFFICES

| COUNTY OFFICE | ADDRESS | PHONE |
|---|---|---|
| Assessor | South Lassen Street<br>Susanville, CA 96130 | 916/257-5331 |
| Clerk<br>  div from 1864<br>  pro from 1864<br>  civ from 1864 | Courthouse<br>Lassen Street<br>Susanville, CA 96130 | 916/257-7191 |
| Courts<br>  Juvenile<br><br>  Superior | Courthouse<br>Susanville, CA 96130<br><br>Courthouse<br>Susanville, CA 96130 | |
| Recorder<br>  b<br>  d<br>  m<br>  lnd | Courthouse<br>Susanville, CA 96130 | 916/257-7231 |

ADOPTION AGENCIES

Children's Home Society
1216 Sheridan Avenue
Chico, CA 95926
916/342-2464

State Dept. of Social Services
California Adoption Service
500 Cohasset Road, Suite 34
Chico, CA 95926
916/891-1986

CEMETERIES

Lassen County Cemetery
Chestnut Street
Susanville, CA 96130
916/257-3038

CHAMBERS OF COMMERCE

Roops Fort Chamber of Commerce
75 N. Weatherlow
Susanville, CA 96130
916/257-4323

COLLEGES & UNIVERSITIES

Lassen College
Highway 139
Susanville, CA 96130

HOSPITALS

Lassen Memorial Hospital
Hospital Lane & West Street
Susanville, CA 96130

County Seat:  Los Angeles

| | | |
|---|---|---|
| 7001 Alhambra | 7035 Glendora | 7068 Palos Verdes |
| 7003 Arcadia | 7038 Hawthorne | 7069 Pasadena |
| 7006 Azusa | 7039 Hermosa Beach | 7071 Pomona |
| 7008 Baldwin Park | 7040 Huntington Park | 7073 Redondo Beach |
| 7012 Belvedere Township | 7042 Inglewood | 7076 San Fernando |
| 7013 Beverly Hills | 7045 Lakewood | 7077 San Gabriel |
| 7014 Burbank | 7047 La Puente | 7078 San Marino |
| 7017 Claremont | 7048 La Verne | 7080 Santa Monica |
| 7019 Compton | 7052 Long Beach | 7081 Sierra Madre |
| 7020 Covina | 7053 Los Angeles | 7082 Signal Hill |
| 7022 Culver City | 7055 Lynwood | 7083 Southgate |
| 7025 Downey | 7057 Manhattan Beach | 7084 South Pasadena |
| 7028 El Monte | 7059 Maywood | 7089 Torrance |
| 7029 El Segundo | 7060 Monrovia | 7093 West Covina |
| 7032 Gardena | 7061 Montebello | 7094 Whittier |
| 7034 Glendale | 7063 Monterey Park | 7097 Rest of County |

## LOS ANGELES COUNTY OFFICES

| COUNTY OFFICE | ADDRESS | PHONE |
|---|---|---|
| Assessor | 500 W. Temple Street<br>Los Angeles, CA 90012 | 213/974-3101 |
| *Clerk<br>  div from 1880<br>  pro from 1850<br>  civ from 1850 | 111 N. Hill Street<br>Los Angeles, CA 90012 | 213/974-5101 |
| Courts<br>  Juvenile<br><br>  Superior | 1601 Eastlake Avenue<br>Los Angeles, CA 90033<br><br>Room 105E, Courthouse<br>111 N. Hill Street<br>Los Angeles, CA 90012<br><br>East District<br>400 Civic Center Plaza<br>Pomona, CA 91766<br><br>Northeast District<br>300 E. Walnut Avenue<br>Pasadena, CA 91101<br><br>Northwest District<br>6230 Sylmar<br>Van Nuys, CA 91401<br><br>South District<br>415 W. Ocean Boulevard<br>Long Beach, CA 90802<br><br>Southeast District<br>12720 Norwalk Blvd.<br>Norwalk, CA 90650<br><br>Southwest District<br>825 Maple Avenue<br>Torrance, CA 90503<br><br>West District<br>1725 Main Street<br>Santa Monica, CA 90401 | |

| | | |
|---|---|---|
| Recorder<br>b<br>d<br>m<br>lnd | 227 N. Broadway Street<br>Los Angeles, CA 90012 | 213/974-6611<br>974-6631 |
| Voter Registration | P. O. Box 30450<br>Los Angeles, CA 90030<br><br>5557 Ferguson Drive<br>City of Commerce, 90022 | 213/721-1100 |

*The Los Angeles County Clerk has adoption decrees. He will provide copies to adoptees upon request. It is suggested than an adoptee request his or her decree and send a blank check labeled "not to exceed $5.00" for each copy requested. The following information must be included with the request: name of adoptee, names of the adoptive parents, adoptee's date and place of birth and approximate date of adoption. When the decree is sent, the adoptee's birthname and names of the birthparents will be inked out.

## ADOPTION AGENCIES

Children's Bureau of Los Angeles
2824 Hyans Street
Los Angeles, CA 90026
213/384-2515

Children's Home Society
Los Angeles District Office
630 S. Shatto Place
Los Angeles, CA 90005
213/388-3184

Children's Home Society
Long Beach Office
920 Atlantic Ave., Suite B
Long Beach, CA 90813
213/436-3201

Children's Home Society
Van Nuys Office
6851 Lennox Avenue
Van Nuys, CA 91405
213/908-5055

Family Ministries
17150 Norwalk Blvd., Suite 111
Cerritos, CA 90701
213/924-5898

Holy Family Services
357 Westlake Ave.
Los Angeles, CA 90057
213/484-1441

Holy Family Services
6851 Lennox Avenue
Van Nuys, CA 91405
213/785-8861

Los Angeles Department of Adoptions
Central Office
2550 W. Olympic Blvd.
Los Angeles, CA 90006
213/381-2761

Covina District Office
274 Badillo Street
Covina, CA 91723
213/967-9541

South Central Dist. Office
644 El Segundo Blvd.
Los Angeles, CA 90059
213/538-5300

Antelope Valley Office
44758 N. Elm Street
Lancaster, CA 93534
805/948-4615

Long Beach Office
1401 Chestnut Ave.
Long Beach, CA 90813
213/599-9269

Van Nuys Office
6640 Van Nuys Blvd., Room 110
Van Nuys, CA 91405
213/873-5674

Vista Del Mar Child-Care Services
3200 Motor Avenue
Los Angeles, CA 90034
213/836-1223

## CEMETERIES

| | | | | |
|---|---|---|---|---|
| All Souls | 4400 Cherry Ave. | Long Beach | 90807 | 213/424-8601 |
| Angeles Abbey | 1515 E. Compton | Compton | 90021 | 631-1141 |
| Beth Israel | 1068 S. Downy Road | Los Angeles | 90023 | 268-7757 |
| Beth Olam | 900 N. Gower St. | Los Angeles | 90038 | 469-2322 |
| Calvary | 4201 Whittier Blvd. | Los Angeles | 90023 | 261-3106 |
| Desert Lawn | 2200 E. Ave S | Palmdale | 93550 | 947-7177 |
| Eden Memorial | 11500 Sepulveda | Mission Hills | 91345 | 361-7161 |
| El Monte | 9263 Valley Blvd. | Rosemead | 91770 | 287-4838 |
| Eternal Valley | 23287 N. Sierra Hwy | Newhall | 91331 | 259-0800 |
| Evergreen | 204 N. Evergreen | Los Angeles | 90033 | 268-6714 |
| Forest Lawn | 21300 E. Via Verde | Covina | 91724 | 966-3671 |
| Forest Lawn | 1712 S. Glendale | Glendale | 91205 | 254-3131 |
| Forest Lawn | 6300 Forest Lawn Dr. | Los Angeles | 90068 | 254-7251 |
| Glenhaven | 13017 N. Lopez Canyon | San Fernando | 91342 | 899-5211 |
| Grand View | 1341 Glenwood Road | Glendale | 91201 | 245-1582 |
| Green Hills | 27501 S. Western Ave. | San Pedro | 90732 | 831-0311 |
| Hillside | 6001 W. Centinela | Los Angeles | 90045 | 776-1931 |
| Hollywood | 6000 Santa Monica Blvd. | Hollywood | 90038 | 469-1181 |
| Holy Cross | 5835 W. Slauson Ave. | Culver City | 90230 | 670-7697 |
| Holy Cross | 444 E. Lexington Ave. | Pomona | 91766 | 627-3602 |
| Home of Peace | 4334 Whittier Blvd. | Los Angeles | 90023 | 388-3161 |
| Inglewood Park | 720 E. Florence | Inglewood | 90001 | 674-1181 |
| Joshua | 808 E. Lancaster | Lancaster | 93534 | 942-8125 |
| La Verne | 1201 B Street | La Vern | 91750 | 593-1415 |
| Lincoln | 16701 S. Central | Compton | 90220 | 636-7141 |
| Live Oak | 200 E. Duarte Road | Monrovia | 91016 | 359-5311 |
| Long Beach | 1095 E. Willow | Long Beach | 90806 | 424-5030 |
| Mountain View | 2400 N. Fair Oaks | Altadena | 91001 | 794-7133 |
| Mt. Carmell | 6501 E. Gage | Commerce | 90040 | 927-1203 |
| Mt. Olive | 7231 E. Slauson | Commerce | 90040 | 721-4729 |
| Mt. Sinai | 5950 Forest Lawn | Los Angeles | 90068 | 466-4171 |
| Oakdale | 1401 S. Grand | Glendora | 91740 | 335-0281 |
| Oakwood | 22600 Lassen | Chatsworth | 91311 | 341-0344 |
| Odd Fellows | 3640 Whittier | Los Angeles | 90023 | 261-6156 |
| Olive Lawn | 13926 S. La Mirada | La Mirada | 90638 | 943-1718 |
| Pacific Crest | 182nd St. & Inglewood | Redondo Beach | 90278 | 370-5891 |
| Paradise | 11541 E. Florence | Santa Fe Springs | 90670 | 864-7316 |
| Park Lawn | 6555 Gage Avenue | Commerce | 90040 | 773-3220 |
| Pomona | 502 E. Franklin | Pomona | 91766 | 622-2029 |
| Queen of Heaven | 2161 S. Fullerton | Rowland Heights | 91748 | 964-1291 |
| Restland | 2301 W. Olive | Burbank | 91506 | 846-3531 |
| Resurrection | 966 N. Portrero Grande | San Gabriel | 91770 | 728-1231 |
| Roosevelt | 18255 S. Vermont | Gardena | 90044 | 329-7887 |
| Rosedale | 1831 W. Washington | Los Angeles | 90007 | 734-3155 |
| Rose Hills | 3900 S. Workman Mill Rd. | Whittier | 90601 | 699-0921 |
| San Fernendo | 11160 Stanwood Ave. | Los Angeles | 90066 | 361-7387 |
| San Gabriel | 601 Roses Road | San Gabriel | 91775 | 282-2764 |
| Sholom | 13017 N. Lopez Canyon | San Fernando | 91342 | 899-5216 |
| Sunnyside | 1095 E. Willow | Long Beach | 90806 | 424-2639 |
| Valhalla | 10621 Victory Blvd. | Hollywood | 91606 | 763-9121 |
| Valley Oaks | 5600 N. Lindero Canyon | Westlake Village | | 889-0902 |
| Verdugo Hills | 7000 Parsons Terrace | Tujunga | 91042 | 352-6123 |
| Westwood | 1218 Glendon Avenue | Los Angeles | 90024 | 474-1579 |
| Wilmington | 605 East O Street | Wilmington | 90709 | 834-4442 |
| Woodlawn | 1727 14th St. | Santa Monica | 90404 | 450-0781 |
| Woodlawn | 1715 W. Greenleaf | Compton | | 636-1696 |

## CHAMBERS OF COMMERCE

| | | | |
|---|---|---|---|
| Agoura Valley | 29439 W. Agoura | Agoura | 91301 |
| Alhambra | 11 S. Second | Alhambra | 91801 |
| Altadena | 2526 N. Elm | Altadena | 91001 |
| Antelope Valley | 44812 N. Elm | Lancaster | 93534 |
| Arcadia | 388 W. Huntington | Arcadia | 91006 |
| Artesia | 18634 S. Pioneer | Artesia | 90701 |
| Avalon/Catalina | Pleasure Pier | Avalon | 90704 |

77

| | | | |
|---|---|---|---|
| Azusa | 213 E. Foothill | Azusa | 91702 |
| Baldwin Park | 14327 E. Ramona | Baldwin Park | 91706 |
| Bell | 4321 E. Gage | Bell | 90201 |
| Bellflower | 9729 E. Flower | Bellflower | 90706 |
| Bell Gardens | 6902 Eastern Ave. | Bell Gardens | 90201 |
| Beverly Hills | 239 S. Beverly Dr. | Beverly Hills | 90035 |
| Bradbury | 600 Winston Ave. | Bradbury | 91010 |
| Burbank | 200 W. Magnolia | Burbank | 91502 |
| Canoga Park | 6633 E. Fallbrook | Canoga Park | |
| Canyon Country | 19333 Soledad Canyon | Saugas | 91350 |
| Carson | 426 W. Carson St. | Carson | 90746 |
| Century City | 2020 Ave. of the Stars | Century City | 90067 |
| Cerritos | 11355 E. South St. | Cerritos | 90701 |
| Chatsworth | 21757 Devonshire | Chatsworth | 91311 |
| City of Commerce | 2615 Senta Ave. | Commerce | 90040 |
| Claremont | 234 Yale Avenue | Claremont | 91711 |
| Compton | 499 E. Compton | Compton | 90221 |
| Covina | 153 E. College | Covina | 91723 |
| Culver City | 9702 Washington | Culver City | 90230 |
| Downey | 8497 E. 2nd | Downey | 90241 |
| Duarte | 2229 E. Huntington | Duarte | 91010 |
| Eagle Rock | 2158 Colorado Blvd. | Eagle Rock | 90041 |
| El Monte | 10820 Valley Mall | El Monte | 91734 |
| El Segundo | 427 Main | El Segundo | 90245 |
| Encino | 4933 Balboa Blvd. | Encino | 91406 |
| Gardena Valley | 1551 W. Redondo Beach | Gardena | |
| Glendale | 200 S. Louise St. | Glendale | 91206 |
| Glendora | 224 N. Glendora Ave. | Glendora | 91740 |
| Hawaiian Gardens | 21527 S. Norwalk | Hawaiian Gdns | 90716 |
| Hawthorne | 12427 S. Hawthorne | Hawthorne | 90250 |
| Hermosa Beach | 1035 Valley Drive | Hermosa Beach | 90254 |
| Highland Park | 540 N. Figueroa | Los Angeles | |
| Hollywood | 6324 Sunset Blvd. | Hollywood | 90028 |
| Huntington Park | 2650 Zoe Ave. | Huntington Pk | 90255 |
| Industry | 255 N. Hacienda Blvd. | Industry | |
| Inglewood | 330 E. Queen Street | Inglewood | 90301 |
| Irwindale | 16244 E. Arrow | Irwindale | 91706 |
| La Canada | 1327 Foothill | La Canada | 91011 |
| La Crescenta | 2709 Foothill | La Crescenta | 91214 |
| Lakewood | 5787 E. South St. | Lakewood | 90713 |
| La Mirada | 15707 E. Imperial | La Mirada | 90638 |
| La Puente | 15917 E. Main St. | La Puente | 91744 |
| Lancaster | 44943 N. 10th St. | Lancaster | 93534 |
| La Verne | 2078 Bonita Ave. | La Verne | 91750 |
| Lawndale | 14704 S. Hawthorne | Lawndale | 90260 |
| Lomita | 24300 Narbonne | Lomita | 90717 |
| Long Beach | 50 Oceangate Plaza | Long Beach | 90802 |
| Los Angeles | 404 S. Bixel St. | Los Angeles | 90051 |
| Lynwood | 11302 Long Beach | Lynwood | 90262 |
| Manhattan Beach | 425 15th Street | Manhattan Beach | 90266 |
| Malibu | 22653 W. Pacific | Malibu | 90265 |
| Marina Del Rey | 4701 Admiralty Way | Marina Del Rey | 90291 |
| Mar Vista | 12932 Venice Blvd. | Mar Vista | 90066 |
| Maywood | 4349B Slauson | Maywood | 90270 |
| Mission Hills | 10646½ Sepulveda | Mission Hills | 91345 |
| Monrovia | 111 W. Colorado | Monrovia | 91016 |
| Montebello | 700 W. Washington | Montebello | 90640 |
| Monterey Park | 163 W. Garvey | Monterey Park | 91754 |
| Montrose | 3808 Ocean View | Montrose | 91020 |
| Newhall/Saugas | 23560 Lyons Ave. | Newhall | 91321 |
| North Hollywood | 5019 Lankershim | North Hollywood | 91601 |
| Northridge | 8946 Tampa Ave. | Northridge | 91324 |
| Norwalk | 12040 E. Foster | Norwalk | 90650 |
| Pacific Palisades | 864 Via de la Paz | Pacific Palisades | 90272 |
| Pacoima | 13517 Van Nuys | Pacoima | 91331 |
| Palmdale | 708 E. Palmdale | Palmdale | 93550 |
| Palos Verdes | 655 Deep Valley Dr. | Rolling Hills | 90204 |
| Panorama City | 8155 Van Nuys Blvd. | Panorama City | 91402 |

| Paramount | 15357 Paramount | Paramount | 90723 |
|---|---|---|---|
| Pasadena | 181 S. Los Robles | Pasadena | 91101 |
| Pico Rivera | 9122 E. Washington | Pico Rivera | 90660 |
| Pomona | 250 S. Garey Ave. | Pomona | 91769 |
| Redondo Beach | 1215 N. Catalina | Redondo Beach | 90277 |
| Reseda | 18210 Sherman Way | Reseda | 91335 |
| Rosemead | 8780 E. Valley | Rosemead | 91770 |
| San Dimas | 111 S. Monte Vista | San Dimas | 91773 |
| San Fernando | 502 S. Brand | San Fernando | 91340 |
| San Gabriel | 534 W. Mission | San Gabriel | 91776 |
| San Marino | 2304 Huntington Dr. | San Marino | 91108 |
| San Pedro | 390 W. 7th Street | San Pedro | 90731 |
| Santa Fe Springs | 11736 E. Telegraph | Sante Fe Springs | 90670 |
| Santa Monica | 606 Broadway | Santa Monica | 90401 |
| Sepulveda | 8722 Sepulveda | Sepulveda | 91343 |
| Sherman Oaks | 14652 Ventura Blvd. | Sherman Oaks | 91403 |
| Sierra Madre | 49 S. Baldwin | Sierra Madre | 91024 |
| Signal Hill | 1919 E. Hill | Signal Hill | 90806 |
| South Gate | 3350 Tweedy Blvd. | South Gate | 90280 |
| South Pasadena | 1424 Mission St. | South Pasadena | 91030 |
| Studio City | 12069 Ventura Place | Studio City | 91604 |
| Sun Valley | 8261 Sunland | Sun Valley | 91352 |
| Sylmar | 13251 Gladstone | Sylmar | 91342 |
| Tarzana | 19318 Ventura | Tarzana | 91356 |
| Temple City | 5827 N. Temple City | Temple City | 91780 |
| Toluca Lake | 10205 Riverside Dr. | Toluca Lake | 91602 |
| Torrance | 3828 W. Carson St. | Torrance | 90503 |
| Van Nuys | 14545 Victory Blvd. | Van Nuys | 91411 |
| Venice | 415 Washington | Venice | 90291 |
| Vernon | 2630 Leonis | Vernon | 90058 |
| Walnut Valley | 370 S. Lemon Ave. | Walnut | 91789 |
| Westchester | 8939 S. Sepulveda | Westchester | 90045 |
| West Covina | 833 W. Christopher | West Covina | 91790 |
| West Hollywood | 1038 N. Fairfax | Los Angeles | 90046 |
| Whittier | 8158 S. Painter | Whittier | 90607 |
| Wilmington | 1316A N. Avalon | Wilmington | 90061 |
| Wilshire | 2961 Wilshire | Wilshire | 90010 |

## COLLEGES & UNIVERSITIES

| Ambassador College | 300 W. Green St. | Pasadena | 91123 |
|---|---|---|---|
| Antelope Valley | 3041 W. Ave. K | Lancaster | 93534 |
| Art Center College | 1700 Lida Pasa | Pasadena | 91103 |
| Azusa Pacific | Hwy 66 at Citrus | Azusa | 91702 |
| Biola College | 13800 Biola Ave. | La Mirada | 90639 |
| Brooks College | 4825 E. Pacific Coast | Long Beach | 90804 |
| Cal Insitute of Technology | 1201 E. California | Pasadena | 91125 |
| California State U. | 3801 W. Temple | Pomona | 91768 |
| California State U. | 1250 Bellflower | Long Beach | 90840 |
| California State U. | 5151 State University | Los Angeles | 90032 |
| California State U. | 18111 Nordhoff St. | Northridge | 91330 |
| Cerritos College | 11110 E. Alondra | Norwalk | 90605 |
| Citrus College | 18824 E. Foothill | Azusa | 91702 |
| Claremont Men's | Bauer Circle | Claremont | 91711 |
| Compton Community | 1111 E. Artesia | Compton | 90221 |
| Don Bosco Technical | 1151 N. San Gabriel | Rosemead | 91770 |
| East Los Angeles College | 1301 Brooklyn Ave. | Monterey Park | 91754 |
| El Camino College | 16007 Crenshaw | Torrance | 90506 |
| Glendale Community | 1500 N. Verdugo | Glendale | 91208 |
| Harvey Mudd College | 12th & Columbia | Claremont | 91711 |
| Hebrew Union College | 3007 University Mall | Los Angeles | 90007 |
| Immaculate Heart | 2021 N. Western | Los Angeles | 90027 |
| Life Bible College | 1100 Glendale Blvd. | Los Angeles | 90026 |
| La Verne College | 1950 Third Street | La Verne | 91750 |
| Long Beach City | 4901 E. Carson St. | Long Beach | 90808 |
| Los Angeles Baptist | Placerita Canyon Rd. | Newhall | 91321 |
| Los Angeles City | 855 N. Vermont Ave. | Los Angeles | 90029 |
| Los Angeles Harbor | 1111 Figueroa Place | Wilmington | 90744 |

| | | | |
|---|---|---|---|
| Los Angeles Pierce | 6201 Winnetka Ave. | Woodland Hills | 91371 |
| Los Angeles Southwest | 11514 S. Western | Los Angeles | 90047 |
| Los Angeles Valley | 5800 Fulton Ave. | Van Nuys | 91401 |
| Loyola Marymount U. | 7101 W. 80th St. | Los Angeles | 90045 |
| Marymount Palos Verdes | 30800 Palos Verdes East | Palos Verdes | 90274 |
| Mount Saint Mary's | 12001 Chalon Road | Los Angeles | 90049 |
| Mount San Antonio | 1100 N. Grand | Walnut | 91789 |
| Northrop University | 1155 W. Arbor Vitae | Inglewood | 90306 |
| Occidental College | 1600 Campus Road | Los Angeles | 90041 |
| Pacific Oaks College | 5 Westmoreland Place | Pasadena | 91106 |
| Pacific States U. | 1516 W. Western Ave. | Los Angeles | 90006 |
| Pasadena City College | 1570 E. Colorado | Pasadena | 91106 |
| Pepperdine University | 24255 Pacific Coast | Malibu | 90265 |
| Pitzer College | | Claremont | 91711 |
| Pomona College | | Claremont | 91711 |
| Rio Hondo College | 3600 Workman Mill | Whittier | 90608 |
| Santa Monica College | 1815 Pearl Street | Santa Monica | 90406 |
| Scripps College | 10th and Columbia | Claremont | 91711 |
| University of Calif. | 405 Hilgard Avenue | Los Angeles | 90024 |
| University of So. Calif. | University Park | Los Angeles | 90007 |
| West Coast University | 440 Shatto Place | Los Angeles | 90020 |
| University of W. Los Angeles | 11000 Washington | Culver City | 90230 |
| West Los Angeles College | 4800 Freshman Drive | Culver City | 90230 |
| Whittier College | 13406 E. Philadelphia | Whittier | 90608 |
| Woodbury University | 1027 Wilshire Blvd. | Los Angeles | 90017 |

## HEALTH DEPARTMENTS

Long Beach City Health Deparment     (birth and death
Vital Statistics     since 1895)
P. O. Box 6157
Long Beach, CA 90806

Pasadena City Health Department     (birth and death
Vital Statistics     since 1890)
100 N. Garfield
Pasadena, CA 91109

## HOSPITALS

| | | | |
|---|---|---|---|
| Alhambra Community | 100 S. Raymond | Alhambra | 91802 |
| Alondra Community | 9246 E. Alondra | Bellflower | 90706 |
| Antelope Valley | 1600 W. Avenue J | Lancaster | 93534 |
| Artesia Community | 18120 S. Pioneer | Artesia | 90701 |
| Athens Park | 250 W. 120th St. | Los Angeles | 90061 |
| Avalon | 5860 Avalon | Los Angeles | 90003 |
| Avalon Municipal | 100 Falls Canyon | Avalon | 90704 |
| Baldwin Park | 14148 E. Francisquito | Baldwin Park | 91706 |
| Bay Harbor | 1437 W. Lomita | Harbor City | 90710 |
| Bella Vista | 5425 E. Pomona | Los Angeles | 90022 |
| Bellflower | 9542 E. Artesia | Bellflower | 90706 |
| Bellwood | 10250 E. Artesia | Bellflower | 90706 |
| Beverly | 309 W. Beverly | Montebello | 90640 |
| Beverly Glen | 10361 W. Pico | Los Angeles | 90064 |
| Broadway | 9500 S. Broadway | Los Angeles | 90003 |
| Brotman | 3828 Delmas Terrace | Culver City | 90230 |
| Burbank | 466 E. Olive | Burbank | 91501 |
| California Medical | 1414 S. Hope St. | Los Angeles | 90015 |
| Canoga Park | 20800 Sherman Way | Canoga Park | 91306 |
| Carson | 23621 S. Main St. | Carson | 90745 |
| Casa Colina | 255 E. Bonita | Pomona | 91767 |
| Cedars-Sinai | 8700 Beverly Blvd. | Los Angeles | 90048 |
| Centinella | 555 E. Hardy St. | Inglewood | 90301 |
| Century City | 2080 Century Park E. | Los Angeles | 90048 |
| Cerritos Gardens | 21530 S. Pioneer | Hawaiian Gardens | 90716 |
| City of Hope | 1500 E. Duarte Road | Duarte | 91010 |

80

| | | | |
|---|---|---|---|
| City View | 3711 Baldwin | Los Angeles | 90031 |
| Community of Gardena | 1246 W. 155th St. | Gardena | 90247 |
| Crenshaw Center | 3831 Stocker | Los Angeles | 90308 |
| Daniel Freeman | 333 N. Prairie | Inglewood | 90301 |
| Dominguez Valley | 3100 S. Susana | Compton | 90221 |
| Downey | 11500 S. Brookshire | Downey | 90241 |
| East Los Angeles | 4060 Whittier | Los Angeles | 90023 |
| Encino | 16237 Ventura | Encino | 91436 |
| Foothill Presbyterian | 250 S. Grand | Glendora | 91740 |
| Fox Hills | 5525 W. Slauson | Los Angeles | 90056 |
| French Hospital | 531 W. College | Los Angeles | 90012 |
| Gardena Medical Center | 2315 W. Compton | Gardena | 90249 |
| Gardena Memorial | 1145 W. Redondo Beach | Gardena | 90247 |
| Garfield | 150 Hampton Ave. | Monterey Park | 91754 |
| Garfield-Cottage | 1410 N. Garey St. | Pomona | 91767 |
| Glendale Community | 800 S. Adams | Glendale | 91205 |
| Glendale Memorial | 1420 S. Central | Glendale | 91204 |
| Glendora | 638 S. Santa Fe | Glendora | 91740 |
| Golden State | 24124 Lyons Ave. | Newhall | 91321 |
| Good Samaritan | 616 S. Witmer St. | Los Angeles | 90017 |
| Granada Hills | 10445 Balboa | Granada Hills | 91344 |
| Great El Monte | 1701 Santa Anita | El Monte | 91733 |
| Harbor UCLA Medical | 1000 W. Carson | Torrance | 90509 |
| Hawthorne Community | 11711 S. Grevillea | Hawthorne | 90250 |
| Hawthorne | 13300 S. Hawthorne | Hawthorne | 90250 |
| Henry Mayo Newhall | 23845 W. McBean | Valencia | 91355 |
| Holly Park | 2501 El Segundo | Hawthorne | 90250 |
| Hollywood Community | 6245 De Longpre | Los Angeles | 90028 |
| Hollywood Presbyterian | 1300 N. Vermont | Los Angeles | 90027 |
| Hollywood West | 1233 N. La Brea | Hollywood | 90038 |
| Holy Cross | 15031 Rinaldi St. | Mission Hills | 91345 |
| Huntington | 100 Congress | Pasadena | 91105 |
| Imperial | 11222 Inglewood | Inglewood | 90304 |
| Inglewood | 426 E. 99th | Inglewood | 90301 |
| Inter-Community | 303 N. 3rd Ave. | Covina | 91723 |
| John Wesley | 2829 S. Grand Ave. | Los Angeles | 90007 |
| Kaiser Foundation | 13652 Cantara | Panorama City | 91402 |
| Kaiser Foundation | 1050 W. Pacific Coast | Harbor City | 90710 |
| Kaiser Foundation | 6041 Cadillac | Los Angeles | 90034 |
| Kaiser Foundation | 4867 Sunset Blvd. | Hollywood | 90027 |
| Kaiser Foundation | 9400 E. Rosecrans | Bellflower | 90702 |
| Martin L. King, Jr. | 12021 S. Wilmington | Willowbrook | 90025 |
| Lakewood | 5300 N. Clark Ave. | Lakewood | 90712 |
| La Mirada | 14900 E. Imperial | La Mirada | 90638 |
| Lancaster | 43830 N. 10th St. | Lancaster | 93534 |
| Lanterman, Frank D. | 3530 Pomona | Pomona | 91766 |
| Lark Ellen | 845 N. Lark Ellen | West Covina | 91791 |
| Las Encinas | 2900 E. Del Mar | Pasadena | 91107 |
| La Vina | 3900 N. Lincoln | Altadena | 91002 |
| Lincoln | 443 S. Soto | Los Angeles | 90033 |
| Little Company of Mary | 4101 Torrance | Torrance | 90503 |
| Long Beach Community | 1720 Termino | Long Beach | 90804 |
| Long Beach General | 2597 Redondo | Long Beach | 90806 |
| Long Beach | 1725 Pacific | Long Beach | 90813 |
| Los Altos | 3340 Los Coyotes | Long Beach | 90808 |
| Los Angeles New | 1177 S. Beverly | Los Angeles | 90035 |
| Marina Mercy | 4650 Lincoln | Marina Del Rey | 90291 |
| Medical Center | 18321 Clark St. | Tarzana | 91356 |
| Memorial Hospital | 2801 Atlantic | Long Beach | 90801 |
| Memorial Hospital | 14850 Roscoe Blvd. | Panorama City | 91402 |
| Methodist Hospital | 300 W. Huntington | Arcadia | 91006 |
| Metropolitan | 2001 S. Hoover | Los Angeles | 90007 |
| Metropolitan State | 11400 S. Norwalk | Norwalk | 90650 |
| Mira Loma | 44900 N. 60th St. W | Lancaster | 93534 |
| Midway | 5925 W. San Vicente | Los Angeles | 90014 |
| Mission | 3111 E. Florence | Huntington Park | 90255 |
| Monrovia | 323 S. Heliotrope | Monrovia | 91016 |
| Monterey Park | 900 S. Atlantic | Monterey Park | 91754 |
| Morningside | 8711 S. Harvard | Los Angeles | 90047 |

| | | | |
|---|---|---|---|
| Newhall | 24237 San Fernando | Newhall | 91321 |
| North Glendale | 1401 W. Glenoaks | Glendale | 91201 |
| Northridge | 18300 Roscoe | Northridge | 91324 |
| Norwalk | 13222 Bloomfield | Norwalk | 90650 |
| Olive View | 14445 Olive View | Sylmar | 91342 |
| Pacific Glen | 712 S. Pacific Ave. | Glendale | 91204 |
| Pacific | 2776 Pacific Ave. | Long Beach | 90801 |
| Pacoima Memorial | 11600 Eldridge | Pacoima | 91331 |
| Palmdale | 1212 E. Ave. S | Palmdale | 93550 |
| Paramount | 16453 S. Colorado | Paramount | 90723 |
| Park Avenue | 1225 N. Park Ave. | Pomona | 91768 |
| Park View | 1021 N. Hoover | Los Angeles | 90029 |
| Parkwood | 7011 Shoup | Canoga Park | 91307 |
| Pasadena | 1845 N. Fair Oaks | Pasadena | 91103 |
| Pico Rivera | 5216 S. Rosemead | Pico Rivera | 90660 |
| Pioneer | 17831 S. Pioneer | Artesia | 90701 |
| Pomona Valley | 1798 N. Garey | Pomona | 91767 |
| Presbyterian | 12401 E. Washington | Whittier | 90602 |
| Queen of Angels | 2301 Bellevue | Los Angeles | 90026 |
| Queen of the Valley | 1115 S. Sunset | West Covina | 91790 |
| Rancho Los Amigos | 7601 E. Imperial Hwy | Downey | 90242 |
| Rio Hondo | 8300 E. Telegraph | Downey | 90240 |
| Riverside | 12629 Riverside Dr. | No. Hollywood | 91637 |
| Riviera | 4025 W. 266th St. | Torrance | 90505 |
| Ross Loos | 1711 W. Temple St. | Los Angeles | 90026 |
| St. Anne's Maternity | 155 N. Occidental | Los Angeles | 90026 |
| St. Francis | 3630 E. Imperial | Lynwood | 90262 |
| St. John's | 1328 22nd | Santa Monica | 90404 |
| St. Joseph | 501 S. Buena Vista | Burbank | 90505 |
| St. Luke's | 2632 E. Washington | Pasadena | 91107 |
| St. Mary | 1050 Linden Ave. | Long Beach | 90801 |
| St. Vincent | 2131 W. 3rd Street | Los Angeles | 90051 |
| San Dimas | 1350 W. Covina | San Dimas | 91773 |
| San Gabriel | 216 S. Santa Anita | San Gabriel | 91776 |
| San Gabriel Valley | 115 E. Broadway | San Gabriel | 91776 |
| San Pedro | 1300 W. 7th Street | San Pedro | 90732 |
| Santa Fe | 610 S. St. Louis | Los Angeles | 90023 |
| Santa Marta | 319 N. Humphreys | Los Angeles | 90022 |
| Santa Monica | 1225 15th Street | Santa Monica | 90404 |
| Santa Teresita | 1210 Royal Oaks Drive | Duarte | 91010 |
| San Vicente | 6000 W. San Vicente | Los Angeles | 90057 |
| Sepulveda | 16111 Plummer | Sepulveda | 91343 |
| Serra | 9449 San Fernando Rd. | Sun Valley | 91352 |
| Sherman Oaks | 4929 Van Nuys Blvd. | Sherman Oaks | 91403 |
| Sierra Madre | 225 W. Sierra Madre | Sierra Madre | 91024 |
| South Bay | 514 N. Prospect | Redondo Beach | 90277 |
| South Hoover | 5700 S. Hoover | Los Angeles | 90037 |
| Studebaker | 13100 Studebaker | Norwalk | 90650 |
| Temple | 235 N. Hoover | Los Angeles | 90004 |
| Torrance | 3330 W. Lomita | Torrance | 90505 |
| US Naval | 7500 E. Carson | Long Beach | 90822 |
| University | 3787 S. Vermont | Los Angeles | 90007 |
| Valley Presbyterian | 15107 Van Owen St. | Van Nuys | 91405 |
| Van Nuys | 14433 Emelita St. | Van Nuys | 91401 |
| Verdugo Hills | 1812 Verdugo | Glendale | 91208 |
| Viewpark | 5035 Coliseum St. | Los Angeles | 90016 |
| Washington | 12101 Washington | Culver City | 90230 |
| West Adams | 2231 S. Western Ave. | Los Angeles | 90018 |
| West Covina | 725 S. Orange Ave. | West Covina | 91790 |
| West Hills | 23023 Sherman Way | Canoga Park | 91307 |
| Westlake | 4415 Lakeview Canyon | Westlake Vill | 91361 |
| West Park | 22141 Roscoe Blvd. | Canoga Park | 91304 |
| Westside | 910 S. Fairfax | Los Angeles | 90036 |
| Westside Community | 2101 Magnolia Ave. | Long Beach | 90806 |
| West Valley | 5333 Balboa Blvd. | Encino | 91316 |
| White Memorial | 1720 Brooklyn Ave. | Los Angeles | 90033 |
| Whittier | 15151 E. Janine Dr. | Whittier | 90605 |
| Woodruff | 3800 Woodruff Ave. | Long Beach | 90808 |
| Woodruff Gables | 17800 S. Woodruff Ave. | Bellflower | 90706 |

*NOTE--To locate files of defunct hospitals check with:

Bureau of Licenses
241 N. Figueroa
Los Angeles, CA 90012
213/974-7961

## LIBRARIES

| | | | | |
|---|---|---|---|---|
| Alamitos | 1836 E. 3rd Street | Long Beach | 90802 | 213/436-6448 |
| *Alhambra LDS | 106 Hillview Ave. | Alhambra | 91803 | 726-8145 |
| Alhambra Main | 410 W. Main Street | Alhambra | 91801 | 289-4216 |
| Alhambra Branch | 2037 W. Fremont | Alhambra | 91003 | 282-5153 |
| Allendale | 1130 S. Marengo | Pasadena | 91106 | 799-2519 |
| Alondra | 11949 Alondra | Norwalk | 90650 | 868-7771 |
| Altadena | 600 E. Mariposa | Altadena | 91001 | 798-0833 |
| Angeles Mesa | 2700 W. 52nd St. | Los Angeles | 90062 | 292-4328 |
| Angelo M Iacaboni | 5020 Clark Ave. | Lakewood | 90712 | 866-1777 |
| Arcadia | 20 W. Duarte Road | Arcadia | 91006 | 446-7111 |
| Architect | 3723 Wilshire Blvd. | Los Angeles | 90010 | 384-8548 |
| Arroya Seco | 2659 N. Lincoln | Altadena | 91001 | 797-5448 |
| Arroyo Regional | 6145 N. Figueroa | Los Angeles | 90042 | 256-3178 |
| Artesia | 18722 S. Clarkdale | Artesia | 90701 | 865-6614 |
| Ascot | 256 W. 70th Street | Los Angeles | 90003 | 759-4817 |
| Atwater | 3229 Glendale | Los Angeles | 90039 | 644-1353 |
| *Augustan Society | 1510 Cravens | Torrance | 90501 | 320-7766 |
| Avalon | 215 Sumner | Avalon | 90704 | 510-1050 |
| Azusa | 729 N. Dalton | Azusa | 91702 | 334-0338 |
| Bach | 4055 Bellflower | Long Beach | 90808 | 421-5411 |
| Baldwin Park | 4181 Baldwin Park | Baldwin Park | 91706 | 962-6947 |
| Bay Shore | 195 Bay Shore Ave. | Long Beach | 90803 | 438-3501 |
| Bell | 4411 E. Gage Ave. | Bell | 90201 | 585-0091 |
| Beverly Hills | 444 N. Rexford Drive | Beverly Hills | 90035 | 550-4721 |
| Bilbrew | 150 E. El Segundo | Los Angeles | 90061 | 538-3350 |
| Brakensiek | 9945 E. Flower | Bellflower | 90706 | 925-5543 |
| Brand | 1601 W. Mountain | Glendale | 91201 | 956-2051 |
| Brentwood | 11820 San Vicente | W. Los Angeles | 90049 | 826-6579 |
| Brewitt | 4036 E. Anaheim St. | Long Beach | 90804 | 438-9200 |
| Buena Vista | 401 N. Buena Vista | Burbank | 91505 | 847-9747 |
| Burbank | 110 N. Glen Oaks | Burbank | 91503 | 847-9737 |
| Burnett | 560 E. Hill Street | Long Beach | 90806 | 591-8614 |
| Cahuenga | 4591 Santa Monica | Los Angeles | 90021 | 664-6418 |
| Canoga Park | 7260 Owensmouth | Los Angeles | 91303 | 887-0320 |
| *Canyon Country LDS | Drycliff & Camp Plen | Canyon Country | 91351 | 251-5539 |
| Canyon Country | 18538 Soledad Canyon | Saugus | 91350 | 251-2720 |
| Carson | 151 E. Carson | Carson | 90745 | 830-0901 |
| Casa Verdugo | 1151 N. Brand Blvd. | Glendale | 91202 | 956-2047 |
| Central | 630 W. 5th Street | Los Angeles | 90071 | 626-7461 |
| *Cerritos LDS | 17909 Bloomfield | Cerritos | 90701 | 868-8927 |
| Charter Oak | 20562 Arrow Highway | Covina | 91724 | 339-2151 |
| Chatsworth | 21052 Devonshire | Los Angeles | 91311 | 341-4276 |
| Chevy Chase | 3301 E. Chevy Chase | Glendale | 91206 | 956-2046 |
| Chinatown | 536 W. College St. | Los Angeles | 90012 | 620-0925 |
| Civic Center | 3301 Torrance | Torrance | 90503 | 328-2251 |
| Claremont | 208 N. Harvard | Claremont | 91711 | 621-4902 |
| Commerce Central | 2262 S. Atlantic | Commerce | 90040 | 268-9351 |
| Compton | 240 W. Compton | Compton | 90220 | 637-0202 |
| Covina | 234 N. 2nd | Covina | 91723 | 967-3935 |
| Crenshaw-Imperial | 11141 Crenshaw | Inglewood | 90303 | 649-7403 |
| Cudahy | 5218 Santa Ana | Cudahy | 90201 | 771-1345 |
| Culver City | 4975 Overland | Culver City | 90230 | 559-1676 |
| Cypress Park | 3320 Pepper | Los Angeles | 90065 | 225-0989 |
| Dana | 3680 Atlantic | Long Beach | 90807 | 424-4828 |
| Del Mar | 3132 N. Del Mar | Rosemead | 91770 | 280-4422 |
| Diamond Bar | 1061 S. Grand | Diamond Bar | 91765 | 595-7418 |
| Dominguez | 2719 E. Cardon St. | Carson | 90810 | 835-8441 |
| Downey | 8490 3rd Street | Downey | 90241 | 923-3256 |
| Duarte | 1301 Buena Vista | Duarte | 91010 | 358-1865 |

| Name | Address | City | Zip | Phone |
|---|---|---|---|---|
| Eagle Rock | 2225 Colorado | Los Angeles | 90041 | 255-6315 |
| East Compton | 4205 E. Compton | Compton | 90221 | 632-6193 |
| East Los Angeles | 4801 E. 3rd Street | Los Angeles | 90063 | 264-0155 |
| *East Pasadena LDS | 770 N. Sierra Madre | Pasadena | 91107 | 351-8517 |
| Echo Park | 515 N. La Veta Ter. | Los Angeles | 90026 | 628-5903 |
| Edgewood | 1435 W. Puente | West Covina | 91740 | 962-4069 |
| El Camino | 4264 E. Whittier | Los Angeles | 90023 | 269-8102 |
| El Dorado | 2900 Studebaker Rd. | Long Beach | 90815 | 429-1814 |
| El Monte | 3224 N. Tyler Ave. | El Monte | 91731 | 444-9506 |
| El Retiro | 126 Vista Del Parque | Torrance | 90505 | 385-0922 |
| El Segundo | 111 W. Mariposa | El Segundo | 90245 | 322-4121 |
| El Sereno | 4990 Huntington Dr. S. | Los Angeles | 90032 | 225-9201 |
| Encino-Tarzana | 18231 Ventura Blvd. | Los Angeles | 91436 | 343-1983 |
| Exposition Park | 3665 S. Vermont | Los Angeles | 90007 | 732-0169 |
| Fairfax | 161 S. Gardner | Los Angeles | 90036 | 936-6191 |
| Fairview | 2101 Ocean Park | Santa Monica | 90405 | 450-0443 |
| Felipe de Neve | 2820 W. 6th Street | Los Angeles | 90057 | 384-7676 |
| Franklin | 2200 E. 1st Street | Los Angeles | 90033 | 263-6901 |
| Gardena | 1731 W. Gardena | Gardena | 90247 | 323-6363 |
| Glendale | 222 E. Harvard | Glendale | 91205 | 956-2020 |
| Glendora | 140 S. Glendora | Glendora | 91740 | 963-4168 |
| Graham | 1900 E. Firestone | Los Angeles | 90001 | 582-3809 |
| Granada Hills | 10640 Petit Ave. | Los Angeles | 91344 | 368-5687 |
| Grandview | 1535 5th Street | Glendale | 91201 | 956-2049 |
| Greenwood | 6130 Greenwood Ave. | Commerce | 90040 | 927-1516 |
| Hacienda Heights | 16010 La Monde | Hacienda Heights | 91745 | 968-9356 |
| Harte | 1595 W. Willow | Long Beach | 90810 | 424-2345 |
| Hastings | 3325 E. Orange Grove | Pasadena | 91107 | 792-0945 |
| Hawaiian Gardens | 121134 Tilbury St. | Hawaiian Gardens | 90716 | 420-2641 |
| Hawthorne | 12700 S. Grevillea | Hawthorne | 90250 | 679-8193 |
| Henderson | 4805 Emerald | Torrance | 90503 | 371-2075 |
| Hermosa Beach | 550 Pier Avenue | Hermosa Beach | 90254 | 374-8973 |
| Hill | 55 S. Hill Avenue | Pasadena | 91106 | 796-1276 |
| Holifield | 1060 S. Greenwood | Montebello | 90640 | 728-0421 |
| Holly Park | 2150 W. 120th St. | Hawthorne | 90250 | 757-1735 |
| Hollydale | 12000 Garfield Ave. | South Gate | 90280 | 634-0156 |
| Hollywood | 1623 Ivar Avenue | Los Angeles | 90028 | 464-3101 |
| *Huntington | | San Marino | 91108 | 792-6141 |
| Huntington Park | 6518 Miles Avenue | Huntington Park | 90255 | 583-1461 |
| Hyde Park | 6527 Crenshaw Blvd. | Los Angeles | 90040 | 750-7241 |
| Immigrant | 5043 Lankershim | No. Hollywood | 91601 | 762-0251 |
| Inglewood | 101 W. Manchester | Inglewood | 90301 | 649-7380 |
| Irwindale | 5050 N. Irwindale | Irwindale | 91706 | 962-5255 |
| Jefferson | 2211 W. Jefferson | Los Angeles | 90018 | 734-8573 |
| John C. Fremont | 6121 Melrose Ave. | Los Angeles | 90038 | 465-9593 |
| John Muir | 1005 W. 64th Street | Los Angeles | 90044 | 759-4184 |
| Junipero Serra | 4255 S. Olive St. | Los Angeles | 90039 | 234-1685 |
| La Canada | 4545 N. Oakwood Ave. | La Canada | 91011 | 790-3330 |
| La Crescenta | 4521 La Crescenta Ave. | La Crescenta | 91214 | 248-5313 |
| *La Crescenta LDS | 4550 Raymond Avenue | La Crescenta | 91214 | 957-0925 |
| Lamanda Park | 140 S. Santa Anita | Pasadena | 91107 | 793-5672 |
| La Mirada | 13800 La Mirada | La Mirada | 90638 | 943-0277 |
| Lancaster | 1150 W. Avenue J | Lancaster | 93534 | 805/948-5029 |
| *Lancaster LDS | 3140 W. Avenue K | Lancaster | 93534 | 805/943-9927 |
| La Pintoresca | 1355 N. Raymond Ave. | Pasadena | 91103 | 213/797-1873 |
| La Puente | 15920 E. Central | La Puente | 91744 | 968-4613 |
| Las Virgenes | 29130 Roadside | Agoura | 91301 | 889-2278 |
| La Verne | 2125 Bonita Ave. | La Verne | 91750 | 593-1418 |
| Lawndale | 14615 Burin Avenue | Lawndale | 90260 | 676-0242 |
| Lennox | 4359 Lennox Blvd. | Lennox | 90304 | 674-0385 |
| Lincoln Heights | 2530 Workman St. | Los Angeles | 90031 | 225-3977 |
| Linda Vista | 1281 Bryant St. | Pasadena | 91103 | 793-1808 |
| Littlerock | 8135 Pearblossom Hwy | Littlerock | 93543 | 944-1277 |
| Live Oak | 4153 Live Oak Ave. | Arcadia | 91006 | 447-5772 |
| Lomita | 24200 Narbonne Ave. | Lomita | 90717 | 539-4515 |
| *Long Beach | 101 Pacific Avenue | Long Beach | 90802 | 436-9225 |
| *Long Beach LDS | 1140 Ximeno | Long Beach | 90814 | 439-3093 |
| Los Altos | 5614 Britton Drive | Long Beach | 90815 | 596-7320 |
| *Los Angeles Main | 630 W. Fifth Street | Los Angeles | 90017 | 626-7461 |

| Name | Address | City | ZIP | Phone |
|---|---|---|---|---|
| *Los Angeles LDS | 10741 Santa Monica Blvd. | Los Angeles | 90025 | 213/474-9990 |
| L. A. County Law | 301 W. 1st Street | Los Angeles | 90012 | 629-3531 |
| Los Feliz | 1939½ Hillhurst Ave. | Los Angeles | 90027 | 664-2903 |
| Los Nietos | 8801 Norwalk Blvd. | Los Angeles | 90606 | 692-2715 |
| Loyola Village | 7114 W. Manchester | Los Angeles | 90045 | 670-5436 |
| Lynwood | 11320 Bullis Road | Lynwood | 90262 | 635-7121 |
| Malabar | 2801 Wabash Blvd. | Los Angeles | 90033 | 268-0874 |
| Malaga Cove Plaza | 2400 Via Campesina | Palos Verdes | 90274 | 377-9584 |
| Malibu | 23519 W. Civic Center | Malibu | 90265 | 456-6438 |
| Manhattan Beach | 1320 Highland Avenue | Manhattan Beach | 90266 | 545-8595 |
| Manhattan Heights | 1560 Manhattan Beach | Manhattan Beach | 90266 | 379-8401 |
| Marina Del Rey | 4533 Admiralty Way | Marina Del Rey | 90291 | 821-3415 |
| Mark Twain | 1325 E. Anaheim St. | Long Beach | 90804 | 591-7412 |
| Mark Twain | 9621 S. Figueroa | Los Angeles | 90003 | 755-4088 |
| Mar Vista | 12006 Venice Blvd. | Los Angeles | 90006 | 390-3454 |
| Maywood | 4323 E. Slauson Avenue | Maywood | 90270 | 589-2713 |
| Memorial | 4625 Olympic Blvd. | Los Angeles | 90019 | 934-0855 |
| Monrovia | 321 S. Myrtle Avenue | Monrovia | 91016 | 358-0174 |
| Montana | 1704 Montana Avenue | Santa Monica | 90403 | 394-7081 |
| Montebello | 1550 Beverly Blvd. | Montebello | 90640 | 722-6551 |
| Monterey Park | 318 Ramona Road | Monterey Park | 91754 | 573-1411 |
| Newhall | 22704 W. 9th Street | Newhall | 91321 | 259-0750 |
| North Glenoaks | 411 N. Irving Drive | Burbank | 91504 | 847-9749 |
| No. Hollywood | 5211 Tujunga Avenue | Los Angeles | 91601 | 766-7185 |
| North Long Beach | 5571 Orange Avenue | Long Beach | 90805 | 422-1927 |
| North Redondo | 2000 Artesia Blvd. | Redondo Beach | 90278 | 374-0218 |
| Northridge | 9051 Darby Avenue | Northridge | 91325 | 886-3640 |
| No. Torrance | 3604 W. Artesia Blvd | Torrance | 90504 | 323-7200 |
| Northwest | 1466 S. McDonnell Ave. | Commerce | 90040 | 265-1787 |
| Northwest Park | 3323 Victory Blvd. | Burbank | 91502 | 847-9750 |
| Norwalk | 12350 Imperial Highway | Los Angeles | 90650 | 868-0775 |
| *Norwalk LDS | 14812 Harvest Avenue | Norwalk | 90650 | |
| Norwood | 4550 N. Peck Road | El Monte | 91732 | 443-3147 |
| Nye | 6600 Del Amo Blvd. | Lakewood | 90713 | 421-8497 |
| Ocean Park | 2601 Main Street | Santa Monica | 90405 | 396-2741 |
| Pacoima | 13605 Van Nuys | Pacoima | 91331 | 899-5203 |
| Palisades | 861 Alma Real Drive | Pacific Palisades | 90272 | 459-2754 |
| Palmdale | 700 E. Palmdale | Palmdale | 93550 | 273-2820 |
| Palms/Rancho Park | 2920 Overland Ave. | Los Angeles | 90064 | 838-2157 |
| Panorama City | 14345 Roscoe Blvd. | Los Angeles | 91402 | 894-4071 |
| Paramount | 16254 S. Colorado | Paramount | 90723 | 630-3159 |
| *Pasadena | 285 E. Walnut Street | Pasadena | 91101 | 577-4066 |
| Pico Rivera | 9001 Mines Avenue | Pico Rivera | 90660 | 692-1254 |
| Pio Pico | 1025 S. Oxford Ave. | Los Angeles | 90006 | 734-9851 |
| *Pomona Public | 625 S. Garey | Pomona | 91766 | 620-2043 |
| Post Avenue | 1345 Post Avenue | Torrance | 90501 | 328-5392 |
| Quartz Hill | 42018 N. 50th St. W | Quartz Hill | 93534 | 943-4517 |
| Redondo Beach | 309 Esplanade | Redondo Beach | 90277 | 376-8723 |
| Rivera | 7828 S. Serapis Ave. | Pico Rivera | 90660 | 949-5485 |
| Robertson | 1719 S. Robertson | Los Angeles | 90025 | 837-1239 |
| Rosemead | 8800 Valley Blvd. | Rosemead | 91770 | 573-5220 |
| Rowland Heights | 1850 Nogales Street | Rowland Heights | 91748 | 964-9488 |
| San Dimas | 145 N. Walnut | San Dimas | 91773 | 599-6738 |
| San Fernando | 102 MacNeil Street | San Fernando | 91340 | 361-6786 |
| San Gabriel | 500 S. Del Mar Ave. | San Gabriel | 91776 | 287-0761 |
| San Marino | 1890 Huntington Drive | San Marino | 91108 | 282-8484 |
| San Pedro | 931 S. Gaffey | San Pedro | 90701 | 831-9211 |
| San Rafael | 1240 Nithsdale | Pasadena | 91105 | 795-7974 |
| Santa Catalina | 999 E. Washington Blvd. | Pasadena | 91104 | 794-1219 |
| Santa Fe Springs | 11700 E. Telegraph Road | Santa Fe Springs | 90670 | 868-7738 |
| Santa Monica | 1343 6th Street | Santa Monica | 90401 | 451-5751 |
| San Vicente | 715 N. San Vicente Blvd. | Los Angeles | 90069 | 652-5340 |
| Satow | 14433 S. Crenshaw Blvd. | Gardena | 90249 | 679-0638 |
| Sherman Oaks | 14245 Moorpark Street | Los Angeles | 91423 | 981-7850 |
| Sierra Madre | 440 W. Sierra Madre | Sierra Madre | 91024 | 355-7186 |
| Sorensen | 11405 E. Rosehedge | Whittier | 90606 | 695-0105 |
| South El Monte | 1430 N. Central | So. El Monte | 91733 | 443-4158 |
| South Pasadena | 1115 El Centro | So. Pasadena | 91030 | 799-9108 |
| South Whittier | 14433 E.Leffingwell | Whittier | 90604 | 941-8111 |

| | | | | |
|---|---|---|---|---|
| Southeast Torrance | 23115 Arlington | Torrance | 90501 | 530-5044 |
| Studio City | 4400 Babcock Ave. | Studio City | 91604 | 769-5212 |
| Sunkist | 840 N. Puente Ave. | La Puente | 91746 | 960-2707 |
| Sunland-Tujunga | 7771 Foothill | Tujunga | 91042 | 352-4481 |
| Sunnyslope | 346 S. Rosemead | Pasadena | 91107 | 792-5733 |
| Sun Valley | 7935 Vineland Ave. | Los Angeles | 91852 | 764-7907 |
| Sylmar | 13059 Glenoaks Blvd. | Sylmar | 91342 | 367-6102 |
| Temple City | 5939 Golden West Ave. | Temple City | 91780 | 285-2136 |
| Tropico | 1501 S. Brand Blvd. | Glendale | 91204 | 956-2050 |
| Valencia | 23743 W. Valencia | Valencia | 91355 | 259-8942 |
| Van Nuys | 6250 Sylmar Avenue | Van Nuys | 91401 | 988-5950 |
| Venice | 610 California Ave. | Venice | 91405 | 821-1769 |
| Vermont Square | 1201 W. 48th Street | Los Angeles | 90291 | 293-7138 |
| Vernon | 4504 S. Central | Los Angeles | 90037 | 234-9106 |
| Victoria Park | 17906 Avalon Blvd. | Carson | 90011 | 327-4830 |
| View Park | 3854 W. 54th Street | Los Angeles | 90043 | 293-5371 |
| Villa Carson | 23317 S. Avalon Blvd. | Carson | 90745 | 830-5561 |
| Vine Avenue | 545 E. Vine Avenue | West Covina | 91790 | 337-4538 |
| Walnut | 134 N. Pierre Road | Walnut | 91789 | 595-0757 |
| Walteria | 3815 W. 242nd Street | Torrance | 90505 | 375-8418 |
| Washington Irving | 1803 S. Arlington | Los Angeles | 90019 | 734-6303 |
| Watts | 1501 E. 103rd | Watts | 90002 | 567-2297 |
| Weaver | 4035 Tweedy Blvd. | South Gate | 90280 | 567-8853 |
| Weingart | 12301 207th Street | Lakewood | 90715 | 865-4615 |
| Westchester | 8946 Sepulveda Eastway | Westchester | 90045 | 645-6082 |
| West Covina | 1601 W. Covina Parkway | West Covina | 91740 | 962-3541 |
| *West Covina LDS | 656 W. Grand | West Covina | 91791 | 331-7117 |
| West Hollywood | 1403 N. Gardner Street | W. Hollywood | 90046 | 876-2741 |
| West Los Angeles | 11360 Santa Monica | W. Los Angeles | 90025 | 477-9546 |
| West Valley | 19036 Vanowen Street | Los Angeles | 90407 | 345-4393 |
| Whittier Central | 7344 S. Washington Ave. | Whittier | 90602 | 698-8181 |
| *Whittier College | | Whittier | 90602 | 698-9531 |
| *Whittier LDS | 7906 S. Pickering | Whittier | 90602 | 698-5556 |
| Whittwood | 10537 S. St. Gertrudes | Whittier | 90603 | 947-5417 |
| Willowbrook | 2326 El Segundo Blvd | Compton | 90222 | 631-4311 |
| Wilshire | 149 N. St. Andrews | Los Angeles | 90004 | 467-7343 |
| Wiseburn | 5335 W. 135th Street | Hawthorne | 90250 | 676-5550 |
| Woodcrest | 1340 W. 106th Street | Los Angeles | 90044 | 757-9373 |
| Woodland Hills | 22200 Ventura Blvd. | Los Angeles | 91364 | 887-0160 |

NOTE***Pacific Telephone maintains a library of
telephone books, mostly from California,
which date back many years. This library
is open to the public and is located at:

PACIFIC TELEPHONE DIRECTORY ARCHIVES
3470 Wilshire Boulevard-at Normandy
Los Angeles, CA 90010
213/480-2901

## PROFESSIONAL ASSOCIATIONS

### BAR ASSOCIATIONS

Beverly Hills Bar
300 S. Beverly Dr.
Beverly Hills, CA 90212

San Fernando Bar
14328 Victory Blvd., Suite 208
Van Nuys, CA 91401

Long Beach Bar
444 W. Ocean Blvd., Suite 500
Long Beach, CA 90802

South Bay Bar Association
826 Maple Avenue
Torrance, CA 90503

Los Angeles County Lawyers Club
412 W. Sixth Street
Los Angeles, CA 90014

Southeast District Bar
8050 E. Florence
Downey, CA 90241

MEDICAL ASSOCIATIONS

| | | | |
|---|---|---|---|
| Antelope Valley Dist. 16 | P. O. Box 2469 | Lancaster | 93534 |
| Arcadia Foothill Dist. 13 | 735 W. Duarte Rd. | Arcadia | 91006 |
| East San Fernando Valley | 14724 Ventura | Sherman Oaks | 91403 |
| Forty-First Medical | 3250 Wilshire #606 | Los Angeles | 90010 |
| Glendale District 4 | 545 W. Glenoaks | Glendale | 91202 |
| Long Beach District 3 | 115 E. Eighth St. | Long Beach | 90813 |
| Los Angeles County | 1925 Wilshire | Los Angeles | 90057 |
| Los Angeles Metropolitan | 1925 Wilshire | Los Angeles | 90057 |
| Pasadena District 2 | 127 N. Madison Ave. | Pasadena | 91101 |
| Pomona District 14 | 1798 N. Garey | Pomona | 91767 |
| San Pedro District 8 | 438 Gaffey Street | San Pedro | 90731 |
| Sherman Oaks District 10 | 14724 Ventura Blvd. | Sherman Oaks | 91403 |
| Torrance SW District 9 | 3655 Lomita Blvd. | Torrance | 90505 |
| West San Fernando Valley | 15910 Ventura Blvd. | Encino | 91436 |
| Whittier District 11 | 13766 E. Philadelphia | Whittier | 90601 |

MADERA COUNTY #20

County Seat: Madera
2001 Chowchilla
2002 Madera
2097 Rest of County

MADERA COUNTY OFFICES

| COUNTY OFFICE | ADDRESS | PHONE |
|---|---|---|
| Assessor | 209 W. Yosemite Avenue<br>Madera, CA 93637 | 209/674-4641 |
| Clerk-Recorder<br>  b   from 1893<br>  d   from 1893<br>  m   from 1893<br>  div from 1893<br>  pro from 1893<br>  civ from 1893<br>  lnd from 1893 | 209 W. Yosemite Avenue<br>Madera, CA 93637 | 209/674-4641 |
| Courts<br>  Juvenile<br><br><br>  Superior | Government Center<br>209 W. Yosemite Avenue<br>Madera, CA 93637<br><br>Government Center<br>209 W. Yosemite Avenue<br>Madera, CA 93637 | |
| Voter Records | 209 W. Yosemite Avenue<br>Madera, CA 93637 | 209/674-4641<br>EX245 |

ADOPTION AGENCIES

Children's Home Society
703 Truxtun Avenue
Bakersfield, CA 93301
805/324-4091

State Dept. of Social Services
California Adoption Service
2400 Glendale Lane, Suite B
Sacramento, CA 95825
916/920-6897

CEMETERIES

| | | | | |
|---|---|---|---|---|
| Arbor Vitae Cemetery | 1301 Roberts Avenue | Madera | 93637 | 209/674-8826 |
| Calvary Cemetery | 28447 Avenue 14 | Madera | 93637 | 674-6052 |
| Chowchilla Cemetery | 23359 Road 14½ | Chowchilla | 93610 | 665-3857 |
| Madera Cemetery District | 40188 Highway 41 | Oakhurst | 93644 | 683-4845 |

CHAMBERS OF COMMERCE

| | | | | |
|---|---|---|---|---|
| Chowchilla District | 115 2nd | Chowchilla | 93610 | 209/665-4818 |
| Eastern Madera County | 49074 Civic Circle | Oakhurst | 93644 | 683-7766 |
| Madera District | 131 W. Yosemite Ave. | Madera | 93637 | 673-3563 |

HOSPITALS

Chowchilla District Memorial
1104 Ventura Avenue
Chowchilla, CA 93610

Madera Community Hospital
27600 Avenue 13½
Madera, CA 93637

LIBRARIES

Oakhurst Branch
49044 Civic Circle
Oakhurst, CA 93644
209/683-4838

Madera County
621 W. Robertson Blvd.
Chowchilla, CA 93610
209/665-2630

County Seat:  San Rafael

| | | | |
|---|---|---|---|
| 2103 | Fairfax | 2111 | San Rafael |
| 2105 | Larkspur | 2112 | Sausalito |
| 2107 | Mill Valley | 2197 | Rest of County |
| 2120 | San Anselmo | | |

## MARIN COUNTY OFFICES

| COUNTY OFFICE | ADDRESS | PHONE |
|---|---|---|
| Assessor | Civic Center<br>Administration Bldg.<br>San Rafael, CA 94903 | 415/479-1100 |
| Clerk<br>  div from 1900<br>  pro from 1880<br>  civ from 1910 | Hall of Justice<br>Civic Center<br>San Rafael, CA 94903 | 415/499-1991 |
| Courts<br>  Juvenile<br><br><br>  Superior | Hall of Justice, Room 151<br>Civic Center<br>San Rafael, CA 94903<br><br>Hall of Justice, Room 151<br>Civic Center<br>San Rafael, CA 94903 | |
| Recorder<br>  b   from 1863<br>  d   from 1863<br>  m   from 1856<br>  1nd from 1852 | Civic Center<br>San Rafael, CA 94903 | 415/499-6092 |
| Voter Records | Hall of Justice<br>Civic Center<br>San Rafael, CA 94903 | 415/479-2221 |

## ADOPTION AGENCIES

Children's Home Society
3200 Telegraph Avenue
Oakland, CA 94609
415/655-7406

Marin County Dept. of Human Services
P. O. Box 4160
Civic Center Branch
San Rafael, CA 94903
415/499-7178

## CEMETERIES

| | | | | |
|---|---|---|---|---|
| Bahia Valley | 650 Bugeia Lane | Novato | 94947 | 415/897-9609 |
| Daphne Fernwood | 301 Tennessee Valley | Mill Valley | 94941 | 383-7100 |
| Mt. Olivet | Los Ranchitos Road | San Rafael | 94903 | 479-9020 |
| Mt. Tamalpais | 2500 W. 5th Avenue | San Rafael | 94901 | 454-3166 |
| Olema | Shoreline Highway | Olema | 94950 | |

## CHAMBERS OF COMMERCE

| | | | |
|---|---|---|---|
| Corte Madera | 500 Tamalpais | Corte Madera | 94925 |
| Larkspur | 537 Magnolia Ave. | Larkspur | 94939 |
| Mill Valley | 85 Throckmorton | Mill Valley | 94941 |
| Novato | 807 De Long Ave. | Novato | 94947 |
| San Anselmo | 120 Sir Francis Drake | San Anselmo | 94960 |
| San Rafael | 633 5th Avenue | San Rafael | 94901 |
| Sausalito | 3030 Bridgeway | Sausalito | 94965 |
| Tiburon Peninsula | P. O. Box 563 | Tiburon | 94920 |

## COLLEGES & UNIVERSITIES

| | | | |
|---|---|---|---|
| College of Marin | College Avenue | Kentfield | 94904 |
| College of Marin | Wharf Road | Bolinas | 94924 |
| College of Pacific | Cliff Street | Dillon Beach | 94929 |
| Dominican College | 1520 Grand Ave. | San Rafael | 94901 |
| Indiana Valley College | 1800 Ignacio Blvd. | Novato | 94947 |
| World College West | P. O. Box 3060 | San Rafael | 94902 |

## HOSPITALS

| | | | |
|---|---|---|---|
| Kaiser Permanente | 99 Montecillo | San Rafael | 94903 |
| Kentfield Medical | 1125B Sir Francis Drake | Kentfield | 94964 |
| Marin General | 250 Bon Air Road | San Rafael | 94904 |
| Novato General | 1625 Hill Road | Novato | 94947 |
| Ross General | 1150 Sir Francis Drake | Ross | 94957 |

## LIBRARIES

| | | | |
|---|---|---|---|
| Belvedere | Post Office Building | Belvedere | 94920 | 415/435-1361 |
| Bolinas | Wharf Road | Bolinas | 94924 | 868-1171 |
| Corte Madera | 707 Meadowsweet | Corte Madera | 94925 | 924-4844 |
| Fairfax | 2097 Sir Francis Drake | Fairfax | 94930 | 453-8092 |
| Inverness | 1 Sir Francis Drake | Inverness | 94937 | 669-1288 |
| Jose del Pina | Sir Francis Drake Blvd. | Ross | 94957 | 453-5218 |
| Larkspur | 400 Magnolia Avenue | Larkspur | 94939 | 924-2405 |
| Marin County | Civic Center | San Rafael | 94901 | 479-5262 |
| Mill Valley | 375 Throckmorton | Mill Valley | 94941 | 388-4245 |
| Novato | 1720 Novato Blvd. | Novato | 94947 | 897-1141 |
| Point Reyes | 4th & A Streets | Point Reyes | 94946 | 663-8375 |
| San Anselmo | 110 Tunstead Ave. | San Anselmo | 94960 | 456-4419 |
| San Geronimo | 7282 Sir Francis Drake | Lagunitas | 94938 | 488-0430 |
| San Rafael | 1100 E Street | San Rafael | 94901 | 456-1118 |
| Sausalito | 420 Litho | Sausalito | 94965 | 332-2325 |
| Stinson Beach | 3470 Shoreline Highway | Stinson Beach | 94970 | 868-0252 |
| Woodacre | 1 Garden Way | Woodacre | 94973 | |

## PROFESSIONAL ASSOCIATIONS

Marin County Bar Association
1010 B Street, Suite 419
San Rafael, CA 94901

Marin Medical Society
4460 Redwood Highway
Box 4344
San Rafael, CA 94903

MARIPOSA COUNTY #22

County Seat: Mariposa
2297 County

MARIPOSA COUNTY OFFICES

| COUNTY OFFICE | ADDRESS | PHONE |
|---|---|---|
| Assessor | P. O. Box 35<br>Bullion Street<br>Mariposa, CA 95338 | 209/966-2332 |
| Clerk<br>  div<br>  pro<br>  civ | Courthouse<br>P. O. Box 247<br>Mariposa, CA 95338 | 209/966-2005 |
| Courts<br>  Juvenile<br><br>  Superior | Courthouse<br>Mariposa, CA 95338<br><br>Courthouse<br>Mariposa, CA 95338 | |
| Recorder<br>  b<br>  d<br>  m<br>  bur | P. O. Box 156<br>Mariposa, CA 95338 | 209/966-5719 |
| Registrar of Voters | P. O. Box 247<br>Mariposa, CA 95338 | 209/966-2005 |

ADOPTION AGENCIES

Children's Home Society
703 Truxtun Avenue
Bakersfield, CA 93301
805/324-4091

State Dept. of Social Services
California Adoption Service
2400 Glendale Lane, Suite B
Sacramento, CA 95825
916/920-6897

HOSPITALS

John C. Fremont Hospital
Hospital Road
Mariposa, CA 95338

PROFESSIONAL ASSOCIATIONS

Merced-Mariposa Medical Society
Bear Creek Plaza
Merced, CA 95340

County Seat: Ukiah
   2301  Fort Bragg
   2303  Ukiah
   2304  Willits
   2397  Rest of County

## MENDOCINO COUNTY OFFICES

| COUNTY OFFICE | ADDRESS | PHONE |
|---|---|---|
| Assessor | State & Stanley<br>Courthouse, Room 117<br>P. O. Box 354<br>Ukiah, CA 95482 | 707/468-4311 |
| Clerk<br>  div from 1858<br>  pro from 1872<br>  civ from 1858 | P. O. Box 148<br>Ukiah, CA 95482 | 707/468-4379 |
| Courts<br>  Juvenile<br><br>  Superior | P. O. Box 303<br>Ukiah, CA 95482<br><br>Courthouse<br>Ukiah, CA 95482 | |
| Recorder<br>  b<br>  d<br>  m<br>  lnd | P. O. Box 148<br>Ukiah, CA 95482 | 707/468-4376 |
| Registrar of Voters | N. State & W. Perkins<br>Ukiah, CA 95482 | 707/468-4371 |

## ADOPTION AGENCIES

Children's Home Society
3200 Telegraph Avenue
Oakland, CA 94609
415/655-7405

State Dept. of Social Services
California Adoption Service
2350 Professional Drive
Santa Rosa, CA 95406
707/545-2921

## CEMETERIES

Russian River Cemetery District
Low Gap Road
Ukiah, CA 95482
707/462-8012

## CHAMBERS OF COMMERCE

Mendocino County
331 N. School
Ukiah, CA 95482
707/462-3091

Ukiah
495 E. Perkins
Ukiah, CA 95482
707/462-4705

## COLLEGES & UNIVERSITIES

Mendocino College
P. O. Box 3000
Ukiah, CA 95482

## HOSPITALS

| | | | |
|---|---|---|---|
| Frank R. Howard Memorial | Madrone & Manzanita | Willits | 95490 |
| Hillside Community | 333 Laws Avenue | Ukiah | 95482 |
| Mendocino Community | 860 N. Bush Street | Ukiah | 95482 |
| Ukiah General | 1120 S. Dora Street | Ukiah | 95482 |

## LIBRARIES

Fort Bragg Library
353 N. Main
Fort Bragg, CA 95437
707/964-2020

Willets
85 E. Commercial
Willets, CA 95490
707/459-5908

MERCED COUNTY #24

County Seat: Merced
2401  Atwater
2405  Los Banos
2406  Merced
2497  Rest of County

MERCED COUNTY OFFICES

| COUNTY OFFICE | ADDRESS | PHONE |
|---|---|---|
| Assessor | 2222 "M" Street<br>Merced, CA 95340 | 209/726-7231 |
| Clerk<br>  div from 1855<br>  pro from 1855<br>  civ from 1855 | Courts Building<br>Merced, CA 95340 | 209/726-7501 |
| Courts<br>  Juvenile<br><br>  Superior | 670 W. 22nd Street<br>Merced, CA 95340<br><br>P. O. Box 2008<br>Merced, CA 95340 | |
| Recorder<br>  b<br>  d<br>  m<br>  bur | 2222 "M" Street<br>Merced, CA 95340 | 209/726-7541 |
| Voter Registration | 2222 "M" Street<br>Merced, CA 95340 | 209/726-7541 |

ADOPTION AGENCIES

Children's Home Society
703 Truxtun Avenue
Bakersfield, CA 93301
805/324-4091

Merced County Human Resources
302 East 15th Street
P. O. Box 112
Merced, CA 95340
209/726-7241

CEMETERIES

| | | | | |
|---|---|---|---|---|
| Evergreen Memorial | 1480 B Street | Merced | 95340 | 209/722-7488 |
| Los Banos Cemetery | 965755 Center Ave. | Los Banos | 93635 | 826-0882 |
| Merced Cemetery District | Childs Avenue & J | Merced | 95340 | 722-2364 |
| Winton Cemetery District | 7651 W. Almond Ave. | Winton | 95388 | 358-3703 |

CHAMBERS OF COMMERCE

| | | | |
|---|---|---|---|
| Los Banos | 402 W. Pachico Blvd. | Los Banos | 93635 |
| Merced | 505 W. 20th | Merced | 95340 |
| Merced County | 732 W. 18th | Merced | 95340 |

COLLEGES & UNIVERSITIES

Merced College
3600 "M" Street
Merced, CA 95340

## HOSPITALS

| | | | |
|---|---|---|---|
| Bloss Memorial | 1691 3rd | Atwater | 95301 |
| Dos Palos Hospital | 2118 Marguerite | Dos Palos | 93620 |
| Los Banos Community | 520 W. 1st Street | Los Banos | 93635 |
| Merced Community | 301 E. 13th St. | Merced | 95340 |
| Mercy Hospital | 2740 M Street | Merced | 95340 |

## LIBRARIES

| | | | | |
|---|---|---|---|---|
| Ballico Branch | 11285 N. Ballico Ave. | Ballico | 95303 | 209/634-4694 |
| Delhi Branch | 16091 W. Locust | Delhi | 95315 | 632-7916 |
| Irwin Hilmar | 20041 W. Falke | Irwin | | 632-0746 |
| Merced County | 399 George Drive | Merced | 95340 | 723-6571 |
| Stevinson | 20085 W. 3rd Avenue | Stevinson | 95374 | 634-5796 |

## PROFESSIONAL ASSOCIATIONS

Merced-Mariposa Medical Society
Bear Creek Plaza
2835 "G" Street
Merced, CA 95340

MODOC COUNTY #25

County Seat: Alturas
2501 Alturas
2597 Rest of County

MODOC COUNTY OFFICES

| COUNTY OFFICE | ADDRESS | PHONE |
|---|---|---|
| Assessor | 204 S. Court<br>P. O. Box 1605<br>Alturas, CA 96101 | 916/233-4168 |
| Clerk<br>  div from 1874<br>  pro from 1874<br>  civ from 1874 | 204 S. Court<br>Alturas, CA 96101 | 916/233-2115 |
| Courts<br>  Juvenile<br><br>  Superior | Courthouse<br>Alturas, CA 96101<br><br>Courthouse<br>Alturas, CA 96101 | |
| Recorder<br>  b<br>  m<br>  d | 204 Court Street<br>Room 107<br>Alturas, CA 96101 | 916/233-2115 |
| Voter Registration | 204 Court Street<br>Alturas, CA 96101 | 916/233-2115 |

ADOPTION AGENCIES

Children's Home Society
1212 Sheridan Avenue
Chico, CA 95926
916/342-2464

State Dept. of Social Services
California Adoption Service
500 Cohasset Road, Suite 34
Chico, CA 95926
916/891-1986

HOSPITALS

Modoc Medical Center
228 McDowell Street
Alturas, CA 96101

Modoc Medical Center
Main & Washington
Adarville, CA 96101

MONO COUNTY #26

County Seat:  Bridgeport
2697  County

MONO COUNTY OFFICES

| COUNTY OFFICE | ADDRESS | PHONE |
|---|---|---|
| Assessor | Courthouse<br>Main Street<br>Bridgeport, CA 93517 | 714/932-7911 |
| Clerk-Recorder<br>  b    from 1861<br>  d    from 1900<br>  m    from 1861<br>  div from 1900<br>  pro from 1900<br>  civ from 1900<br>  lnd from 1864<br>  bur from 1900 | P. O. Box 537<br>Bridgeport, CA 93517 | 714/932-7911<br>EX292 |
| Courts<br>  Juvenile<br><br>  Superior | Courthouse<br>Bridgeport, CA 93517<br><br>Courthouse<br>Bridgeport, CA 93517 | |

ADOPTION AGENCIES

Children's Home Society
703 Truxtun Avenue
Bakersfield, CA 93301
805/324-4091

State Dept. of Social Services
California Adoption Service
2400 Glendale Lane, Suite B
Sacramento, CA 95825
916/920-6897

HOSPITALS

Mono General Hospital
Twin Lakes Road
Box 356
Bridgeport, CA 93517

MONTEREY COUNTY #27

County Seat: Salinas
    2702  Carmel by the Sea
    2711  Monterey
    2712  Pacific Grove
    2714  Salinas
    2797  Rest of County

MONTEREY COUNTY OFFICES

| COUNTY OFFICE | ADDRESS | PHONE |
|---|---|---|
| Assessor | P. O. Box 570<br>Salinas, CA 93901 | 408/433-4756 |
| Clerk | 1200 Aguajito Road<br>Salinas, CA 93901 | 408/372-8081 |
| Courts<br>  Juvenile<br><br>  Superior | P. O. Box 2135<br>Salinas, CA 93901<br><br>Courthouse<br>Salinas, CA 93901 | |
| Recorder | P. O. Box 29<br>Salinas, CA 93902 | 408/424-8611<br>EX228 |
| Registrar of Voters | 201 Main Street<br>Salinas, CA 93902 | 408/424-7621 |

ADOPTION AGENCIES

Children's Home Society
444 Pearl Street
Monterey, CA 93940
408/373-4126

Monterey County Dept. of Social Services
1352 Natividad Road
P. O. Box 299
Salinas, CA 93901
408/757-2911

CEMETERIES

| | | | |
|---|---|---|---|
| Chinese Cemetery | Natividad Road | Salinas | 93906 |
| El Carmelo | Asilomar & Lighthouse | Pacific Grove | 93950 |
| Garden of Memories | 768 Abbott Street | Salinas | 93901 |
| Mission Memorial | La Salle & South | Seaside | 93955 |
| San Carlos | Fremont Street | Monterey | 93940 |

CHAMBERS OF COMMERCE

| | | | |
|---|---|---|---|
| King City | 203 Broadway | King City | 93930 |
| Marina | 2174 Reindollar | Marina | 93933 |
| Pacific Grove | Forest & Central | Pacific Grove | 93950 |
| Salinas | 119 E. Alisal | Salinas | 93901 |
| Seaside | 505 Broadway Ave. | Seaside | 93955 |

## COLLEGES & UNIVERSITIES

| | | | |
|---|---|---|---|
| Hartnell College | 156 Homestead Ave. | Salinas | 93901 |
| Monterey Institute | P. O. Box 1978 | Monterey | 93940 |
| Monterey Peninsula | 980 Fremont | Monterey | 93940 |

## HOSPITALS

| | | | |
|---|---|---|---|
| Alisal Community | 333 Sanborn Road | Salinas | 93905 |
| Eskaton Monterey | 576 Hartnell St. | Monterey | 93940 |
| George L. Mee | 300 Canal Street | King City | 93930 |
| Monterey Peninsula | 23625 WR Holman | Monterey | 93940 |
| Natividad | 1611 Natividad | Salinas | 93906 |
| Salinas Valley | 450 E. Romie Lane | Salinas | 93901 |

## LIBRARIES

| | | | |
|---|---|---|---|
| Castroville | 16665 Merritt | Castroville | 95012 |
| East Salinas | 1207 E. Market | Salinas | 93905 |
| El Gabilan | 1400 N. Main | Salinas | 93906 |
| Gonzales | 349 Belden | Gonzales | 93926 |
| Greenfield | 131 El Camino Real | Greenfield | 93927 |
| Harrison | Ocean & Lincoln | Carmel | 93923 |
| John Steinbeck | 110 W. San Luis | Salinas | 93901 |
| King City | 212 N. Vanderhurst | King City | 93930 |
| Marina Branch | 371 Carmel Ave. | Marina | 93933 |
| Monterey | Madison & Pacific | Monterey | 93940 |
| Pacific Grove | Forest & Central | Pacific Grove | 93950 |
| Prunedale | 8075 San Miguel Canyon | Prunedale | 93907 |
| Seaside | 550 Harcourt | Seaside | 93955 |
| *Seaside LDS | 1024 Noche Buena | Seaside | 93955 |
| Soledad | 179 Main Street | Soledad | |

## PROFESSIONAL ASSOCIATIONS

Monterey County Medical Society
P. O. Box 308
Salinas, CA 93901

NAPA COUNTY  #28

County Seat:  Napa
2802  Napa
2897  Rest of County

NAPA COUNTY OFFICES

| COUNTY OFFICE | ADDRESS | PHONE |
|---|---|---|
| Assessor | 725 Coombs Street<br>Napa, CA 94558 | 707/253-4466 |
| Clerk<br>  div from 1850<br>  pro from 1850<br>  civ from 1850 | P. O. Box 880<br>Napa, CA 94558 | 707/253-4481 |
| Courts<br>  Juvenile<br><br>  Superior | Courthouse<br>Napa, CA 94558<br><br>Courthouse<br>Napa, CA 94558 | |
| Recorder<br>  b<br>  d<br>  m<br>  lnd | 821 Coombs Street<br>Napa, CA 94558 | 707/253-4246 |
| Voter Registration | P. O. Box 880<br>Napa, CA 94558 | 707/253-4321 |

ADOPTION AGENCIES

Children's Home Society
3200 Telegraph Avenue
Oakland, CA 94609
415/655-7406

State Dept. of Social Services
California Adoption Service
2350 Professional Drive
Santa Rosa, CA 95406
707/545-2921

CEMETERIES

| | | | | |
|---|---|---|---|---|
| Napa Valley Memorial | 2383 Napa-Vallejo | Napa | 94558 | 707/255-3433 |
| St. Helena Cemetery Asso. | 2461 Spring | St. Helena | 94574 | 963-3544 |
| Tulocay Cemetery | Coombsville Road | Napa | 94558 | 252-4727 |

CHAMBERS OF COMMERCE

Calistoga Chamber of Commerce
1139 Lincoln Avenue
Calistoga, CA 94515

Napa Chamber of Commerce
1900 Jefferson
Napa, CA 94558

COLLEGES & UNIVERSITIES

Napa College
2277 Napa-Vallejo Highway
Napa, CA 94558

100

## HOSPITALS

| | | | |
|---|---|---|---|
| Napa State Hospital | P. O. Box A | Imola | 94558 |
| Queen of the Valley | 1000 Traucas St. | Napa | 94558 |
| St. Helena Hospital | Sanitarium & Sunnyside | Deer Park | 94576 |

## LIBRARIES

| | | | |
|---|---|---|---|
| Calistoga | 1108 Myrtle | Calistoga | 94515 |
| Napa City and County | 1150 Division | Napa | 94558 |
| St. Helena | 1492 Library Lane | St. Helena | 94574 |

## PROFESSIONAL ASSOCIATIONS

Napa County Medical Society
1041 Lincoln
P. O. Box 2158
Napa, CA 94558

NEVADA COUNTY #29

County Seat: Nevada City
2901 Grass Valley
2902 Nevada City
2997 Rest of County

NEVADA COUNTY OFFICES

| COUNTY OFFICE | ADDRESS | PHONE |
|---|---|---|
| Assessor | 201 Church Street<br>Nevada City, CA 95959 | 916/265-2461 |
| Clerk-Recorder<br>b    from 1873<br>d    from 1873<br>m    from 1856<br>div from 1880<br>pro from 1880<br>civ from 1880<br>lnd from 1856 | 201 Church Street<br>Nevada City, CA 95959 | 916/265-2461 |
| Courts<br>  Juvenile<br><br>  Superior | Courthouse<br>Nevada City, CA 95959<br><br>Courthouse<br>Nevada City, CA 95959 | |
| Election Clerk | 201 Church Street<br>Nevada City, CA 95959 | 916/265-2461<br>EX 254 |

ADOPTION AGENCIES

Children's Home Society
121 E. Orangeburg Avenue
Modesto, CA 95350
209/521-5237

State Dept. of Social Services
California Adoption Service
500 Cohasset Road, Suite 34
Chico, CA 95926
916/891-1986

CEMETERIES

Truckee Cemetery District
Old Highway 40
Truckee, CA 95734
916/587-6553

CHAMBERS OF COMMERCE

Grass Valley Chamber of Commerce
151 Mill
Grass Valley, CA 95945

HOSPITALS

Sierra Nevada Memorial Miners Hospital
Highway 20 and Glasson Way
Grass Valley, CA 94945

LIBRARIES

| | | | | |
|---|---|---|---|---|
| Grass Valley | 207 Mill | Grass Valley | 94945 | 916/273-4117 |
| Nevada City | North Pine | Nevada City | 95959 | 265-4604 |
| Nevada County | Donner Pass Road | Truckee | 587-3062 | 587-3062 |

County Seat: Santa Ana

| | | | |
|---|---|---|---|
| 3001 | Anaheim | 3011 | Laguna Beach |
| 3003 | Brea | 3012 | La Habra |
| 3004 | Buena Park | 3015 | Newport Beach |
| 3005 | Costa Mesa | 3016 | Orange |
| 3008 | Fullerton | 3020 | Santa Ana |
| 3009 | Garden Grove | 3021 | Seal Beach |
| 3010 | Huntington Beach | 3097 | Rest of County |

## ORANGE COUNTY OFFICES

| COUNTY OFFICE | ADDRESS | PHONE |
|---|---|---|
| Assessor | 630 N. Broadway<br>P. O. Box 149<br>Santa Ana, CA 92702 | 714/834-2727 |
| Clerk<br>  div from 1889<br>  pro from 1889<br>  civ from 1889 | 700 Civic Center Dr. W<br>P. O. Box 838<br>Santa Ana, CA 92702 | 714/834-2223 |
| Courts<br>  Juvenile<br><br><br>  Superior | 301 South Manchester<br>Orange, CA 92668<br><br>Courthouse<br>Santa Ana, CA 92702 | |
| Recorder<br>  b  from 1889<br>  d  from 1889<br>  m  from 1889<br>  lnd from 1889 | 630 N. Broadway<br>P. O. Box 238<br>Santa Ana, CA 92702 | 714/834-2500 |
| Voter Registration | 1300 S. Grand Avenue<br>P. O. Box 11298<br>Santa Ana, CA 92711 | 714/834-3262 |

## ADOPTION AGENCIES

Children's Home Society
300 S. Sycamore Street
Santa Ana, CA 92701
714/542-1147

Latter Day Saints Adoptions
505 North Tustin, Suite 214
Santa Ana, CA 92705
714/973-4764

Holy Family Services
1403 S. Main Street
Santa Ana, CA 92707
714/835-5551

Orange County Adoptions
1920 E. 17th Street
Santa Ana, CA 92701
714/834-4321

## CEMETERIES

| | | | | |
|---|---|---|---|---|
| Anaheim | 1400 E. Sycamore | Anaheim | 92805 | 714/533-4928 |
| Ascension | 24754 Trabuco Road | El Toro | 92630 | 837-1331 |
| El Toro | 25751 Trabuco Road | El Toro | 92630 | 951-8244 |
| Fairhaven Memorial | 1702 E. Fairhaven | Santa Ana | 92701 | 633-1442 |
| Forest Lawn | 4471 Lincoln Ave. | Cypress | 90630 | 828-3131 |
| Good Shepherd | 17952 Beach Blvd. | Huntington Beach | 92647 | 847-8546 |
| Harbor Rest/Mt. Olive | 1625 Gisler | Costa Mesa | 92626 | 545-5554 |
| Holy Sepulcher | 7820 Santiago Canyon | Orange | 92669 | 532-6551 |

| | | | | |
|---|---|---|---|---|
| Loma Vista Memorial | 701 E. Bastanchury | Fullerton | 92635 | 525-1575 |
| Magnolia Memorial | 12241 Magnolia St. | Garden Grove | 92641 | 539-1771 |
| Melrose Abbey | 2303 S. Manchester | Anaheim | 92802 | 634-1981 |
| Memory Garden | 455 W. Central | Brea | 92621 | 529-3961 |
| Pacific View | 3500 Pacific View | Newport Beach | 92625 | 644-2700 |
| Santa Ana Cemetery | 1919 E. Santa Clara | Santa Ana | 92701 | |
| Westminster Memorial | 14801 Beach Blvd. | Westminster | 92683 | 893-2421 |

## CHAMBERS OF COMMERCE

| | | | | |
|---|---|---|---|---|
| Balboa Island | 333 Marine | Balboa Island | 92662 | 714/675-6871 |
| Brea | 770 S. Brea Blvd. | Brea | 92621 | 529-4938 |
| Buena Park | 6696 Beach Blvd. | Buena Park | 90620 | 521-0261 |
| Corona Del Mar | 2855 E. Coast Highway | Corona Del Mar | 92625 | 673-4050 |
| Costa Mesa | 2690 Harbor Blvd. | Costa Mesa | 92627 | 969-0536 |
| Cypress | 9471 Walker Street | Cypress | 90630 | 827-2430 |
| Dana Point | 34102 St. Violet Lantern | Dana Point | 92629 | 496-1555 |
| Fountain Valley | 10525 Slater Avenue | Fountain Valley | 92708 | 962-4441 |
| Fullerton | 219 E. Commonwealth | Fullerton | 92632 | 871-3100 |
| Garden Grove | 11400 Stanford Ave. | Garden Grove | 92640 | 638-7950 |
| Huntington Beach | 18582 Beach Blvd. | Huntington Beach | 92648 | 962-6661 |
| Laguna Beach | 357 Glenneyre Street | Laguna Beach | 92651 | 494-1018 |
| La Habra | 301 W. La Habra Blvd. | La Habra | 90631 | 992-4702 |
| La Palma | 7822 Walker Street | La Palma | 90623 | 523-7700 |
| Newport Beach | 1470 Jamboree Road | Newport Beach | 92660 | 644-8211 |
| Orange | 633 E. Chapman Ave. | Orange | 92666 | 638-3581 |
| Orange County | 1 City Boulevard W. | Anaheim | 92668 | 634-2900 |
| Placentia | 119 N. Bradford Ave. | Placentia | 92670 | 528-1873 |
| Saddleback Valley | 25200 E. La Paz Road | Laguna Hills | 92653 | 837-3000 |
| San Clemente | 1100 N. El Camino Real | San Clemente | 92672 | 492-1131 |
| San Juan Capistrano | 31882 Camino Capistrano | San Juan Capistrano | 92675 | 493-4700 |
| Santa Ana | 1616 E. 4th Street | Santa Ana | 92707 | 541-5353 |
| Tustin | 615 E. 1st Street | Tustin | 92680 | 544-5341 |
| Westminster | 14491 Beach Boulevard | Westminster | 92683 | 898-9648 |
| Yorba Linda | 4897 Lakeview Avenue | Yorba Linda | 92686 | 993-5820 |

## COLLEGES & UNIVERSITIES

| | | | |
|---|---|---|---|
| Cal State Fullerton | | Fullerton | 92634 |
| Chapman | 333 N. Glassell St. | Orange | 92606 |
| Christ College | 1530 Concordia | Irvine | 92715 |
| Coastline College | 10231 Slater Ave. | Fountain Valley | 92708 |
| Cypress College | 9200 Valley View | Cypress | 90630 |
| Fullerton College | | Fullerton | 92631 |
| Golden West College | 15744 Golden West | Huntington Beach | 92647 |
| Orange Coast College | 2701 Fairview Road | Costa Mesa | 92626 |
| Pacific Christian | 2500 E. Nutwood | Fullerton | 92631 |
| Saddleback Community | 28000 Marguerita Pkwy | Mission Viejo | 92675 |
| Santa Ana College | | Santa Ana | 92706 |
| University of Calif. | | Irvine | 92664 |
| West Coast University | 550 S. Main Street | Orange | 92668 |

## HOSPITALS

| | | | |
|---|---|---|---|
| Anaheim Doctors | 1660 W. Broadway | Anaheim | 92802 |
| Anaheim General | 3350 W. Ball Road | Anaheim | 92804 |
| Anaheim Memorial | 1111 W. La Palma | Anaheim | 92801 |
| Beach Community | 5742 Beach Blvd. | Buena Park | 90621 |
| Brea Community | 380 W. Central Ave. | Brea | 92621 |
| Canyon General | 441 Lakeview Ave. | Anaheim | 92807 |
| Chapman General | 2601 E. Chapman | Orange | 92669 |
| Costa Mesa | 301 Victoria | Costa Mesa | 92627 |
| Doctors of Santa Ana | 1901 College Ave. | Santa Ana | 92706 |
| Esperanza | 16850 E. Bastanchury | Yorba Linda | 92686 |
| Fairview State | 2501 Harbor Blvd. | Costa Mesa | 92626 |
| Fountain Valley | 17100 Euclid | Fountain Valley | 92708 |
| Fullerton | 100 E. Valley View | Fullerton | 92632 |
| Garden Park | 950 S. Gilbert St. | Anaheim | 92804 |

| Good Samaritan | 1025 S. Anaheim | Anaheim | 92805 |
| Hoag Memorial | 301 Newport Blvd. | Newport Beach | 92663 |
| Huntington | 17772 Beach Blvd. | Huntington Beach | 92647 |
| La Habra | 1251 W. Lambert Road | La Habra | 90631 |
| La Palma | 7901 Walker Avenue | La Palma | 90623 |
| Lincoln | 6850 Lincoln Blvd. | Buena Park | 91506 |
| Los Alamitos | 3751 Katella Ave. | Los Alamitos | 90721 |
| Martin Luther | 1825 W. Romneya Dr. | Anaheim | 92801 |
| Mercy General | 2701 S. Bristol | Santa Ana | 92704 |
| Mission | 27802 Puerta Real | Mission Viejo | 92691 |
| Pacifica | 18792 Delaware | Huntington Beach | 92648 |
| Palm Harbor | 12601 Garden Grove | Garden Grove | 92643 |
| Placentia | 1301 N. Rose Drive | Placentia | 92670 |
| Riverview | 1901 N. Fairview | Santa Ana | 92706 |
| Saddleback | 24451 Via Estrada | Laguna Hills | 92653 |
| St Joseph | 1100 W. Steward Drive | Orange | 92668 |
| St Jude | 101 E. Valencia Mesa | Fullerton | 92635 |
| San Clemente | 654 Camino De Los Mares | San Clemente | 92672 |
| Santa Ana | 600 E. Washington Ave. | Santa Ana | 92701 |
| Santa Ana-Tustin | 1001 N. Tustin Ave. | Santa Ana | 92705 |
| South Coast | 31872 Coast Highway | So. Laguna | 92677 |
| Stanton | 7770 Katella Avenue | Stanton | 90680 |
| Tustin | 14662 Newport Ave. | Tustin | 92680 |
| University Irvine | 101 The City Drive | Orange | 92668 |
| West Anaheim | 3033 W. Orange Ave. | Anaheim | 92804 |
| Westminster | 200 Hospital Circle | Westminster | 92683 |

## LIBRARIES

| *Anaheim LDS | 440 N. Loara | Anaheim | 92801 | 714/635-2471 |
| Anaheim Public | 500 W. Broadway | Anaheim | 92805 | 999-1880 |
| Balboa | 100 E. Balboa | Newport Beach | 92661 | 640-2241 |
| Banning Annex | 9281 Banning | Huntington Beach | 92646 | 962-6664 |
| Brea | 642 S. Brea | Brea | 92621 | 671-1922 |
| Buena Park | 7150 La Palma | Buena Park | 90620 | |
| Chapman | 9182 Chapman Ave. | Garden Grove | 92641 | 539-2115 |
| Corona Del Mar | 420 Marigold | Newport Beach | 92625 | 640-2191 |
| Costa Mesa | 1855 W. Park | Costa Mesa | 92627 | 646-8845 |
| Cypress | 5331 Orange Ave. | Cypress | 90680 | 826-0350 |
| Dana Niguel | 33840 Niguel Road | Dana Point | 92629 | 496-5517 |
| El Modena | 380 S. Hewes | Orange | 92669 | 639-7181 |
| Euclid | 1340 S. Euclid St. | Anaheim | 92802 | 533-0160 |
| Fountain Valley | 17565 Los Alamos | Fountain Valley | 92708 | 962-1324 |
| Fullerton | 353 Commonwealth | Fullerton | 92631 | 738-6333 |
| Garden Grove | 11200 Stanford | Garden Grove | 92640 | 530-0711 |
| Graham Annex | 15882 Graham | Huntington Beach | 92649 | 894-1307 |
| Haskett | 2540 W. Broadway | Anaheim | 92804 | 821-0551 |
| Hunt | 201 S. Basque Ave. | Fullerton | 92633 | 871-9450 |
| *Huntington Beach | 7111 Talbert Ave. | Huntington Beach | 92648 | 842-4481 |
| Laguna Beach | 363 Glenneyre St. | Laguna Beach | 92651 | 497-1733 |
| La Habra | Civic Center | La Habra | 90631 | 526-7728 |
| La Palma | 7842 Walker | La Palma | 90623 | 523-8585 |
| Leisure World | 2300 Beverly Manor | Seal Beach | 90740 | 213/598-2431 |
| Los Alamitos-Rossmoor | 12700 Montecito Rd. | Seal Beach | 90740 | 213/430-1048 |
| Main Annex | 525 Main Street | Huntington Beach | 92648 | 714/960-3344 |
| Mariners | 2005 Dover Drive | Newport Beach | 92660 | 640-2141 |
| McFadden | 2627 W. McFadden | Santa Ana | 92704 | 834-4085 |
| Mesa Verde | 2969 Mesa Verde Drive | Costa Mesa | 92626 | 546-5274 |
| Mission Viejo | 24851 Chrisanta Drive | Mission Viejo | 92691 | 830-7100 |
| *Mission Viejo LDS | 23850 Los Alisos | Mission Viejo | 92691 | 495-2742 |
| Newhope | 122 N. Newhope St. | Santa Ana | 92703 | |
| Orange | 101 N. Center St. | Orange | 92666 | 532-0391 |
| Orange County | 431 S. The City Drive | Orange | 92668 | 634-7841 |
| *Orange LDS | 674 Yorba Street | Orange | 92669 | 997-7710 |
| Placentia | 411 E. Chapman | Placentia | 92670 | 528-1906 |
| San Clemente | 233 Avenida Granada | San Clemente | 92672 | 492-3493 |

| | | | | |
|---|---|---|---|---|
| Santa Ana | 26 Civic Center Plaza | Santa Ana | 92701 | 834-4013 |
| *Sherman Foundation | 2647 E. Coast Hwy | Corona Del Mar | 92625 | 673-1880 |
| Silverado | 28192 Silverado Canyon | Silverado | 92676 | 649-2216 |
| Stanton | 7850 Katella Avenue | Stanton | 90680 | 898-3300 |
| Sunkist | 901 S. Sunkist Street | Anaheim | 92806 | 956-3501 |
| Taft | 740 E. Taft Avenue | Orange | 92665 | 532-0421 |
| Tustin | 345 E. Main Street | Tustin | 92680 | 544-7725 |
| University Park | 4512 Sandburg Way | Irvine | 92715 | 552-1602 |
| Villa Park | 17865 Santiago Blvd. | Villa Park | 92667 | 998-0861 |
| Westminster | 8180 13th Street | Westminster | 92683 | 893-5057 |
| *Westminster LDS | 10332 Bolsa Avenue | Westminster | 92683 | 531-0591 |
| Wilson Branch | 707 Electric Avenue | Seal Beach | 90740 | 213/431-3584 |
| Yorba Linda | 18262 Lemon Drive | Yorba Linda | 92686 | 777-2873 |

PROFESSIONAL ASSOCIATIONS

Orange County Bar Association
17291 Irvine Boulevard
Tustin, CA 92680

Orange County Medical Association
300 S. Flower
P. O. Box 1297
Orange, CA 92668

## PLACER COUNTY  #31

County Seat:  Auburn
3101  Auburn
3106  Roseville
3197  Rest of County

## PLACER COUNTY OFFICES

| COUNTY OFFICE | ADDRESS | PHONE |
|---|---|---|
| Assessor | Administration Center<br>145 Fulweiler Avenue<br>Auburn, CA 95603 | 916/823-4336 |
| Clerk<br>  b   from 1873<br>  d   from 1873<br>  m   from 1873<br>  div from 1851<br>  pro from 1851<br>  civ from 1851<br>  lnd from 1851 | Courthouse, Room 34<br>P. O. Box 1547<br>Auburn, CA 95603 | 916/823-4471 |
| Courts<br>  Juvenile<br><br><br><br>  Superior | 560 Elm Street<br>Auburn, CA 95603<br><br>Administration Center<br>P. O. Box 1177<br>Tahoe City, CA 95730<br><br>Courthouse, Room 34<br>P. O. Box 1547<br>Auburn, CA 95603 | |
| Election Dept. | 175 Fulweiler Avenue<br>Auburn, CA 95603 | 916/823-4346 |
| Recorder | P. O. Box 1547<br>Auburn, CA 95603 | 916/823-4621 |

## ADOPTION AGENCIES

Children's Home Society
121 E. Orangeburg Ave., Suite 11
Modesto, CA 95350
209/521-5237

Placer County Welfare
Adoption Division
11519 B. Avenue
Auburn, CA 95603
916/823-4788

## CEMETERIES

| | | | | |
|---|---|---|---|---|
| Auburn Cemetery District | Collins Drive | Auburn | 95603 | 916/885-5922 |
| Newcastle Cemetery District | Taylor Road | Newcastle | 95658 | 663-2104 |
| Rocklin Cemetery District | 4090 Kannasto | Rocklin | 95677 | 642-2760 |

## CHAMBERS OF COMMERCE

Auburn Area Chamber of Commerce
1101 High
Auburn, CA 95603

## HOSPITALS

Auburn Faith Hospital
11815 Education Street
Auburn, CA 95603

Roseville Community Hospital
333 Sunrise Avenue
Roseville, CA 95678

## LIBRARIES

| | | | | |
|---|---|---|---|---|
| Applegate | 17870 Applegate Road | Applegate | 95703 | 916/878-2721 |
| Auburn-Placer | 350 Nevada | Auburn | 95603 | 823-4391 |
| Kings Beach | 296 Deer | Kings Beach | 95719 | 546-2021 |
| Lincoln | 590 5th | Lincoln | 95648 | 645-8744 |
| Loomis | Library Drive | Loomis | 95650 | 652-7061 |
| Penryn | Masonic Bldg. | Penryn | 95663 | 663-3621 |
| Placer | 714 N. Lake Blvd. | Tahoe City | 95730 | 583-3382 |
| Rocklin | 3935 Rocklin Road | Rocklin | 95677 | 624-3133 |

PLUMAS COUNTY #32

County Seat:  Quincy
3297  County

PLUMAS COUNTY OFFICES

| COUNTY OFFICE | ADDRESS | PHONE |
|---|---|---|
| Assessor | No. 1 Main Street<br>P. O. Box 1016<br>Quincy, CA 95971 | 916/283-2380 |
| Clerk<br>  div from 1860<br>  pro from 1860<br>  civ from 1860 | 520 W. Main<br>Quincy, CA 95971 | 916/283-1060 |
| Courts<br>  Juvenile<br><br>  Superior | Courthouse<br>Quincy, CA 95971<br><br>Courthouse<br>Quincy, CA 95971 | |
| Recorder<br>  b<br>  d<br>  m | P. O. Box 706<br>Quincy, CA 95971 | 916/283-2940 |
| Voter Records | P. O. Box 207<br>Quincy, CA 95971 | 916/283-1060 |

ADOPTION AGENCIES

Children's Home Society
1216 Sheridan Avenue
Chico, CA 95926
916/342-2464

State Dept. of Social Services
California Adoption Service
500 Cohasset Road, Suite 34
Chico, CA 95926
916/891-1986

CEMETERIES

Quincy Cemetery District
S. Redburg Avenue
East Quincy, CA 95971
916/283-2616

CHAMBERS OF COMMERCE

Plumas County Chamber of Commerce
500 Jackson
Quincy, CA 95971
916/283-2045

COLLEGES & UNIVERSITIES

Feather River College
Highway 70 North
Quincy, CA 95971

## HOSPITALS

| | | | |
|---|---|---|---|
| Eastern Plumas District | 500 1st Avenue | Portola | 96122 |
| Feather River District | 174 Hot Springs Road | Greenville | 95947 |
| Plumas District | Meadow Valley Star Route | Quincy | 95971 |
| Seneca District | Brentwood Drive | Chester | 96020 |

## LIBRARIES

| | | | | |
|---|---|---|---|---|
| Chester Branch | 1st Avenue | Chester | 96020 | 916/258-2742 |
| Plumas County | 171 Nevada | Portola | 96122 | 832-4241 |
| Quincy Branch | 445 Jackson | Quincy | 95971 | 283-0780 |

RIVERSIDE COUNTY #33

County Seat: Riverside

| | | | |
|---|---|---|---|
| 3301 | Banning | 3309 | Hemet |
| 3302 | Beaumont | 3311 | Indio |
| 3303 | Blythe | 3316 | Palm Springs |
| 3305 | Coachella | 3318 | Riverside |
| 3306 | Corona | 3397 | Rest of County |

RIVERSIDE COUNTY OFFICES

| COUNTY OFFICE | ADDRESS | PHONE |
|---|---|---|
| Assessor | 4080 Lemon Street<br>P. O. Box 907<br>Riverside, CA 92502 | 714/787-6331 |
| Clerk<br>  div from 1893<br>  pro from 1893<br>  civ from 1893 | 4050 Main Street<br>Riverside, CA 92501 | 714/787-6151 |
| Courts<br>  Juvenile<br><br>  Superior | P. O. Box 1748<br>Indio, CA 92201<br><br>Courthouse<br>P. O. Box 431<br>Riverside, CA 92502 | |
| Recorder<br>  b  from 1893<br>  d  from 1893<br>  m  from 1893<br>  1nd | 4080 Lemon<br>P. O. Box 751<br>Riverside, CA 92501 | 714/787-2026 |
| Voter Registration | 4175 Main Street<br>Riverside, CA 92501 | 714/787-2921 |

ADOPTION AGENCIES

Children's Home Society  Riverside County Dept. of Adoptions
4353 B Main Street       3707 Sunnyside Drive
Riverside, CA 92501      Riverside, CA 92506
714/686-7603             714/682-4171

CEMETERIES

| | | | | |
|---|---|---|---|---|
| Coachella Valley | 82897 52nd Avenue | Coachella | 92236 | 714/398-3221 |
| Corona | Rimpau Corner | Corona | 91720 | 737-5910 |
| Crestlawn | 11500 Arlington | Riverside | 94805 | 689-1441 |
| Desert Lawn | 11251 Desert Lawn | Calimesa | 92320 | 795-2451 |
| Elsinore Valley | 18170 Collier Ave. | Lake Elsinore | 92330 | 674-2418 |
| Evergreen | 4414 14th | Riverside | 92501 | 683-1840 |
| Green Acres | 11715 Cedar Avenue | Bloomington | 92316 | 877-2311 |
| Mountain View | 1315 Edgar Avenue | Beaumont | 92223 | 845-3303 |
| Olivewood | 3300 Central Ave. | Riverside | 92506 | 683-6611 |
| Palm Springs | 69920 Ramon Road | Palm Springs | 92264 | 328-3316 |
| Perris Valley | 915 N. Perris Blvd. | Perris | 92370 | 657-2352 |
| Riverside National | 22492 Van Buren | Riverside | 92504 | |
| San Jacinto Valley | 24900 Santa Fe St. | Hemet | 92343 | 658-4923 |
| Stewart Sunnyslope | 1st & Pennsylvania | Beaumont | 92223 | 845-1336 |
| Sunnyslope | 2201 N. San Gorgonio | Banning | 92220 | 849-3725 |

## CHAMBERS OF COMMERCE

| | | | | |
|---|---|---|---|---|
| Arlington | 4261 Main Street | Riverside | 92501 | 714/683-7100 |
| Banning | 78 N. Murray St. | Banning | 92226 | 849-2781 |
| Beaumont | 560 E. 6th St. | Beaumont | 92223 | 845-1292 |
| Blythe | 227 E. Hobsonway | Blythe | 92225 | 922-8166 |
| Cathedral City | 36399 Cathedral Canyon | Cathedral City | 92234 | 328-1213 |
| Coachella | 1258 6th Street | Coachella | 92236 | 398-5111 |
| Corona | 904 E. 6th Street | Corona | 91720 | 737-3350 |
| Desert Hot Springs | 13440 Palm Drive | Desert Hot Springs | 92240 | 329-6403 |
| Hemet | 528 E. Florida | Hemet | 92343 | 658-3211 |
| Idyllwild | 54200 N. Circle Dr. | Idyllwild | 92349 | 659-3259 |
| Indio | 82503 Highway 111 | Indio | 92201 | 347-0676 |
| Jurupa | 5563 Mission Blvd. | Rubidoux | 92509 | 686-2860 |
| Lake Elsinore Valley | 132 W. Graham Ave. | Lake Elsinore | 92330 | 674-2577 |
| La Sierra | 4261 Main Street | Riverside | 92501 | 683-7100 |
| Mead Valley | 19199 Clark St. | Mead Valley | 92370 | 657-9129 |
| Moreno Valley | 12540 Headcock St. | Sunnymead | 92388 | 653-4400 |
| Murrieta | 24757 1st Avenue | Murrieta | 92362 | 677-5522 |
| Norco | 3900 Acacia Avenue | Norco | 91760 | 737-2531 |
| Palm Desert | 74004 Highway 111 | Palm Desert | 92260 | 346-6111 |
| Palm Springs | 190 W. Amado Road | Palm Springs | 92262 | 683-7100 |
| Perris Valley | 100 N. D Street | Perris | 92370 | 657-3555 |
| Rancho Mirage | 42339 Bob Hope Drive | Rancho Mirage | 92270 | 346-1022 |
| Riverside | 4261 Main Street | Riverside | 92501 | 683-7100 |
| San Jacinto | 249 E. Main Street | San Jacinto | 92383 | 654-9246 |
| Sun City Area | 28031 Bradly Road | Sun City | 92381 | 679-1290 |
| Thousand Palms | 72715 La Canada Way | Thousand Palms | 92276 | 343-9911 |

## COLLEGES & UNIVERSITIES

| | | | |
|---|---|---|---|
| California Baptist | 8432 Magnolia Ave. | Riverside | 92504 |
| College of the Desert | 43-500 Monterey St. | Palm Desert | 92260 |
| Mount San Jacinto | 21-400 Highway 79 | San Jacinto | 92383 |
| Palo Verde College | 811 W. Chanslorway | Blythe | 92225 |
| Riverside City | 4800 Magnolia Ave. | Riverside | 92506 |
| U. of California | | Riverside | 92521 |
| U. of Calif-Fine Arts | 52500 Temecula Road | Idyllwild | 92349 |

## HOSPITALS

| | | | |
|---|---|---|---|
| Circle City | 730 Magnolia Ave. | Corona | 91729 |
| Community of Valleys | 2224 Ruby Drive | Perris | 92370 |
| Corona Community | 812 S. Washburn | Corona | 91720 |
| Desert | 1151 N. Via Miraleste | Palm Springs | 92262 |
| Eisenhower Medical | 39000 Bob Hope Drive | Palm Desert | 92260 |
| Hemet Valley | 1116 E. Latham | Hemet | 92343 |
| Indio Community | 47111 Monroe Street | Indio | 92201 |
| Knollwood | 5900 Brockton Avenue | Riverside | 92506 |
| Mission Valley | 21220 Walnut Street | Lake Elsinore | 92330 |
| Palo Verde | 250 N. First Street | Blythe | 92225 |
| Parkview Community | 3865 Jackson Street | Riverside | 92503 |
| Riverside | 4455 Magnolia Avenue | Riverside | 92501 |
| Riverside General | 9851 Magnolia Avenue | Riverside | 92503 |
| San Gorgonio Pass | 600 N. Highland Springs | Banning | 92220 |
| Valley Memorial | 82485 Miles Avenue | Indio | 92201 |

## LIBRARIES

| | | | | |
|---|---|---|---|---|
| Arlington | 9556 Magnolia | Arlington | 92503 | 714/689-6612 |
| Banning | 21 W. Nicolet | Banning | 92220 | 849-3192 |
| Beaumont | 125 E. 8th Street | Beaumont | 92223 | 845-1357 |
| Cabazon | 50171 Ramona | Cabazon | 92230 | 849-4082 |
| Casa Blanca | 2985 Madison St. | Riverside | 92504 | 688-3825 |
| Cathedral City | 68715 A Street | Cathedral City | 92234 | 328-4262 |
| Coachella | 1515 6th Street | Coachella | 92236 | 398-5148 |
| Corona | 650 S. Main | Corona | 91720 | 736-2381 |

| | | | |
|---|---|---|---|
| Desert Hot Springs | 11691 West Drive | Desert Hot Springs 92240 | 329-5926 |
| Glen Avon | 9010 Mission Blvd. | Riverside 92509 | 685-8121 |
| Hemet | 510 E. Florida | Hemet 92343 | 658-7293 |
| Highgrove | 937 W. Center St. | Riverside 92507 | 682-1507 |
| Idyllwild | 54962 Pine Crest | Idyllwild 92349 | 659-2300 |
| Indio | 200 Civic Center Mall | Indio 92201 | 347-2383 |
| Lake Elsinore | 400 W. Graham Ave. | Lake Elsinore 92330 | 674-4517 |
| Lake Tamarisk | Lake Tamarisk Drive | Desert Center 92239 | 227-3273 |
| La Sierra | 4600 La Sierra Blvd. | Riverside 92505 | 688-7740 |
| Marcy | 3711 Central Avenue | Riverside 92506 | 682-5524 |
| Mecca-North Shore | 91280 2nd Street | Mecca 92254 | 396-2363 |
| Murray | 100 S. Palm Canyon | Palm Springs 92262 | 323-8296 |
| Norco | 2634 Hamner Avenue | Norco 91760 | 735-5329 |
| Nuview | 29540 Nuevo Road | Nuevo 92367 | 657-4769 |
| Palm Desert | 45480 Portola Ave. | Palm Desert 92660 | 346-6552 |
| Palm Desert | 77-800 California Ave. | Palm Desert 92660 | 345-1745 |
| Palm Springs | 300 S. Sunrise Way | Palm Springs 92262 | 232-8291 |
| Palo Verde Valley | 125 W. Chanslorway | Blythe 92225 | 922-5371 |
| Perris | 424 D Street | Perris 92370 | 657-2358 |
| Rancho California | 27585 Ynez Road | Temecula 92390 | 676-5316 |
| *Riverside | 3581 7th | Riverside 92501 | 787-7201 |
| *Riverside LDS | 5900 Grand Ave. | Riverside 92504 | 784-1918 |
| *Riverside LDS | 4375 Jackson Street | Riverside 92503 | 687-5542 |
| Rubidoux | 5763 Tilton Ave. | Rubidoux 92509 | 682-5485 |
| San Jacinto | 316 E. Main Street | San Jacinto 92383 | 654-7450 |
| Sun City | 28081 Bradley Road | Sun City 92381 | 679-3534 |
| Sunnymead | 24092 Postal Avenue | Sunnymead 92388 | 653-5500 |
| Valle Vista | 43975 E. Florida Ave. | Valle Vista 92507 | 927-2611 |

## PROFESSIONAL ASSOCIATIONS

Riverside County Bar Association
3765 Tenth Street
Riverside, CA 92501

Riverside County Medical Association
6833 Indian
Riverside, CA 92506

SACRAMENTO COUNTY #34

County Seat: Sacramento
3408 North Sacramento
3409 Sacramento
3497 Rest of County

## SACRAMENTO COUNTY OFFICES

| COUNTY OFFICE | ADDRESS | PHONE |
|---|---|---|
| Assessor | 700 H. Street<br>Sacramento, CA 95814 | 916/440-5271 |
| Clerk<br>  div from 1880<br>  pro from 1880<br>  civ from 1880 | 720 Ninth Street<br>Sacramento, CA 95814 | 916/440-5522 |
| Courts<br>  Juvenile<br><br>  Superior | 9601 Kiefer Boulevard<br>Sacramento, CA 95827<br><br>Courthouse<br>Sacramento, CA 95814 | |
| Health Agency<br>  Vital Statistics | 3701 Branch Center Road<br>Sacramento, CA 95826 | 916/366-2145 |
| Recorder<br>  b<br>  d<br>  m<br>  lnd | 901 "G" Street<br>P. O. Box 839<br>Sacramento, CA 95804 | 916/440-6326 |
| Registrar of Voters | 3700 Branch Center Road<br>Sacramento, CA 95827 | 916/366-2051 |

## ADOPTION AGENCIES

Children's Home Society
3731 "T" Street
Sacramento, CA 95816
916/452-4672

Sacramento County Adoptions
3701 Branch Center Road
Sacramento, CA 95827
916/366-2367

Latter Day Saints Adoptions
3000 Auburn Blvd., Suite #1
Sacramento, CA 95821
916/488-6111

## CEMETERIES

| | | | | |
|---|---|---|---|---|
| Arlington Memorial | Elder Creek Road | Sacramento | 95826 | 916/ |
| Bellview | Elder Creek Road | Sacramento | 95826 | |
| Calvary | 7101 Verner Avenue | Sacramento | 95841 | 332-0533 |
| Camellia Memorial | 10221 Jackson Road | Walsh Station | 95832 | 363-9431 |
| City Cemetery | 10th and Broadway | Sacramento | 95817 | |
| East Lawn | 43rd & Folsom | Sacramento | 95819 | 455-3033 |
| East Lawn Sierra | 6700 Verner Avenue | Sacramento | 95841 | 332-5398 |
| East Lawn Southgate | 9189 Stockton Blvd. | Elk Grove | 95624 | 422-4114 |
| Elder Creek | Elder Creek Road | Sacramento | 95826 | |
| Elk Grove | Bond & Waterman | Elk Grove | 95624 | |
| Fair Oaks | 7780 Olive Street | Fair Oaks | 95628 | 966-1613 |
| Franklin | Hood Franklin Road | Franklin | 94558 | |

| Home of Peace | 5700 El Paraiso | Sacramento | 95824 | 393-1535 |
|---|---|---|---|---|
| Lakeside | 507 Scott Street | Folsom | 95630 | 985-2295 |
| Masonic Lawn | 2700 Riverside Blvd. | Sacramento | 95818 | 443-7796 |
| Mt. Vernon | 8201 Greenback Lane | Fair Oaks | 95628 | 967-1251 |
| Odd Fellow Lawn | 2720 Riverside Blvd. | Sacramento | 95818 | 443-8598 |
| Rocklin | 4090 Kannasto St. | Rocklin | 95677 | 624-2760 |
| Sacramento County | 21st Avenue | Sacramento | 95826 | |
| Sacramento | 6100 Stockton Blvd. | Sacramento | 95824 | 421-1171 |
| St. Josephs | 2615 21st Street | Sacramento | 95820 | 455-8324 |
| St. Marys | 6700 21st Avenue | Sacramento | 95820 | 452-2831 |
| St. Rose Catholic | Franklin Blvd. | Sacramento | 95823 | |
| San Joaquin | Stockton & Sheldon | Sacramento | 95838 | |
| Sunset Lawn | 4701 Marysville Blvd. | Sacramento | 95838 | 922-5833 |
| Sylvan | Ramona Lane & Auburn | Citrus Heights | 95610 | |

## CHAMBER OF COMMERCE

Sacramento Metropolitan Chamber of Commerce
P. O. Box 1017
Sacramento, CA 95805

## COLLEGES & UNIVERSITIES

| | | | |
|---|---|---|---|
| American River College | 4700 College Oak Dr. | Sacramento | 95841 |
| California State U. | 6000 "J" Street | Sacramento | 95819 |
| Cosumnes River College | 8401 Center Pkwy | Sacramento | 95823 |
| Missionary Baptist | 2351 Wyda Way | Sacramento | 95825 |
| Sacramento City | 3835 Freeport Blvd. | Sacramento | 95822 |

## HOSPITALS

| | | | |
|---|---|---|---|
| American River | 4747 Engle Road | Carmichael | 95608 |
| Community of Sacramento | 2251 Hawthorne | N. Sacramento | 95838 |
| Kaiser Foundation | 2025 Morse Avenue | Sacramento | 95825 |
| Mercy Children's | 3994 H Street | Sacramento | 95819 |
| Mercy Sacramento | 4001 J Street | Sacramento | 95819 |
| Mercy San Juan | 6501 Coyle Avenue | Carmichael | 95608 |
| Methodist | 7500 Timberlake Way | Elk Grove | 95624 |
| Sacramento Medical | 2315 Stockton Blvd. | Sacramento | 95817 |
| Sutter General | 2820 L Street | Sacramento | 95816 |
| Sutter Memorial | 52nd and F Streets | Sacramento | 95819 |
| Twin Lakes | 223 Fargo Way | Folsom | 95630 |

## LIBRARIES

| | | | | |
|---|---|---|---|---|
| Arcade | 2443 Marconi Ave. | Sacramento | 95821 | 916/483-5061 |
| Arden | 891 Watt Avenue | Arden | 95825 | 483-6361 |
| Broderick | 904 Sacramento | Broderick | 95605 | 372-0700 |
| Carmichael | 5604 Marconi Ave. | Carmichael | 95608 | 483-6055 |
| Central | 828 I Street | Sacramento | 95814 | 449-5203 |
| Coloma Way | 1299 Coloma Way | Roseville | 95678 | 782-4090 |
| Cooledge | 5681 Freeport | Sacramento | 95822 | 421-1222 |
| Courtland | River Road | Courtland | 95615 | 775-1113 |
| Del Paso Heights | 920 Grand Avenue | Sacramento | 95838 | 927-1133 |
| Elk Grove | 8980 Elk Grove | Elk Grove | 95624 | 685-4798 |
| Fair Oaks | 11601 Fair Oaks | Fair Oaks | 95628 | 966-5740 |
| Folsom | 311 Market Street | Folsom | 95630 | 985-2780 |
| Fruitridge | 4612A 44th Street | Sacramento | 95820 | |
| Galt | 380 Civic Drive | Galt | 95632 | 745-2066 |
| Gillis | 4001 60th Street | Sacramento | 95820 | 455-2985 |
| Isleton | 101 C Street | Isleton | 95641 | 777-6638 |
| King Regional | 7340 24th St. Bypass | Sacramento | 95822 | 421-3151 |
| McClatchy | 2112 22nd Street | Sacramento | 95818 | 455-8153 |

| | | | | |
|---|---|---|---|---|
| McKinley | 601 Alhambra Blvd. | Sacramento | 95816 | 442-0598 |
| North Highlands | 3601 Plymouth Drive | No. Highlands | 95660 | 331-0675 |
| North Sacramento | 492 Arden Way | Sacramento | 95815 | 927-0652 |
| Oak Park | 3301 5th Street | Sacramento | 95818 | 455-8522 |
| Rancho Cordova | 9845 Folsom Blvd. | Rancho Cordova | 95670 | 362-0641 |
| Rio Linda | 902 Oak Lane | Rio Linda | 95673 | 991-4515 |
| Roseville | 557 Lincoln Street | Roseville | 95678 | 783-7158 |
| *Sacramento LDS | 2745 Eastern Avenue | Sacramento | 95821 | 487-2090 |
| Southgate | 6132 66th Avenue | Sacramento | 95823 | 421-6327 |
| Sylvan | 6700 Auburn Blvd. | Citrus Heights | 95610 | 961-1734 |
| Walnut Grove | 14185 River Road | Walnut Grove | 95690 | 776-1412 |
| West Sacramento | 1212 Merkley Avenue | W. Sacramento | 95818 | 371-5612 |

PROFESSIONAL ASSOCIATIONS

Sacramento County Bar Association
901 "H" Street, Suite 101
Sacramento, CA 95514

SAN BENITO COUNTY #35

County Seat: Hollister
3501 Hollister
3597 Rest of County

SAN BENITO COUNTY OFFICES

| COUNTY OFFICE | ADDRESS | PHONE |
|---|---|---|
| Assessor | Courthouse<br>Hollister, CA 95023 | 408/637-5561 |
| Clerk/Recorder<br>　b　 from 1874<br>　d　 from 1874<br>　m　 from 1874<br>　div from 1874<br>　pro from 1874<br>　bur from 1874<br>　civ from 1874<br>　lnd from 1874 | 440 5th Street<br>Room 206<br>Courthouse<br>Hollister, CA 95023 | 408/637-3786 |
| Courts<br>　Juvenile<br><br>　Superior | 470 Fifth Street<br>Hollister, CA 95023<br><br>Courthouse<br>Hollister, CA 95023 | |
| Elections Clerk | Courthouse, Room 208<br>Hollister, CA 95023 | 408/637-1057 |

ADOPTION AGENCIES

Children's Home Society
1010 Ruff Drive
San Jose, CA 95110
408/293-8940

State Dept. of Social Services
California Adoption Service
2400 Glendale Lane, Suite B
Sacramento, CA 95825
916/920-6897

CEMETERIES

Calvary Cemetery
1100 Hillcrest Road
Hollister, CA 95023
916/637-0131

CHAMBER OF COMMERCE

San Juan Bautista
319 3rd Street
San Juan Bautista, CA 95045

HOSPITALS

Hazel Hawkins Memorial
300 Canal Street
Hollister, CA 95023

San Benito Hospital District
911 Sunset Drive
Hollister, CA 95023

LIBRARIES

San Benito County Library
470 5th
Hollister, CA 95023

San Juan Bautista City Library
801 2nd
San Juan Bautista, CA 95045

County Seat:  San Bernardino

| | | | |
|---|---|---|---|
| 3601 | Barstow | 3617 | Redlands |
| 3604 | Chino | 3618 | Rialto |
| 3605 | Colton | 3619 | Upland |
| 3614 | Needles | 3607 | Rest of County |
| 3615 | Ontario | | |

### SAN BERNARDINO COUNTY OFFICES

| COUNTY OFFICE | ADDRESS | PHONE |
|---|---|---|
| Assessor | 172 W. Third Street<br>San Bernardino, CA 92401 | 714/383-2717 |
| Clerk<br>m   from 1887<br>div from 1856<br>pro from 1856<br>civ from 1853<br>ins from 1887<br>ine from 1887<br>lnd from 1854<br>crm from 1853<br>grd from 1856 | 351 N. Arrowhead Avenue<br>San Bernardino, CA 92401 | 714/383-1313 |
| Courts<br>  Juvenile<br><br><br>  Superior | County Civic Center<br>175 W. Fifth Street<br>San Bernardino, CA 92401<br><br>Courthouse<br>San Bernardino, CA 92402<br><br>1540 N. Mountain Avenue<br>Ontario, CA 91762 | |
| Recorder<br>b from 1853<br>d from 1853<br>m from 1857 | 172 W. Third Street<br>San Bernardino, CA 92401 | 714/383-1361 |
| Registrar of Voters | 777 E. Rialto Avenue<br>San Bernardino, CA 92415 | 714/383-1811 |

### ADOPTION AGENCIES

Children's Home Society
4353 Main Street
Riverside, CA 92501
714/686-7603

San Bernardino County Adoptions
670 E. Gilbert Street
San Bernardino, CA 92404
714/383-1514

San Bernardino County Adoptions
325 East "C" Street
Ontario, CA 91764
714/988-1066

## CEMETERIES

| | | | | |
|---|---|---|---|---|
| Bellevue | 1240 W. "G" Street | Ontario | 91762 | 714/984-3611 |
| Desert View | 11500 Amargosa Road | Hesperia | 92345 | 244-9366 |
| Green Acres | 11715 Cedar Avenue | Bloomington | 92316 | 877-2311 |
| Hermosa | 900 N. Meridian Ave. | Colton | 92324 | 825-3110 |
| Hillside | 1540 Alessandro Road | Redlands | 92373 | 793-2361 |
| Montecito | Waterman & Barton | Colton | 92324 | 825-3024 |
| Mountain Valley | 60121 29 Palms Highway | Joshua Tree | 92252 | 366-9210 |
| Mt. View | Waterman & Highland | San Bernardino | 92404 | 882-2943 |
| Pioneer | 211 E. 9th Street | San Bernardino | 92401 | 885-6385 |
| Rialto | 2nd St. & Willow Ave. | Rialto | 92376 | |
| Riverview | San Clemente & Hwy 95 | Needles | 92363 | |
| Victor Valley | 11th and "C" | Victorville | 92392 | 245-4291 |

## CHAMBERS OF COMMERCE

| | | | |
|---|---|---|---|
| Adelanto | 11713 Bartlett | Adelanto | 92301 |
| Alta Loma | 8520 Avalon Court | Alta Loma | 91701 |
| Apple Valley | 18144 Highway 18 | Apple Valley | 92307 |
| Barstow | 270 E. Virgina | Barstow | 92811 |
| Big Bear | 520 Bartlett | Big Bear Lake | 92315 |
| Chino | 13141 Central Ave. | Chino | 91710 |
| Colton | 620 N. La Cadena | Colton | 92324 |
| Crestline | 23440 Crest Forest | Crestline | 92325 |
| Cucamonga | 9354 Foothill | Cucamonga | 91730 |
| Fontana | 8610 Wheeler Ave. | Fontana | 92335 |
| Hesperia | 17142 Main Street | Hesperia | 92345 |
| Joshua Tree | 61857 29 Palms Hwy | Joshua Tree | 92252 |
| Lake Arrowhead | 322 N. Highway 173 | Lake Arrowhead | 92352 |
| Loma Linda | 25682 Barton Road | Loma Linda | 92354 |
| Lucerne Valley | 32750 Old Woman Springs | Lucerne Valley | 92356 |
| Montclair | 10268 Central Avenue | Montclair | 91763 |
| Morongo Valley | 49730 29 Palms Hwy | Morongo Valley | 92256 |
| Needles | Front & "G" Streets | Needles | 92363 |
| Ontario | 123 W. "D" Street | Ontario | 91762 |
| Redlands | 347 N. Orange Street | Redlands | 92373 |
| Rialto | 120 N. Riverside Ave. | Rialto | 92376 |
| Running Springs | 31930 Hilltop Blvd. | Running Springs | 92382 |
| San Bernardino | 546 W. 6th Street | San Bernardino | 92410 |
| Twentynine Palms | 73629 29 Palms Hwy | Twentynine Palms | 92277 |
| Upland | 886 W. Foothill Blvd. | Upland | 91786 |
| Victorville | 14173 Greentree Blvd. | Victorville | 92392 |
| Wrightwood | 1300 Evergreen Road | Wrightwood | 92397 |
| Yucaipa Valley | 34968 Avenue "H" | Yucaipa | 92399 |
| Yucca Valley | 56297 29 Palms Hwy | Yucca Valley | 92284 |

## COLLEGES & UNIVERSITIES

| | | | |
|---|---|---|---|
| Barstow College | 2700 Barstow Road | Barstow | 92311 |
| California State | 5500 State College | San Bernardino | 92407 |
| Chaffey College | 5885 Haven Avenue | Alta Loma | 91701 |
| Crafton Hills | 11711 Sand Canyon | Yucaipa | 92399 |
| Loma Linda U. | | Loma Linda | 92354 |
| San Bernardino Valley | 701 S. Mount Vernon | San Bernardino | 92403 |
| University of Redlands | 1200 E. Colton Ave. | Redlands | 92373 |
| Victor Valley College | P. O. Drawer OO | Victorville | 92392 |

## HOSPITALS

| | | | |
|---|---|---|---|
| Barstow | 555 S. 7th Street | Barstow | 92311 |
| Bear Valley | 41870 Garstin | Big Bear Lake | 92315 |
| Chino General | 5451 Walnut Avenue | Chino | 91710 |
| Doctors | 5000 San Bernardino | Montclair | 91763 |
| Hi Desert | 6601 White Feather | Joshua Tree | 92252 |
| Kaiser | 9961 Sierra Avenue | Fontana | 92335 |
| Loma Linda | 25333 Barton Road | Loma Linda | 92354 |

| Montclair | 5050 San Bernardino | Montclair | 91763 |
|---|---|---|---|
| Mountains | Highway 173 | Lake Arrowhead | 92352 |
| Needles | 1401 Bailey Avenue | Needles | 92363 |
| Ontario | 550 N. Monterey Ave. | Ontario | 91764 |
| Patton State | 3102 E. Highland | Highland | 92346 |
| Pettis | 11201 Benton | Loma Linda | 92354 |
| Redlands | 350 Terracina Blvd. | Redlands | 92373 |
| St. Bernardines | 2101 N. Waterman Ave. | San Bernardino | 92404 |
| St. Mary Desert | 18300 Highway 18 | Apple Valley | 92307 |
| San Antonio | 999 San Bernardino | Upland | 91786 |
| San Bernardino | 1500 W. 17th Street | San Bernardino | 92411 |
| San Bernardino County | 780 E. Gilbert | San Bernardino | 92404 |
| Santa Fe | 995 W. 5th Street | San Bernardino | 92407 |
| Trona | 82824 Trona Road | Trona | 93562 |
| Victor Valley | 15248 11th Street | Victorville | 92392 |

## LIBRARIES

| Adelanto | 11744 Bartlett | Adelanto | 92301 | 714/246-5661 |
|---|---|---|---|---|
| Apple Valley | 22051 Highway 18 | Apple Valley | 92307 | 247-2022 |
| Barstow | 304 E. Buena Vista | Barstow | 92311 | 256-8481 |
| *Barstow LDS | 2571 Barstow Road | Barstow | 92311 | 252-4117 |
| Big Bear Lake | 40940 Big Bear Blvd. | Big Bear Lake | 92315 | 866-4190 |
| Bloomington | 10145 Orchard Street | Bloomington | 92316 | 877-1453 |
| Chino | 13180 Central Avenue | Chino | 91710 | 628-1604 |
| Coddington | 1003 E. Highland Ave. | San Bernardino | 92404 | 882-8816 |
| Colton | 380 N. Lacadena Drive | Colton | 92324 | 825-1585 |
| Crestline | 607 Forest Shade | Crestline | 92325 | 338-3294 |
| Eastbase Line | 27167 E. Baseline St. | Highland | 92346 | 862-8549 |
| Fontana | 8334 Emerald Avenue | Fontana | 92335 | 822-2321 |
| Hesperia | 16170 Walnut Street | Hesperia | 92345 | 244-4898 |
| Inghram | 1505 W. Highland Ave. | San Bernardino | 92411 | 887-4494 |
| Joshua Tree | 6430 Park Boulevard | Joshua Tree | 92252 | 366-8615 |
| Lake Arrowhead | 27248 Blue Jay Mall | Lake Arrowhead | 92352 | 337-3118 |
| Loma Linda | 11215 Mountain View | Loma Linda | 92354 | 796-8621 |
| Lucerne Valley | Old Woman Springs Rd. | Lucerne Valley | 92356 | 248-7521 |
| Mentone | 1868 Mentone Blvd. | Mentone | 92359 | 794-2657 |
| Montclair | Civic Center-Fremont | Montclair | 91763 | 624-4671 |
| Needles | 1111 Bailey Avenue | Needles | 92363 | 326-2623 |
| Ontario | 215 E. "C" Street | Ontario | 91764 | 984-2758 |
| Rancho Cucamonga | 9191 Base Line Ave. | Cucamonga | 91730 | 987-3107 |
| Redlands | 125 W. Vine Street | Redlands | 92373 | 793-2201 |
| Rialto | 251 W. 1st Street | Rialto | 92376 | 875-0144 |
| Rowe | 108 E. Marshall Blvd. | San Bernardino | 92404 | 883-3411 |
| Running Springs | 31976 Hilltop Blvd. | Running Springs | 92382 | 867-2554 |
| San Bernardino | 104 W. 4th Street | San Bernardino | 92401 | 383-1734 |
| *San Bernardino LDS | 7000 Central Avenue | San Bernardino | 92408 | 862-9972 |
| San Bernardino Main | 401 N. Arrowhead | San Bernardino | 92461 | 889-0264 |
| Trona | 82805 Mountain View | Trona | 93562 | 372-5847 |
| Twentynine Palms | 6078 Adobe Road | 29 Palms | 92277 | 367-9519 |
| Upland | 450 N. Euclid Avenue | Upland | 91786 | 982-1561 |
| *Upland LDS | 785 N. San Antonio | Upland | 91786 | 985-8821 |
| Victorville | 15011 Circle Drive | Victorville | 92392 | 245-4222 |
| Villasenor | 1244 W. 9th Street | San Bernardino | 92411 | 884-9696 |
| Yucaipa | 12040 5th Street | Yucaipa | 92349 | 797-9316 |
| Yucca Valley | 57098 29 Palms Hwy | Yucca Valley | 92284 | 365-2387 |

## PROFESSIONAL ASSOCIATIONS

San Bernardino County Medical Society
P. O. Box 5216
San Bernardino, CA 92412

SAN DIEGO COUNTY #37 and #80

County Seat:  San Diego
    8003  Chula Vista          8015  National City
    8004  Coronado             8017  Oceanside
    8006  El Cajon             8020  San Diego
    8009  Escondido            8097  Rest of County
    8012  La Mesa

## SAN DIEGO COUNTY OFFICES

| COUNTY OFFICE | ADDRESS | PHONE |
|---|---|---|
| Assessor | 1600 Pacific Highway<br>San Diego, CA 92101 | 714/236-3073 |
| Clerk<br>  div from 1855<br>  pro from 1855<br>  civ from 1855 | 220 W. Broadway<br>P. O. Box 128<br>San Diego, CA 92112 | 714/236-3275 |
| Courts<br>  Juvenile<br><br><br>  Superior | 2901 Meadowland Drive<br>P. O. Box 23096<br>San Diego, CA 92123<br><br>Courthouse<br>220 Broadway<br>San Diego, CA 92101 | |
| Health Care Services<br>  Vital Statistics | 1700 Pacific Hwy, Room 101<br>San Diego, CA 92101 | 714/236-2296 |
| Recorder<br>  b<br>  d<br>  m<br>  lnd | P. O. Box 1750<br>1600 Pacific Highway<br>San Diego, CA 92112 | 714/236-2695 |
| Registrar of Voters | 5201-I Ruffin Road<br>San Diego, CA 92123 | 714/565-5800 |

## ADOPTION AGENCIES

Children's Home Society
7695 Cardinal Court
San Diego, CA 92123
714/278-7800

San Diego County Adoptions
6950 Levant Street
San Diego, CA 92111
714/560-2301

Latter Day Saints
5821 Linda Paseo
San Diego, CA 92115
714/287-4410

San Diego County Adoptions
516 Cassidy Street, Suite B
Oceanside, CA 92045
714/433-5151

San Diego County Adoptions
5106 Federal Blvd., Room 201
San Diego, CA 92113
714/263-7707

## CEMETERIES

| | | | | |
|---|---|---|---|---|
| Cypress View | 3953 Imperial | San Diego | 92113 | 714/264-3169 |
| El Camino | 9450 Carroll Canyon | San Diego | 92121 | 453-2121 |
| Eternal Hills | 1999 El Camino Real | Oceanside | 92054 | 757-2020 |
| Glen Abbey | P. O. Box 607 | Chula Vista | 92012 | 422-0118 |
| Greenwood | 43rd & Market | San Diego | 92121 | 264-3131 |
| Holy Cross | 4470 Hilltop Drive | San Diego | 92101 | 264-3127 |
| La Vista | 3191 Orange Avenue | National City | 92050 | 475-7770 |

## CHAMBERS OF COMMERCE

| | | | | |
|---|---|---|---|---|
| Alpine | 2157 Alpine Blvd. | Alpine | 92001 | 714/445-2722 |
| Borrego Springs | Palm Canyon Road | Borrego Springs | 92004 | 767-5555 |
| Cardiff by the Sea | 154 Aberdeen Drive | Cardiff | 92007 | 436-0431 |
| Carlsbad | Elm Avenue | Carlsbad | 92008 | 729-1181 |
| Chula Vista | 233 4th Avenue | Chula Vista | 92010 | 420-6602 |
| Coronado | 720 Orange Avenue | Coronado | 92118 | 435-9260 |
| Del Mar | 1049 Camino Del Mar | Del Mar | 92014 | 755-4844 |
| El Cajon | 109 Rea Avenue | El Cajon | 92020 | 440-6161 |
| Encinitas | 1st Street | Encinitas | 92024 | 753-6041 |
| Escondido | 720 N. Broadway | Escondido | 92025 | 745-2125 |
| Fallbrook | 300 N. Main | Fallbrook | 92028 | 728-5845 |
| Imperial Beach | 825 Coronado Ave. | Imperial Beach | 92032 | 424-3151 |
| Julian | P. O. Box 413 | Julian | 92036 | 765-0273 |
| Lakeside | 9815 Maine Avenue | Lakeside | 92040 | 561-1031 |
| La Mesa | 8155 University Ave. | La Mesa | 92041 | 465-7700 |
| Lemon Grove | 3415 Imperial Ave. | Lemon Grove | 92045 | 469-9621 |
| National City | 711 A Avenue | National City | 92050 | 477-9339 |
| Oceanside | 510 4th Street | Oceanside | 92054 | 722-1534 |
| Old San Diego | 2547 San Diego Ave. | San Diego | 92110 | 291-4903 |
| Poway | 13255 Poway Road | Poway | 92064 | 748-0082 |
| Ramona | 729 Main Street | Ramona | 92065 | 789-1311 |
| San Diego | 110 W. C Street | San Diego | 92101 | 232-0124 |
| San Diego East | 3865 43rd Street | San Diego | 92105 | 283-6777 |
| San Diego Junior | 702 Ash Street | San Diego | 92101 | 234-4197 |
| San Marcos | 245 N. Rancho Santa Fe | San Marcos | 92069 | 744-1270 |
| Santee | 10315 Mission Gorge | Santee | 92071 | 449-6572 |
| San Ysidro | 421 W. San Ysidro Blvd. | San Ysidro | 92073 | 428-2258 |
| Solana Beach | 210 W. Plaza | Solana Beach | 92075 | 755-4775 |
| South Bay | 1720 Palm Avenue | San Diego | 92154 | 429-9063 |
| Spring Valley | 10783 Jamacha Blvd. | Spring Valley | 92114 | 466-5736 |
| Vista | 117 S. Santa Fe | Vista | 92083 | 726-1122 |

## COLLEGES & UNIVERSITIES

| | | | |
|---|---|---|---|
| Christian Heritage | 2100 Greenfield Drive | El Cajon | 92021 |
| Cuyamaca College | 2950 Jamacha Road | El Cajon | 92020 |
| Grossmont College | Grossmont College Dr. | El Cajon | 92020 |
| Mira Costa College | Barnard Drive | Oceanside | 92054 |
| National University | 4141 Camino del Rio | San Diego | 92108 |
| Palomar College | 1140 W. Mission | San Marcos | 92069 |
| Point Loma | 3900 Lomaland Drive | San Diego | 92106 |
| San Diego Community | 1425 Russ Boulevard | San Diego | 92101 |
| San Diego Community | 7250 Mesa College Dr. | San Diego | 92111 |
| San Diego Community | 10440 Black Mountain | San Diego | 92126 |
| Southwestern | 900 Otay Lakes Road | Chula Vista | 92010 |
| United States U. | 10455 Pomerado Road | San Diego | 92131 |
| University of Calif. | P. O. Box 109 | La Jolla | 92093 |
| University of San Diego | Alcala Park | San Diego | 92110 |

## HOSPITALS

| | | | |
|---|---|---|---|
| Alvarado Community | 6655 Alvarado Road | San Diego | 92120 |
| Bay General | 435 H Street | Chula Vista | 92010 |
| Cabrillo | 3475 Kenyon Street | San Diego | 92110 |
| Centre City | 120 Elm Street | San Diego | 92101 |

| | | | |
|---|---|---|---|
| Childrens | 8001 Frost Street | San Diego | 92123 |
| Clairemont | 5255 Mount Etna | San Diego | 92117 |
| College Park | 6666 Montezuma | San Diego | 92115 |
| Community | 751 Dora Lane | Chula Vista | 92010 |
| Community | 446 26th Street | San Diego | 92113 |
| Coronado | 250 Prospect | Coronado | 92118 |
| El Cajon Valley | 1688 E. Main Street | El Cajon | 92021 |
| Fallbrook | 624 E. Elder Street | Fallbrook | 92028 |
| Grossmont | 5555 Grossmont | La Mesa | 92041 |
| Heartland | 203 Travelodge Dr. | El Cajon | 92020 |
| Hillside | 1940 El Cajon Blvd. | San Diego | 92104 |
| Kaiser | 4647 Zion Avenue | San Diego | 92120 |
| Mercy | 4077 5th Avenue | San Diego | 92103 |
| Mission Bay | 3030 Bunker Hill | San Diego | 92109 |
| Mt. Helix | 7050 Parkway Drive | La Mesa | 92041 |
| Tri-City | 1100 5th Avenue | Oceanside | 92054 |
| Palomar | 550 E. Grand Avenue | Escondido | 92025 |
| Paradise Valley | 2400 E. 4th Street | National City | 92050 |
| Pomerado | 15615 Pomerado Road | Poway | 92064 |
| Scripps Clinic | 10666 N. Torrey Pine | La Jolla | 92037 |
| Scripps Memorial | 9888 Genesee Avenue | La Jolla | 92037 |
| Scripps | 354 Santa Fe Drive | Encinitas | 92024 |
| Sharp | 7901 Frost Street | San Diego | 92123 |
| Tri-City | 4002 Vista Way | Oceanside | 92024 |
| University | 225 Dickinson St. | San Diego | 92103 |
| Villa View | 5550 University Ave. | San Diego | 92105 |

## LIBRARIES

| | | | | |
|---|---|---|---|---|
| Alpine | 2130 Arnold Way | Alpine | 92001 | 714/445-4221 |
| Balboa | 4255 Mt. Abernathy | Balboa | 92117 | 277-4133 |
| Beckworth | 721 San Pasqual | San Diego | 92113 | 264-1288 |
| Benjamin | 5188 Zion Street | San Diego | 92120 | 583-2428 |
| Bonita-Sunnyside | 5047 Central | Bonita | 92002 | 475-4642 |
| Borrego | 652 Palm Canyon | Borrego Springs | 92004 | 767-5761 |
| Campo-Morena | 31466 Highway 94 | Campo | 92006 | 478-5945 |
| Cardiff | 2143 Newcastle | Cardiff | 92007 | 753-4027 |
| Carlsbad | 1250 Elm Avenue | Carlsbad | 92008 | 729-7933 |
| Casa De Oro | 9628 Campo Road | Spring Valley | 92077 | 463-3236 |
| Castle Park | 1592 3rd Avenue | Chula Vista | 92011 | 427-1151 |
| Chula Vista | 365th F Street | Chula Vista | 92010 | 575-5062 |
| Clairemont | 2920 Burgener Blvd. | San Diego | 92110 | 276-1140 |
| College Heights | 4710 College Ave. | San Diego | 92115 | 583-6810 |
| Coronado | 640 Orange Avenue | Coronado | 92118 | 435-4187 |
| Crest | 105 Juanita Lane | El Cajon | 92021 | 442-7083 |
| Del Mar | 1050 Camino Del Mar | Del Mar | 92014 | 755-1666 |
| Descanso | Viejas Grande & Oak | Descanso | 92016 | 445-5279 |
| East San Diego | 4089 Fairmount Ave. | San Diego | 92105 | 283-3632 |
| El Cajon | 202 E. Lexington | El Cajon | 92020 | 579-4454 |
| Encinitas | 540 Cornish Drive | Encinitas | 92024 | 753-7376 |
| Escondido | 239 S. Kalmia | Escondido | 92025 | 741-4683 |
| *Escondido LDS | 609 N. Citrus | Escondido | 92027 | 741-8441 |
| Fallbrook | 124 S. Mission Road | Fallbrook | 92028 | 728-2373 |
| Fletcher Hills | 576 Garfield Avenue | El Cajon | 92020 | 466-1132 |
| Imperial Beach | 810 Imperial Beach | Imperial Beach | 92032 | 424-6981 |
| Jacumba | 44511 Old Highway 80 | Jacumba | 92034 | 766-4608 |
| Julian | 4th & Washington | Julian | 92036 | 765-0370 |
| La Jolla | 1006 Wall Street | La Jolla | 92037 | 459-5174 |
| Lakeside | 9839 Vine Street | Lakeside | 92040 | 443-1811 |
| La Mesa | 8055 University Avenue | La Mesa | 92041 | 469-2151 |
| Lemon Grove | 8073 Broadway | Lemon Grove | 92045 | 463-9819 |
| Lincoln Acres | 2725 Granger Avenue | National City | 92050 | 475-9880 |
| Linda Vista | 6960 Linda Vista Road | San Diego | 92111 | 277-3637 |
| Logan Heights | 811 South 28th Street | San Diego | 92102 | 239-6580 |
| Mira Mesa | 8450 Mira Mesa Blvd. | San Diego | 92126 | 271-8410 |
| Mission Hills | 925 W. Washington | San Diego | 92103 | 296-2660 |
| National City | 200 E. 12th Street | National City | 92050 | 474-8211 |

| | | | | |
|---|---|---|---|---|
| Normal Heights | 4121 Adams Avenue | San Diego | 92116 | 283-3733 |
| North Clairemont | 4616 Clairemont | San Diego | 92117 | 274-4610 |
| North Park | 3795 31st Street | San Diego | 92104 | 283-4535 |
| Oak Park | 2902 54th Street | San Diego | 92105 | 262-8249 |
| Ocean Beach | 4801 Santa Monica | San Diego | 92107 | 223-8757 |
| Oceanside | 615 4th Street | Oceanside | 92054 | 433-9011 |
| Otay Mesa | 2925 Coronado Lane | San Diego | 92154 | 424-5871 |
| Pacific Beach | 4606 Ingraham Street | San Diego | 92109 | 273-9581 |
| Paradise Hills | 5922 Rancho Hills | San Diego | 92139 | 479-3538 |
| Pine Valley | 28857 Highway 80 | Pine Valley | 92062 | 473-8022 |
| Point Loma | 2130 Poinsettia | San Diego | 92107 | 223-1161 |
| Potrero | 24955 Library Lane | Potrero | 92063 | 478-5978 |
| Poway | 13264 Poway Road | Poway | 92064 | 748-2411 |
| Ramona | 1406 Montecito | Ramona | 92065 | 789-0430 |
| Rancho Bernardo | 16840 Bernardo Center | San Diego | 92128 | 487-2146 |
| Rancho Santa Fe | Avenida De Acacias | RanchoSanta Fe | 92067 | 756-2512 |
| San Carlos | 7265 Jackson Drive | San Diego | 92119 | 461-4480 |
| *San Diego | 820 E. Street | San Diego | 92101 | 236-5800 |
| San Diego | 5555 Overland Avenue | San Diego | 92123 | 656-5100 |
| *San Diego LDS | 3705 Tenth Avenue | San Diego | 92103 | 295-9808 |
| San Marcos | 131 W. Richmar Road | San Marcos | 92069 | 744-0707 |
| Santee | 10515 Mission Gorge | Santee | 92071 | 448-1863 |
| San Ysidro | E. Park & San Ysidro | San Ysidro | 92073 | 428-2111 |
| Serra Mesa | 3440 Sandrock Road | San Diego | 92123 | 278-0640 |
| Skyline Hills | 480 S. Meadowbrook | San Diego | 92114 | 479-5835 |
| Solana Beach | 155 S. Highway 101 | Solana Beach | 92075 | 755-1404 |
| Spring Valley | 1043 Elkelton Blvd. | Spring Valley | 92077 | 463-3006 |
| University | 4155 Governor Drive | La Jolla | 92037 | 453-5722 |
| University Heights | 4193 Park Boulevard | San Diego | 92103 | 296-4514 |
| Valencia Park | 101 50th Street | San Diego | 92102 | 264-8370 |
| Valley Center | 29115 Valley Center Rd. | Valley Center | 92082 | 749-1305 |
| Vista | 325 S. Melrose Drive | Vista | 92083 | 724-5507 |
| Woodlawn Park | 115 Spruce Road | Chula Vista | 92011 | 426-8111 |

## PROFESSIONAL ASSOCIATIONS

San Diego County Bar
1200 Third Ave., Suite 604
San Diego, CA 92101

San Diego County Medical
3702 Ruffin Road
San Diego, CA 92123

SAN FRANCISCO COUNTY  #38 and #90

County Seat:  San Francisco
9097  All of County

SAN FRANCISCO COUNTY OFFICES

| COUNTY OFFICE | ADDRESS | PHONE |
|---|---|---|
| Assessor | Room 101, City Hall<br>San Francisco, CA 94102 | 415/558-4351 |
| Clerk<br>  div from 1906<br>  pro from 1906<br>  civ from 1906 | Room 313, City Hall<br>San Francisco, CA 94102 | 415/558-4082 |
| Courts<br>  Juvenile<br><br>  Superior | 375 Woodside Avenue<br>San Francisco, CA 94127<br><br>480 City Hall<br>San Francisco, CA 94102 | |
| Department of Health<br>  b<br>  d<br>  bur | 101 Grove Street<br>San Francisco, CA 94102 | 415/558-3581 |
| Recorder<br>  m | Room 155, City Hall<br>San Francisco, CA 94102 | 415/558-3417 |
| Registrar of Voters | Room 155, City Hall<br>San Francisco, CA 94102 | 415/558-3417 |

ADOPTION AGENCIES

Children's Home Society
3000 California Street
San Francisco, CA 94115
415/922-2803

Dept. of Social Services
Adoption Services
170 Otis Street
San Francisco 94103
415/558-3765

CEMETERIES

| Hills of Eternity | 2266 California | 94115 | 415/346-1720 |
|---|---|---|---|
| Salem | 625 Brotherhood Way | 94132 | 586-8833 |
| San Francisco National | Presidio of San Francisco | 94118 | 561-2008 |

CHAMBERS OF COMMERCE

Greater San Francisco Chamber of Commerce
465 California Street, 9th Floor
San Francisco, CA 94104

COLLEGES & UNIVERSITIES

| Cal. Institute of Asian Studies | 3494 21st Street | San Francisco | 94110 |
|---|---|---|---|
| Cal. School of Psychology | 2450 17th Street | San Francisco | 94110 |
| City College of San Francisco | 50 Phelan Avenue | San Francisco | 94112 |
| Cogswell College | 600 Stockton St. | San Francisco | 94108 |
| Golden Gate University | 536 Mission St. | San Francisco | 94105 |
| Heald Engineering College | 1215 Van Ness | San Francisco | 94109 |
| Lincoln University | 281 Masonic Ave. | San Francisco | 94118 |
| Lone Mountain | 2800 Turk Blvd. | San Francisco | 94118 |

| New College of California | 777 Valencia | San Francisco | 94110 |
| San Francisco Art Institute | 800 Chestnut Street | San Francisco | 94133 |
| San Francisco Conservatory of Music | 1201 Ortega Street | San Francisco | 94122 |
| San Francisco State University | 1600 Holloway Ave. | San Francisco | 94132 |
| Simpson College | 801 Silver Avenue | San Francisco | 94134 |
| University of California | 501 Parnassus Ave. | San Francisco | 94122 |
| University of San Francisco | Golden Gate & Parker | San Francisco | 94117 |
| U. Of California College of Law | 198 Mc Allister St. | San Francisco | 94102 |

## HOSPITALS

| Chinese Hospital | 835 Jackson St. | San Francisco | 94133 |
| French Hospital | Geary & 5th Ave. | San Francisco | 94118 |
| Kaiser | 2425 Geary Blvd. | San Francisco | 94115 |
| Laguna Honda | 375 Laguna Honda | San Francisco | 94116 |
| Letterman Army | Presidio | San Francisco | 94129 |
| Marshall Hale | 3773 Sacramento | San Francisco | 94118 |
| Mount Zion | 1600 Divisadero | San Francisco | 94115 |
| Pacific | Clay & Buchanan | San Francisco | 94115 |
| Presbyterian | 2333 Buchanan | San Francisco | 94115 |
| Ralph K. Davies | Castro & Duboce | San Francisco | 94114 |
| St. Francis | 900 Hyde Street | San Francisco | 94109 |
| St. Josephs | 355 Buena Vista | San Francisco | 94117 |
| St. Lukes | 3555 Army Street | San Francisco | 94110 |
| St. Marys | 450 Stanyar St. | San Francisco | 94117 |
| San Francisco General | 1001 Portrero | San Francisco | 94110 |
| U.S. Public Health | 15th Ave. & Lake | San Francisco | 94118 |
| U. of California | | San Francisco | 94143 |

## LIBRARIES

| Anna Waden | 5075 3rd Street | San Francisco | 94124 | 415/468-1323 |
| Anza | 550 37th Avenue | San Francisco | 94121 | 752-1960 |
| Bernal | 500 Cortland Ave. | San Francisco | 94110 | 285-1744 |
| Business | 530 Kearny St. | San Francisco | 94108 | 558-3946 |
| Chinatown | 1135 Powell St. | San Francisco | 94133 | 989-6770 |
| Communications | 3150 Sacramento | San Francisco | 94115 | 558-4034 |
| Eureka Valley | 3555 16th Street | San Francisco | 94114 | 626-1132 |
| Excelsior | 4400 Mission St. | San Francisco | 94112 | 586-4075 |
| Glen Park | 653 Chenery St. | San Francisco | 94131 | 586-4144 |
| Golden Gate | 1801 Green St. | San Francisco | 94123 | 346-9273 |
| Ingleside | 387 Ashton St. | San Francisco | 94112 | 586-4156 |
| Marina | Chestnut & Webster | San Francisco | 94132 | 346-9336 |
| Merced | 155 Winston Drive | San Francisco | 94132 | 586-4246 |
| Mission | 3359 24th Street | San Francisco | 94110 | 824-2810 |
| Noe Valley | 451 Jersey Street | San Francisco | 94114 | 285-2788 |
| North Beach | 2000 Mason Street | San Francisco | 94133 | 391-9473 |
| Ocean View | 111 Broad Street | San Francisco | 94112 | 586-4193 |
| Ortega | 3223 Ortega St. | San Francisco | 94122 | 681-1848 |
| Park | 1833 Page Street | San Francisco | 94117 | 752-4620 |
| Parkside | 1200 Taraval St. | San Francisco | 94116 | 566-4647 |
| Portola | 2434 San Bruno | San Francisco | 94134 | 468-2232 |
| Potrero | 1616 20th Street | San Francisco | 94107 | 285-3022 |
| Richmond | 351 9th Avenue | San Francisco | 94118 | 752-1240 |
| *San Francisco | Civic Center | San Francisco | 94102 | 558-3191 |
| Sunset | 1305 18th Avenue | San Francisco | 94122 | 566-4552 |
| Visitacion | 45 Leland Avenue | San Francisco | 94134 | 239-5270 |
| Western Addition | 1550 Scott | San Francisco | 94115 | 346-9531 |
| West Portal | 190 Lenox Way | San Francisco | 94127 | 566-4584 |

## PROFESSIONAL ASSOCIATIONS

San Francisco Bar Association  San Francisco Lawyers Club
220 Bush Street                1255 Post Street
San Francisco, CA 94104        San Francisco, CA 94109

San Francisco Medical Society
250 Masonic Avenue
San Francisco, CA 94118

SAN JOAQUIN COUNTY #39

County Seat:  Stockton
    3902  Lodi                  3907  Tracy
    3903  Manteca               3997  Rest of County
    3905  Stockton

## SAN JOAQUIN COUNTY OFFICES

| COUNTY OFFICE | ADDRESS | PHONE |
|---|---|---|
| Assessor | 306 E. Main Street<br>Courthouse<br>Stockton, CA 95202 | 209/946-0200 |
| Clerk<br>  div from 1851<br>  pro from 1851<br>  civ from 1851 | P. O. Box 810<br>222 E. Weber Avenue<br>Stockton, CA 95202 | 209/944-3201 |
| Courts<br>  Juvenile<br><br>  Superior | Courthouse<br>Stockton, CA 95202<br><br>Room 302<br>222 E. Weber Avenue<br>Stockton, CA 95202 | |
| Recorder<br>  b<br>  d<br>  m<br>  lnd | 24 S. Hunter Street<br>Room 304<br>Stockton, CA 95202 | 209/944-2522 |
| Registration-Elections | 119 E. Weber Avenue<br>Stockton, CA 95202 | 209/944-2671 |

## ADOPTION AGENCIES

Children's Home Society
121 E. Orangeburg Avenue
Modesto, CA 95350
209/521-5237

Dept. of Public Assistance
Adoptions Department
300 N. Harrison
Stockton, CA 95203
209/466-6061

## CEMETERIES

| Cherokee Memorial | Highway 99 at Harney | Lodi | 95240 | 209/369-1981 |
|---|---|---|---|---|
| Lodi Memorial | 5668 E. Pine Street | Lodi | 95240 | 368-6541 |
| Park View | E. French Camp Road | Manteca | 95336 | 982-1611 |
| San Joaquin Catholic | Cemetery Lane | Stockton | 95204 | 466-6202 |

## CHAMBERS OF COMMERCE

Mexican American Chamber of Commerce
1201 N. Center
Stockton, CA 95202

Stockton Chamber of Commerce
1105 N. El Dorado
Stockton, CA 95202

## COLLEGES & UNIVERSITIES

| Humphreys College | 6650 Inglewood Street | Stockton | 95207 |
| San Joaquin Delta | 5151 Pacific Avenue | Stockton | 95207 |
| U. of the Pacific | 3601 Pacific Avenue | Stockton | 95211 |

## HOSPITALS

| Dameron | 525 W. Acacia | Stockton | 95203 |
| Lodi Community | 800 S. Lower Sacramento | Lodi | 95240 |
| Lodi Memorial | 975 S. Fairmont Avenue | Lodi | 95240 |
| Manteca | 300 Cottage Avenue | Manteca | 95336 |
| Oak Park | 2510 N. California | Stockton | 95204 |
| San Joaquin | Hospital Road | Stockton | 95201 |
| St. Josephs | 1800 N. California | Stockton | 95204 |
| Stockton State | 510 E. Magnolia Street | Stockton | 95202 |
| Tracy Community | 1420 Tracy Boulevard | Tracy | 95376 |

## LIBRARIES

| Central Library | 605 N. El Dorado | Stockton | 95202 | 209/944-8415 |
| Fair Oaks Branch | 2125 E. Main | Stockton | 95205 | 464-2171 |
| Southeast Branch | 2326 S. Airport Way | Stockton | 95206 | 463-8025 |
| Margaret Troke | 502 W. Benjamin Holt | Stockton | 95207 | 952-0814 |

## PROFESSIONAL ASSOCIATIONS

San Joaquin County Bar          San Joaquin County Medical
301 E. Weber Avenue             445 W. Acacia
Stockton, CA 95202              Stockton, CA 95201

SAN LUIS OBISPO COUNTY #40

County Seat:  San Luis Obispo
    4003  El Paso de Robles (Paso Robles)
    4009  San Luis Obispo
    4097  Rest of County

SAN LUIS OBISPO COUNTY OFFICES

| COUNTY OFFICE | ADDRESS | PHONE |
|---|---|---|
| Assessor | Palm & Osos<br>San Luis Obispo, CA 93401 | 805/544-5643 |
| Clerk<br>  div from 1854<br>  pro from 1854<br>  civ from 1854 | Courthouse Annex, Room 202<br>San Luis Obispo, CA 93408 | 805/549-5241 |
| Courts<br>  Juvenile<br><br>  Superior | Courthouse<br>San Luis Obispo, CA 93401<br><br>Courthouse Annex, Room 202<br>San Luis Obispo, CA 93401 | |
| Recorder<br>  b<br>  d<br>  m<br>  lnd | 1000 Monterey Street<br>Room 102<br>San Luis Obispo, CA 93408 | 805/549-5432 |
| Voter Registration | Courthouse Annex, Room 202<br>San Luis Obispo, CA 93408 | 805/549-5235 |

ADOPTION AGENCIES

Children's Home Society
1941 Johnson Avenue, Suite K
San Luis Obispo, CA 93401
805/541-1474

County Social Services
1185 Islay Street
San Luis Obispo, CA 93401
805/543-5700

CEMETERIES

| | | | | |
|---|---|---|---|---|
| Arroyo Grande Cemetery Dist. | 895 Frontage Road | Arroyo Grande | 93420 | 805/489-2475 |
| Atascadero Cemetery District | Mercedes Avenue | Atascadero | 93422 | 466-1242 |
| Cayucos Morro Bay | Highway 1 | Cayucos | 93430 | 995-3898 |
| Los Osos Valley | 2260 Los Osos Valley | San Luis Obispo | 93401 | 528-1500 |
| Paso Robles Cemetery Dist. | Nacimiento Lake Dr. | Paso Robles | 93446 | 238-4544 |

COLLEGES & UNIVERSITIES

California State Polytechnic University
San Luis Obispo, CA 93407

Cuesta College
P. O. Box J
San Luis Obispo, CA 93406

## HOSPITALS

| | | | |
|---|---|---|---|
| Arroyo Grande | 345 S. Halcyon Road | Arroyo Grande | 93420 |
| French Hospital | 1911 Johnson Avenue | San Luis Obispo | 93401 |
| Paso Robles | 15th St. Box 367 | Paso Robles | 93446 |
| San Luis Obispo | 2180 Johnson Avenue | San Luis Obispo | 93401 |
| Sierra Vista | 1010 Murray Street | San Luis Obispo | 93401 |
| Twin Cities | 1500 Las Tablas Road | Templeton | 93465 |

## LIBRARIES

| | | | |
|---|---|---|---|
| Arroyo Grande | 127 Bridge | Arroyo Grande | 93420 |
| Cambria | 4036 Bruton Dr. | Cambria | 93428 |
| Grover City | 111 S. 9th | Grover City | 93433 |
| Halcyon | S. Halcyon Road | Halcyon | 93420 |
| Morro Bay | 410 Morro Bay | Morro Bay | 93442 |
| Paso Robles | 12th and Park | Paso Robles | 93446 |
| Santa Margarita | Murphy Ave. & 1st | Santa Margarita | 93453 |
| Shell Beach | Veterans Bldg. | Shell Beach | 93449 |
| South Bay | 809 Los Osos Valley | Los Osos | 93402 |

County Seat: Redwood City

| | | | |
|---|---|---|---|
| 4101 | Atherton | 4114 | Redwood City |
| 4103 | Belmont | 4115 | San Bruno |
| 4105 | Burlingame | 4116 | San Carlos |
| 4107 | Daly City | 4117 | San Mateo |
| 4110 | Hillsborough | 4119 | So. San Francisco |
| 4112 | Menlo Park | 4197 | Rest of County |
| 4113 | Millbrae | | |

## SAN MATEO COUNTY OFFICES

| COUNTY OFFICE | ADDRESS | PHONE |
|---|---|---|
| Assessor | 2200 Broadway<br>Redwood City, CA 94063 | 415/364-5600 |
| Clerk-Recorder<br>  b   from 1866<br>  d   from 1866<br>  m   from 1866<br>  div from 1880<br>  pro from 1850<br>  civ from 1880<br>  1nd from 1850 | Hall of Justice & Records<br>Redwood City, CA 94063 | 415/364-5600 |
| Courts<br>  Juvenile<br><br>  Superior | 21 Tower Road<br>Belmont, CA 94002<br><br>Courthouse<br>Redwood City, CA 94063 | |
| Voter Registration | 40 Tower Road<br>Belmont, CA 94002 | 415/573-2081 |

## ADOPTION AGENCIES

Children's Home Society
3200 Telegraph Avenue
Oakland, CA 94609
415/655-7406

San Mateo Social Services
225 37th Avenue
San Mateo, CA 94403
415/573-2823

## CEMETERIES

| | | | | 415/ |
|---|---|---|---|---|
| Catholic | Main St. & Highway 92 | Half Moon Bay | 94019 | |
| Chinese | Callan Boulevard | Daly City | 94015 | 992-4581 |
| Cypress Lawn | Mission Boulevard | Colma | 94014 | 755-0580 |
| Eternal Home | El Camino Real | Colma | 94014 | 755-5236 |
| Golden Gate | Sneath Lane | San Bruno | 94066 | 761-1646 |
| Greek Orthodox | El Camino Real | Colma | 94014 | 755-6939 |
| Greenlawn | El Camino Real | Colma | 94014 | 755-7622 |
| Hills of Eternity | El Camino Real | Colma | 94014 | 756-3633 |
| Holy Cross | Mission Road | Colma | 94014 | 756-2060 |
| Home of Peace | El Camino Real | Colma | 94014 | 755-4700 |
| Italian | El Camino Real | Colma | 94014 | 755-1511 |
| Japanese | El Camino Real | Colma | 94014 | 755-3747 |
| Odd Fellows | El Camino Real | Colma | 94014 | 755-7622 |

| Olivet | 1601 Hillside Blvd. | Colma | 94014 | 755-0322 |
| St. John's | Parrott Drive | San Mateo | 94402 | |
| Salem | El Camino Real | Colma | 94014 | 755-5296 |
| Serbian | 1801 Hillside Blvd. | Colma | 94014 | 755-2453 |
| Skylawn | Skyline Boulevard | San Mateo | 94402 | 349-4411 |
| Woodlawn | Junipero Serra Blvd. | Colma | 94015 | 755-1727 |

## CHAMBERS OF COMMERCE

| | | | |
|---|---|---|---|
| Belmont City | 944 Ralston Avenue | Belmont | 94002 |
| Brisbane | 42 Visitacion Ave. | Brisbane | 94005 |
| Burlingame | 306 Lorton Avenue | Burlingame | 94010 |
| Daly City | 312 90th Street | Daly City | 94015 |
| Foster City | 1291 E. Hillsdale | Foster City | 94404 |
| Half Moon Bay | 625 Miramontes | Half Moon Bay | 94019 |
| Menlo Park | 1100 Merrill St. | Menlo Park | 94025 |
| Millbrae | 348 Broadway | Millbrae | 94030 |
| Pacifica | 80 Eureka Square | Pacifica | 94044 |
| Redwood City | 1006 Middlefield | Redwood City | 94063 |
| San Bruno | 440 San Mateo Ave. | San Bruno | 94066 |
| San Carlos | 666 Elm Street | San Carlos | 94070 |
| San Mateo | 2031 Pioneer Court | San Mateo | 94403 |
| So. San Francisco | 65 Arroyo Drive | So. San Francisco | 94080 |

## COLLEGES & UNIVERSITIES

| | | | |
|---|---|---|---|
| Canada College | 4200 Farm Hill | Redwood City | 94061 |
| College of Notre Dame | 1500 Ralston Ave. | Belmont | 94002 |
| College of San Mateo | 1700 W. Hillsdale | San Mateo | 94402 |
| Menlo College | El Camino Real | Atherton | 94025 |
| Skyline College | 3300 College Dr. | San Bruno | 94066 |

## HOSPITALS

| | | | |
|---|---|---|---|
| H. D. Chope | 222 W. 39th Avenue | San Mateo | 94402 |
| Half Moon Bay | Etheldore at Marine | Moss Beach | 94038 |
| Kaiser-Permanente | 1150 Veterans Blvd. | Redwood City | 94063 |
| Kaiser-Permanente | 1200 El Camino Real | So. San Francisco | 94080 |
| Mary's Help | 1900 Sullivan Avenue | Daly City | 94015 |
| Mills | 100 S. San Mateo Dr. | San Mateo | 94401 |
| Peninsula | 1783 El Camino Real | Burlingame | 94010 |
| Sequoia | Alameda de las Pulgas | Redwood City | 94061 |

## LIBRARIES

| | | | | |
|---|---|---|---|---|
| Atherton | 2 Station Lane | Atherton | 94025 | 415/328-2422 |
| Bayshore | 2960 Geneva Ave. | Daly City | 94014 | 467-5477 |
| Belmont | 1110 Alameda De las Pulgas | Belmont | 94002 | 591-8286 |
| Brisbane | 245 Visitacion Avenue | Brisbane | 94005 | 467-2060 |
| Burlingame | 480 Primrose Road | Burlingame | 94010 | 344-7107 |
| Burlingame | 1800 Easton Drive | Burlingame | 94010 | 343-1794 |
| E. Palo Alto | 2415 University Avenue | Palo Alto | 94303 | 321-7712 |
| Fair Oaks | 2600 Middlefield | Redwood City | 94063 | 364-5050 |
| Foster City | 600 Foster City Blvd. | Foster City | 94404 | 574-4842 |
| Grand Avenue | 440 Grand Avenue | So. San Francisco | 94080 | 877-8530 |
| Half Moon Bay | 620 Correas Avenue | Half Moon Bay | 94019 | 726-2316 |
| Hillsdale | 205 W. Hillsdale | San Mateo | 94403 | 574-6960 |
| Marina | 1530 Susan Court | San Mateo | 94403 | 574-6970 |
| Menlo Park | Alma & Ravenswood | Menlo Park | 94025 | 326-4421 |
| *Menlo Park LDS | 1105 Valparaise Ave. | Menlo Park | 94025 | 325-5289 |
| Millbrae | 1 Library Avenue | Millbrae | 94030 | 697-7607 |

| Mission | 6351 Mission Street | Daly City | 94014 | 992-3032 |
|---|---|---|---|---|
| Pacifica | Hilton & Palmetto Avenue | Pacifica | 94044 | 355-5196 |
| Portola Valley | 765 Portola Road | Portola Valley | 94025 | 851-0560 |
| Redwood City | 881 Jefferson Avenue | Redwood City | 94063 | 369-3737 |
| San Bruno | 701 Angus Avenue West | San Bruno | 94066 | 588-7726 |
| San Carlos | 655 Chestnut Street | San Carlos | 94070 | 591-0341 |
| San Mateo | 55 W. 3rd Avenue | San Mateo | 94402 | 574-6950 |
| San Mateo County | 25 Tower Road | San Mateo | 94402 | 573-2056 |
| Schaberg | 2140 Euclid Avenue | Redwood City | 94061 | 368-8628 |
| Serramonte | 40 Wembley Drive | Daly City | 94015 | 878-8900 |
| Westlake | 275 Southgate Avenue | Daly City | 94015 | 992-2414 |
| West Orange | 840 W. Orange Avenue | So. San Francisco | 94080 | 877-8525 |
| Woodside | 3140 Woodside Road | Woodside | 94062 | 851-0147 |

## PROFESSIONAL ASSOCIATIONS

San Mateo County Bar          San Mateo County Medical Society
333 Bradford Street           3080 La Selva
Redwood City, CA 94063        San Mateo, CA 94403

SANTA BARBARA COUNTY  #42

County Seat:  Santa Barbara

4205  Lompoc
4208  Santa Barbara
4209  Santa Maria
4297  Rest of County

SANTA BARBARA COUNTY OFFICES

| COUNTY OFFICE | ADDRESS | PHONE |
|---|---|---|
| Assessor | 105 E. Anapamu Street<br>Room 204<br>Santa Barbara, CA 93101 | 805/966-1611 |
| Clerk<br>  m   from 1850<br>  div from 1850<br>  pro from 1850<br>  civ from 1850 | P. O. Drawer CC<br>Santa Barbara, CA 93102 | 805/963-7180 |
| Courts<br>  Juvenile<br><br><br><br><br>  Superior | 4500 Hillister Avenue<br>Santa Barbara, CA 93110<br><br>P. O. Box 1068<br>Santa Maria, CA 93454<br><br>Courthouse<br>Santa Barbara, CA 93104<br><br>P. O. Box 1068<br>Santa Maria, CA 93454 | |
| Recorder<br>  b from 1878<br>  d from 1878 | P. O. Drawer CC<br>Santa Barbara, CA 93102 | 805/963-7180 |
| Registrar of Voters | County Courthouse<br>P. O. Drawer CC<br>Santa Barbara, CA 93102 | 805/963-7190 |

ADOPTION AGENCIES

Children's Home Society
824 Bath Street
Santa Barbara, CA 93101
805/962-9191

County Welfare Dept.
35 W. Micheltorena St.
Santa Barbara, CA 93101
805/963-6151

Children's Home Society
Santa Maria Office
210 W. Main Street, Suite 6
Santa Maria, CA 93454
805/925-0330

134

## CEMETERIES

| | | | |
|---|---|---|---|
| Calvary | 199 Hope Avenue | Santa Barbara | 93110 |
| Carpinteria | 1550 Cravens Lane | County | 93013 |
| Goleta | 44 S. San Antonio | County | 93117 |
| Guadalupe | Guadalupe & Main | Guadalupe | 93434 |
| Lompoc Evergreen | S. 'C' Street | Lompoc | 93436 |
| Santa Barbara | E. Cabrillo Blvd. | Santa Barbara | 93110 |
| Santa Maria | 730 E. Stowell Rd. | Santa Maria | 93454 |

## CHAMBERS OF COMMERCE

| | | | |
|---|---|---|---|
| Goleta Valley | 5902 Calle Real | County | 93117 |
| Lompoc Valley | 119 E. Cypress | Lompoc | 93436 |
| Santa Barbara | 1301 Santa Barbara | Santa Barbara | 93101 |
| Santa Maria | 614 S. Broadway | Santa Maria | 93455 |

## COLLEGES & UNIVERSITIES

| | | | |
|---|---|---|---|
| Allan Hancock | 800 S. College Dr. | Santa Maria | 93454 |
| Brooks Institute | 2190 Alston Road | Santa Barbara | 93108 |
| Santa Barbara City | 721 Cliff Drive | Santa Barbara | 93109 |
| U. of California | | Santa Barbara | 93106 |
| Westmont College | 955 La Paz Road | Santa Barbara | 93108 |

## HOSPITALS

| | | | |
|---|---|---|---|
| Cottage | Pueblo at Bath | Santa Barbara | 93105 |
| Goleta Valley | 351 S. Patterson | County | 93017 |
| Lompoc | 508 E. Hickory | Lompoc | 93436 |
| Marian | 1400 E. Church St. | Santa Maria | 93454 |
| St. Francis | 601 E. Micheltorena | Santa Barbara | 93103 |
| Santa Barbara | 300 N. San Antonio | County | 93110 |
| Santa Ynez Valley | 700 Alamo Pintado | County | |
| Valley Community | 505 E. Plaza Drive | Santa Maria | 93454 |

## LIBRARIES

| | | | |
|---|---|---|---|
| Carpinteria | 5141 Carpinteria | Carpinteria | 93013 |
| Central | 40 E. Anapamu | Santa Barbara | 93101 |
| Eastside | 1102 E. Montecito | Santa Barbara | 93103 |
| Goleta | 500 N. Fairview | County | 93117 |
| *Goleta LDS | 478 Cambridge | Goleta | 93117 |
| Guadalupe | 1005 Guadalupe | Guadalupe | 93434 |
| Lompoc | 501 E. North Ave. | Lompoc | 93436 |
| *Lompoc LDS | 1312 W. Prune | Lompoc | 93436 |
| Los Alamos | 405 Helena St. | County | 93440 |
| Montecito | 1482 E. Valley Rd. | County | 93105 |
| Orcutt | 156 F. Union Ave. | County | 93455 |
| Santa Maria | 420 S. Broadway | Santa Maria | 93455 |
| Solvang | 1745 Mission Dr. | County | 93463 |
| Vandenburg | 3755 Constellation | County | 93437 |

## PROFESSIONAL ASSOCIATIONS

Santa Barbara County Medical Society
Nine E. Pedragosa
Santa Barbara, CA 93101

County Seat:  San Jose

| | | | |
|---|---|---|---|
| 4303 | Gilroy | 4311 | San Jose |
| 4306 | Los Gatos | 4312 | Santa Clara |
| 4309 | Mountain View | 4314 | Sunnyvale |
| 4310 | Palo Alto | 4397 | Rest of County |

## SANTA CLARA COUNTY OFFICES

| COUNTY OFFICE | ADDRESS | PHONE |
|---|---|---|
| Assessor | 70 W. Hedding Street<br>San Jose, CA 95110 | 408/299-4347 |
| Clerk<br>   pro from 1850 | 191 N. First Street<br>San Jose, CA 95113 | 408/299-2964 |
| Courts<br>   Juvenile | 840 Guadalupe Parkway<br>San Jose, CA 95110 | |
| Superior | 191 N. First Street<br>San Jose, CA 95113 | |
| Recorder<br>   b    from 1873<br>   d    from 1873<br>   m    from 1850<br>   lnd from 1846 | 70 W. Hedding Street<br>San Jose, CA 95110 | 408/299-2483 |
| Registrar of Voters | 1555 Berger Drive<br>P. O. Box 1147<br>San Jose, CA 95108 | 408/298-7400 |

## ADOPTION AGENCIES

Children's Home Society
1010 Ruff Drive
San Jose, CA 95110
408/293-8940

Dept. of Social Services
Children's Services
100 N. Winchester Blvd.
Santa Clara, CA 95050
408/299-3311

## CEMETERIES

| | | | | |
|---|---|---|---|---|
| Alta Mesa | 695 Arastradero | Palo Alto | 94306 | 408/493-1041 |
| Calvary Catholic | 2655 Madden Avenue | San Jose | 95116 | 258-2940 |
| Gate of Heaven | 22555 Cristo Rey | Los Altos | 94022 | 738-2121 |
| Los Gatos | 2255 Los Gatos | Los Gatos | 95030 | 356-4151 |
| Madronia | 14766 Oak Street | Saratoga | 95070 | 867-3717 |
| Masonic | Hecker Pass Hwy | Gilroy | 95020 | 842-2948 |
| Mission City | Winchester Blvd. | Santa Clara | | 984-3090 |
| Oak Hill | 300 Curtner Avenue | San Jose | 95125 | 297-2447 |
| St. Mary's | Hecker Pass Hwy | Gilroy | 95020 | 847-5151 |
| Santa Clara | 490 Lincoln Street | Santa Clara | 95050 | 296-4656 |

## CHAMBERS OF COMMERCE

| | | | |
|---|---|---|---|
| Campbell | 328 E. Campbell | Campbell | 95008 |
| Cupertino | 10381 S. De Anza | Cupertino | 95014 |
| Gilroy | 7780 Monterey | Gilroy | 95020 |
| Los Altos | 321 University | Los Altos | 94022 |
| Los Gatos | 5 Montebello Way | Los Gatos | 95030 |
| Milpitas | 1 N. Main Street | Milpitas | 95035 |
| Morgan Hill | 17334 Monterey | Morgan Hill | 95037 |
| Mountain View | 580 Castro St. | Mountain View | 94041 |
| Palo Alto | 2 Palo Alto Square | Palo Alto | 94301 |
| San Jose | 1 Paseo de San Antonio | San Jose | 95113 |
| Santa Clara | 1515 El Camino Real | Santa Clara | 95050 |
| Saratoga | 20460 Saratoga | Saratoga | 95070 |
| Sunnyvale | Murphy & W. Olive | Sunnyvale | 94086 |

## COLLEGES & UNIVERSITIES

| | | | |
|---|---|---|---|
| De Anza | 21250 Stevens Creek | Cupertino | 95014 |
| Evergreen Valley | 3095 Yerba Buena | San Jose | 95135 |
| Foothill | 12345 S. El Monte | Los Altos Hills | 94022 |
| Gavilan | 5055 Santa Teresa | Gilroy | 95020 |
| Lincoln | 1050 Park Avenue | San Jose | 95126 |
| San Jose City | 2100 Moorpark Ave. | San Jose | 95128 |
| San Jose State | 125 S. 7th Street | San Jose | 95112 |
| Stanford | Junipero Serra Blvd. | Palo Alto | 94304 |
| U. of Santa Clara | 820 Alviso Street | Santa Clara | 95050 |
| West Valley | 14000 Fruitvale Ave. | Saratoga | 95070 |
| West Valley | 44 E. Latimer Avenue | Campbell | 95008 |

## HOSPITALS

| | | | |
|---|---|---|---|
| Alexian | 225 N. Jackson | San Jose | 95116 |
| El Camino | 2500 Grant Road | Mountain View | 95050 |
| Good Samaritan | 2425 Samaritan | San Jose | 95124 |
| Kaiser Permanente | 900 Kiely Blvd. | Santa Clara | 95051 |
| O'Connor | 2105 Forest Avenue | San Jose | 95128 |
| San Jose | 675 E. Santa Clara | San Jose | 95112 |
| Santa Clara Valley | 751 S. Bascom Ave. | San Jose | 95128 |
| Stanford University | 300 Pasteur Drive | Palo Alto | 94304 |
| Wheeler | 651 6th Street | Gilroy | 95020 |

## LIBRARIES

| | | | | |
|---|---|---|---|---|
| Almaden | 6455 Camden Avenue | San Jose | 95120 | 408/268-7600 |
| Alum Rock | 75 S. White Road | Alum Rock | | 251-1280 |
| Alviso | 1060 Taylor Street | Alviso | 95002 | 263-3626 |
| Berryessa | 3311 Noble Avenue | San Jose | 95132 | 272-3554 |
| Biblioteca | 937 Locust Street | San Jose | 95110 | 294-1237 |
| Calabazas | 1230 S. Blaney | San Jose | 95121 | 996-1535 |
| Calaveras | 78 S. Dempsey Road | Milpitas | 95035 | 262-1171 |
| Cambrian | 1780 Hillsdale | San Jose | 95124 | 269-5062 |
| Campbell | 70 N. Central Ave. | Campbell | 95008 | 378-8122 |
| Childrens | 1276 Harriet Avenue | Palo Alto | 94301 | 329-2134 |
| College Terrace | 2300 Wellesley | Palo Alto | 94306 | 329-2298 |
| Community | 160 S. Main Street | Milpitas | 95035 | 262-0351 |
| Cupertino | 10400 Torre Avenue | Cupertino | 95014 | 253-6212 |
| Downtown | 270 Forrest Avenue | Palo Alto | 94301 | 329-2641 |
| E. San Jose | 1102 E. Santa Clara | San Jose | 95116 | 998-2069 |
| Educational Park | 1776 Educational Park | San Jose | 95133 | 272-3662 |
| Empire | 491 E. Empire Street | San Jose | 95112 | 286-5627 |
| Evergreen | 2635 Aborn Road | San Jose | 95121 | 238-4433 |
| Gilroy | 7387 Rosanna Street | Gilroy | 95020 | 842-8207 |

| | | | | |
|---|---|---|---|---|
| Hillview | 2255 Ocala Avenue | San Jose | 95148 | 272-3100 |
| Los Altos | 13 S. San Antonio | Los Altos | 94022 | 948-7683 |
| Los Gatos | 110 E. Main Street | Los Gatos | 95030 | 354-6891 |
| Mission | Lexington & Main | Santa Clara | 95050 | 984-3154 |
| Mitchell | 3700 Middlefield Road | Palo Alto | 94303 | 329-2586 |
| Morgan Hill | 17575 Peak Avenue | Morgan Hill | 95037 | 779-3196 |
| Mountain View | 585 Franklin Street | Mountain View | 95050 | 968-6595 |
| Northside | 1015 Hidden Lake Dr. | Sunnyvale | 94086 | 734-0876 |
| Palo Alto | 1213 Newell Road | Palo Alto | 94303 | 329-2436 |
| Pearl | 4270 Pearl Avenue | San Jose | 95136 | 265-7833 |
| Rosegarden | 1580 Naglee Avenue | San Jose | 95126 | 998-1511 |
| San Jose | 180 W. San Carlos | San Jose | 95113 | 277-4000 |
| *San Jose LDS | 1336 Cherry Street | San Jose | 95125 | 292-3527 |
| Santa Clara | 2635 Homestead Road | Santa Clara | 95051 | 984-3097 |
| *Santa Clara | 1095 N. 7th St. | San Jose | 95112 | 293-2326 |
| *Santa Clara LDS | 875 Quince Avenue | Santa Clara | 95051 | 241-1449 |
| Saratoga | 13650 Saratoga Ave. | Saratoga | 95070 | 867-6126 |
| Seventrees | 3597 Cas Drive | San Jose | 95111 | 629-4535 |
| Sunnyhills | 115 Dixon Road | Milpitas | 95035 | 262-4200 |
| Sunnyvale | 665 W. Olive Avenue | Sunnyvale | 94086 | 245-9171 |
| Village | 14410 Oak Street | Saratoga | 95070 | 867-3893 |
| West Valley | 1243 San Tomas Aquino | San Jose | 95117 | 244-4747 |
| Willow Glen | 1157 Minnesota Ave. | San Jose | 95125 | 998-2022 |
| Woodland | 1975 Grant Frontage | Los Altos | 94022 | 969-6030 |

PROFESSIONAL ASSOCIATIONS

Santa Clara County Bar
111 N. Market Street #712
San Jose, CA 95113

Santa Clara County Medical Society
700 Empey Way
San Jose, CA 95128

County Seat:  Santa Cruz
>    4405   Santa Cruz
>    4408   Watsonville
>    4497   Rest of County

## SANTA CRUZ COUNTY OFFICES

| COUNTY OFFICE | ADDRESS | PHONE |
|---|---|---|
| Assessor | 701 Ocean Street<br>P. O. Box 552<br>Santa Cruz, CA 95060 | 408/425-2331 |
| Clerk-Recorder<br>  b   from 1873<br>  d   from 1873<br>  m   from 1852<br>  bur from 1905<br>  div from 1850<br>  pro from 1850<br>  civ from 1850<br>  lnd from 1850<br>  nat from 1866 | 701 Ocean Street<br>Room 230<br>Santa Cruz, CA 95060 | 408/425-2217 |
| Courts<br>  Juvenile<br><br>  Superior | Courthouse<br>Santa Cruz, CA 95060<br><br>701 Ocean Avenue<br>Santa Cruz, CA 95060 | |
| Voter Registration | 701 Ocean Avenue<br>Room 210<br>Santa Cruz, CA 95060 | 408/425-2173 |

## ADOPTION AGENCIES

Children's Home Society
1010 Ruff Drive
San Jose, CA 95110
408/293-8940

Dept. of Social Services
Santa Cruz County
545 Ocean View Avenue
Santa Cruz, CA 95060
408/425-2451

## CEMETERIES

| | | | | |
|---|---|---|---|---|
| Holy Cross | | Rodriguez | 95074 | 408/475-3222 |
| Pajaro Valley | Hecker Pass Road | Watsonville | 95076 | 724-7544 |
| Santa Cruz | 66 Marin | Watsonville | 95076 | 722-0310 |
| Soquel | 3680 Old San Jose | Soquel | 95073 | 476-2888 |

## CHAMBERS OF COMMERCE

| | | | |
|---|---|---|---|
| Aptos | 9063 B Soquel Drive | Aptos | 95003 |
| Capitola | 410 Capitola Avenue | Capitola | 95010 |
| San Lorenzo Valley | 1011 Cedar | Santa Cruz | 95060 |
| Santa Cruz | Church & Center | Santa Cruz | 95060 |
| Scotts Valley | 4603 Scotts Valley | Scotts Valley | 95066 |
| Soquel | 3131 Porter | Soquel | 95013 |
| Watsonville | 444 Main Street | Watsonville | 95076 |

## COLLEGES & UNIVERSITIES

| Bethany Bible | 800 Bethany Drive | Santa Cruz | 95066 |
| Cabrillo College | 6500 Soquel Drive | Aptos | 95003 |
| U. Of California | | Santa Cruz | 95060 |

## HOSPITALS

| Community | 610 Frederick St. | Santa Cruz | 95060 |
| Dominican | 1555 Soquel Drive | Santa Cruz | 95065 |
| Star Lodge Center | 5271 Scotts Valley | Scotts Valley | 95066 |
| Watsonville | Green Valley Road | Watsonville | 95076 |

## LIBRARIES

| Aptos | 7695 Soquel Drive | Aptos | 95003 | 408/688-5688 |
| Ben Lomond | 9525 Mill Blvd. | Ben Lomond | 95005 | 336-5639 |
| Boulder Creek | Central Avenue | Boulder Creek | 95006 | 338-6340 |
| Capitola | 411 Capitola | Capitola | 95010 | 475-6547 |
| Felton | 6299 Gushee | Felton | 95018 | 335-4052 |
| Freedom | 24 Holly Drive | Freedom | 95019 | 724-6672 |
| La Selva | 314 Estrella Ave. | La Selva | 95076 | 684-1061 |
| Porter | 3050 Porter | Soquel | 95073 | 475-3326 |
| Scotts Valley | 7 Camp Evers Lane | Scotts Valley | 95066 | 438-2855 |
| Watsonville | 310 Union Street | Watsonville | 95076 | |

SHASTA COUNTY #45

County Seat: Redding
4504 Redding
4597 Rest of County

## SHASTA COUNTY OFFICES

| COUNTY OFFICE | ADDRESS | PHONE |
|---|---|---|
| Assessor | Courthouse, Room 115<br>Court and Yuba<br>Redding, CA 96001 | 916/246-5501 |
| Clerk<br>  div from 1880<br>  pro from 1880<br>  civ from 1880 | P. O. Box 880<br>Redding, CA 96001 | 916/246-5631 |
| Courts<br>  Juvenile<br><br>  Superior | Room B-11, Courthouse<br>Redding, CA 96001<br><br>Courthouse<br>Redding, CA 96001 | |
| Recorder<br>  b<br>  d<br>  m | Courthouse, Room 102<br>Redding, CA 96001 | 916/246-5671 |
| Voter Registrarion | 1656 Yuba<br>Redding, CA 96001 | 916/246-5731 |

## ADOPTION AGENCIES

Children's Home Society
1050 Yuba Street
Redding, CA 96001
916/243-9041

Shasta County Adoption Agency
2460 Hospital Lane
1830 Yuba Street (mailing)
Redding, CA 96001
916/246-5791

## CEMETERIES

| | | | | |
|---|---|---|---|---|
| Cottonwood Cemetery Dist. | 1st Street | Cottonwood | 96022 | 916/347-3521 |
| Lawncrest Memorial | 1522 E. Cypress | Enterprise | 96001 | 222-1587 |
| Mt. Shasta | Lassen Lane | County | | 926-2353 |
| Redding Cemetery | Continental & Eureka | Redding | 96001 | 241-2256 |

## CHAMBERS OF COMMERCE

| | | | |
|---|---|---|---|
| Anderson | 2086 N. Balls Ferry | Anderson | 96007 |
| Redding | 1135 Pine Ridge | Redding | 96003 |
| Shasta Dam | 5248A Shasta Dam | Central Valley | 96019 |

## COLLEGES & UNIVERSITIES

Shasta College
1065 N. Old Oregon Trail
Redding, CA 96001

141

## HOSPITALS

| | | | |
|---|---|---|---|
| Mayers Memorial | Highway 299 E. | Fall River Mills | 96028 |
| Memorial | 1450 Liberty | Redding | 96001 |
| Mercy Medical | Clairmont Heights | Redding | 96001 |
| Shasta General | 2630 Hospital Lane | Redding | 96001 |

## LIBRARIES

| | | | | |
|---|---|---|---|---|
| Anderson | 3200 W. Center | Anderson | 96007 | 916/365-7685 |
| Central Valley | 4204 Shasta Dam | Central Valley | 96019 | 275-1918 |
| Cottonwood | 2341 Front | Cottonwood | 96022 | 347-4575 |
| Shasta County | 1855 Shasta | Redding | 96001 | 246-5756 |
| *Shasta County LDS | 3410 Churn Creek | Redding | 96002 | 243-9595 |

## PROFESSIONAL ASSOCIATIONS

Shasta-Trinity County Medical Society
P. O. Box 959
Redding, CA 96001

SIERRA COUNTY #46

County Seat:  Downieville
4697  County

SIERRA COUNTY OFFICES

| OFFICE | ADDRESS | PHONE |
|---|---|---|
| Assessor | Courthouse<br>Downieville, CA 95936 | 916/289-3271 |
| Clerk-Recorder<br>  b   from 1852<br>  d   from 1852<br>  m   from 1852<br>  div from 1852<br>  pro from 1852<br>  civ from 1852<br>  voting records | P. O. Drawer "D"<br>Downieville, CA 95936 | 916/289-3271 |
| Courts<br>  Juvenile<br><br>  Superior | Courthouse<br>Downieville, CA 95936<br><br>Courthouse<br>Downieville, CA 95936 | |

ADOPTION AGENCIES

Children's Home Society
121 E. Orangeburg Ave., Suite 11
Modesto, CA 95350
209/521-5237

State Dept. of Social Services
California Adoption Service
500 Cohasset Road
Chico, CA 95926
916/891-1986

HOSPITALS

Sierra Valley District Hospital
309 West 3rd Street
Loyalton, CA 96118

143

SISKIYOU COUNTY #47

County Seat: Yreka
4710 Yreka
4797 Rest of County

SISKIYOU COUNTY OFFICES

| COUNTY OFFICE | ADDRESS | PHONE |
|---|---|---|
| Assessor | 4th and Lane Streets<br>Yreka, CA 96097 | 916/842-3531 |
| Clerk-Recorder<br>b<br>d<br>m<br>bur<br>div from 1852<br>pro from 1852<br>civ from 1852<br>voter records | Courthouse<br>P. O. Box 8<br>Yreka, CA 96097 | 916/842-3531 |
| Courts<br>  Juvenile<br><br><br>  Superior | Courthouse<br>P. O. Box 780<br>Yreka, CA 96097<br><br>Courthouse<br>Yreka, CA 96097 | |

ADOPTION AGENCIES

Children's Home Society
1216 Sheridan Avenue
Chico, CA 95926
916/342-2464

State Dept. of Social Services
California Adoption Service
500 Cohasset Road, Suite 34
Chico, CA 95926
916/891-1986

CEMETERIES

Shasta Valley Cemetery District
Evergreen Lane
Yreka, CA 96097
916/842-4933

CHAMBERS OF COMMERCE

Dunsmuir Chamber of Commerce
4841 Dunsmuir Avenue
Dunsmuir, CA 96025
916/235-2177

COLLEGES & UNIVERSITIES

College of the Siskiyous
800 College Avenue
Weed, CA 96094

## HOSPITALS

| | |
|---|---|
| Mount Shasta Community | Siskiyou General |
| 914 Pine Street | 818 S. Main |
| Mount Shasta, CA 96067 | Yreka, CA 96097 |

## LIBRARIES

| | | | |
|---|---|---|---|
| Dunsmuir | 5714 Dunsmuir Avenue | Dunsmuir | 96025 |
| Montague | 1030 13th | Montague | 96064 |
| Mount Shasta | 515 E. Alma | Mount Shasta | 96067 |
| *Siskiyou | 719 4th | Yreka | 96097 |

County Seat:  Fairfield
    4801  Benicia           4808  Vallejo
    4803  Fairfield        4897  Rest of County
    4807  Vacaville

## SOLANO COUNTY OFFICES

| COUNTY OFFICE | ADDRESS | PHONE |
|---|---|---|
| Assessor | Courthouse Annex<br>Fairfield, CA 94533 | 707/429-6281 |
| Clerk<br>  div from 1850<br>  pro from 1850<br>  civ from 1850 | Hall of Justice<br>P. O. Box "I"<br>Fairfield, CA 94533 | 707/429-6412 |
| Courts<br>  Juvenile<br><br>  Superior | 2000 W. Texas Street<br>Fairfield, CA 94533<br><br>600 Union Avenue<br>P. O. Box I<br>Fairfield, CA 94533 | |
| Recorder<br>  b<br>  d<br>  m<br>  bur | Courthouse<br>Fairfield, CA 94533 | 707/429-6271 |
| Voter Registration | P. O. Box "I"<br>Fairfield, CA 94533 | 707/429-6201 |

## ADOPTION AGENCIES

Children's Home Society    Public Welfare Dept.
3200 Telegraph Avenue      Solano County
Oakland, CA 94609          355 Tuolumne Street
415/655-7406              Vallejo, CA 94590
                      707/553-5351

## CEMETERIES

| | | | | |
|---|---|---|---|---|
| Fairmont | 1901 Union Avenue | Fairfield | 94533 | 707/425-1288 |
| Silveyville | South 1st | Dixon | 95620 | 678-5578 |
| Suisun-Fairfield | Union Avenue | Fairfield | 94533 | 425-1622 |
| Sunrise | 2201 Sacramento | Vallejo | 94590 | 643-5190 |
| Vacaville-Elmira | Elmira Road | Vacaville | 95688 | 448-7206 |

## CHAMBERS OF COMMERCE

Vallejo Chamber of Commerce
2 Florida Street
Vallejo, CA 94590

## COLLEGES & UNIVERSITIES

California Maritime Academy
P. O. Box 1392
Vallejo, CA 94590

Solano Community College
Suisun City, CA 94585

## HOSPITALS

| Broadway | 525 Oregon Street | Vallejo | 94590 |
|---|---|---|---|
| Cal Medical | | Vacaville | 95688 |
| Fairfield | 1234 Empire St. | Fairfield | 94533 |
| Intercommunity | 1800 Pennsylvania | Fairfield | 94533 |
| Kaiser | 975 Sereno Drive | Vallejo | 94590 |
| Vallejo | 300 Hospital Dr. | Vallejo | 94590 |

## LIBRARIES

| Dixon | 135 E. B Street | Dixon | 95620 | 707/678-5447 |
|---|---|---|---|---|
| Fairfield | 1150 Kentucky | Fairfield | 94533 | 429-6631 |
| *Fairfield LDS | 2700 Camrose | Fairfield | 94533 | 425-2027 |
| Vacaville | | Vacaville | 95688 | 448-1010 |

## PROFESSIONAL ASSOCIATIONS

Solano County Medical Society
927 Amador
Vallejo, CA 94590

County Seat:  Santa Rosa

| | | | |
|---|---|---|---|
| 4905 | Healdsburg | 4909 | Sebastopol |
| 4906 | Petaluma | 4997 | Rest of County |
| 4908 | Santa Rosa | | |

## SONOMA COUNTY OFFICES

| COUNTY OFFICE | ADDRESS | PHONE |
|---|---|---|
| Assessor | 2555 Mendocino Avenue<br>Santa Rosa, CA 95401 | 707/527-2293 |
| Clerk<br>  div from 1850<br>  pro from 1850<br>  civ from 1850 | 600 Administration Drive<br>Santa Rosa, CA 95402 | 707/527-2651 |
| Courts<br>  Superior | Hall of Justice<br>Room 100 J<br>2555 Mendocino Avenue<br>Santa Rosa, CA 95401 | |
| Recorder<br>  b<br>  d<br>  m<br>  bur<br>  lnd | P. O. Box 6124<br>585 Fiscal Drive<br>Santa Rosa, CA 95406 | |
| Registrar of Voters | 600 Administration Drive<br>Santa Rosa, CA 95402 | 707/527-2614 |

## ADOPTION AGENCIES

Children's Home Society
1211 College Avenue
Santa Rosa, CA 95404
707/523-2442

State Dept. of Social Services
California Adoption Service
2350 Professional Drive
Santa Rosa, CA 95406
707/545-2921

## CEMETERIES

| | | | | |
|---|---|---|---|---|
| Calvary Catholic | 2930 Bennett Valley | Santa Rosa | 95404 | 707/546-6290 |
| Cypress Hill | 430 Magnolia Ave. | Petaluma | 94952 | 762-6683 |
| Santa Rosa | 1900 Franklin Ave. | Santa Rosa | 95404 | 542-1580 |

## CHAMBERS OF COMMERCE

| | | | |
|---|---|---|---|
| Bodega Bay | Highway 1 | Bodega Bay | 94922 |
| Cloverdale | P. O. Box 476 | Cloverdale | 95425 |
| Cotati | 315 E. Cotati Avenue | Rohnert Park | 94928 |
| Forestville | 1st and Front Streets | Forestville | 95436 |
| Healdsburg | 217 Healdsburg Ave. | Healdsburg | 95448 |
| Petaluma | 314 Western Avenue | Petaluma | 94952 |

| | | | |
|---|---|---|---|
| Rohnert Park | 7300 Commerce Blvd. | Rohnert Park | 94928 |
| Russian River | 14034 Armstrong Woods | Guerneville | 95446 |
| Santa Rosa | 637 1st Street | Santa Rosa | 95404 |
| Sebastopol | 7765 Healdsburg Ave. | Sebastopol | 95472 |
| Sonoma Valley | 461 1st Street West | Sonoma | 95476 |

## COLLEGES & UNIVERSITIES

California State College
1801 East Cotati Avenue
Rohnert Park, CA 94928

Santa Rosa Junior College
1501 Mendocino Avenue
Santa Rosa, CA 95401

## HOSPITALS

| | | | |
|---|---|---|---|
| Community | 3325 Chanate Road | Santa Rosa | 95404 |
| Healdsburg | 1375 University | Healdsburg | 95448 |
| Hillcrest | 450 Hayes Lane | Petaluma | 94952 |
| Palm Drive | 501 Petaluma | Sebastopol | 95472 |
| Santa Rosa | 465 A. Street | Santa Rosa | 95401 |
| Santa Rosa | 1165 Montgomery | Santa Rosa | 95405 |
| Sonoma State | Arnold Drive | Eldridge | 95431 |
| Sonoma Valley | 347 Andrieux St. | Sonoma | 95476 |
| Warrack Medical | 4700 Hoen Avenue | Santa Rosa | 95405 |

## LIBRARIES

| | | | | |
|---|---|---|---|---|
| Cloverdale | 401 N. Cloverdale | Cloverdale | 95425 | 707/894-5271 |
| Forestville | 107 1st Street | Forestville | 95436 | 887-7654 |
| Guerneville | First & Church | Guerneville | 95446 | 869-3417 |
| Healdsburg | 221 Matheson St. | Healdsburg | 95448 | 433-3772 |
| Monte Rio | Main Street | Monte Rio | 95462 | 865-2711 |
| Northwest | 150 Coddington Center | Santa Rosa | 95401 | 546-2265 |
| Occidental | 73 Main Street | Occidental | 95465 | 874-3080 |
| Petaluma | 100 Fairgrounds Drive | Petaluma | 94952 | 763-9801 |
| Rohnert Park | 6600 Hunter Drive | Rohnert Park | 94928 | 528-9121 |
| Sebastopol | 7140 Bodega Avenue | Sebastopol | 95472 | 823-7691 |
| Santa Rosa | 3rd and E Streets | Santa Rosa | 95404 | 545-0831 |
| *Santa Rosa LDS | 1725 Peterson Lane | Santa Rosa | 95401 | 525-0399 |
| Sonoma | 755 W. Napa | Sonoma | 95476 | 996-5217 |
| Sonoma Law | 2555 Mendocino Avenue | Santa Rosa | 95401 | 527-2668 |

## PROFESSIONAL ASSOCIATIONS

Sonoma County Medical Association
2466 Mendocino Avenue
Santa Rosa, CA 95401

County Seat:  Modesto

| | | | |
|---|---|---|---|
| 5005 | Modesto | 5015 | Turlock |
| 5009 | Oakdale | 5097 | Rest of County |
| 5011 | Riverbank | | |

## STANISLAUS COUNTY OFFICES

| COUNTY OFFICE | ADDRESS | PHONE |
|---|---|---|
| Assessor | 1100 H Street<br>Courthouse<br>Box 1068<br>Modesto, CA 95353 | 209/526-6461 |
| Clerk<br>  div from 1854<br>  pro from 1854<br>  civ from 1854 | P. O. Box 1008<br>Modesto, CA 95353 | 209/526-6416 |
| Courts<br>  Juvenile<br><br><br>  Superior | P. O. Box 1098<br>1100 I Street<br>Modesto, CA 95353<br><br>P. O. Box 1098<br>Modesto, CA 95353 | |
| Recorder<br>  b<br>  d<br>  m | P. O. Box 1008<br>Modesto, CA 95353 | 209/526-6310 |
| Registrar of Voters | 800 11th<br>Modesto, CA 95354 | 209/526-6313 |

## ADOPTION AGENCIES

Children's Home Society
121 E. Orangeburg Ave., Suite 11
Modesto, CA 95350
209/521-5237

Welfare Department
Stanislaus County
921 County Center
Modesto, CA 95355
209/526-6816

## CEMETERIES

| | | | | |
|---|---|---|---|---|
| Acacia Memorial | 801 Scenic Drive | Modesto | 95350 | 209/522-0452 |
| Ceres Cemetery Asso. | E. Whitmore Ave. | Ceres | 95307 | 537-9013 |
| Escalon Cemetery Dist. | 28320 E. River | Escalon | 95320 | 838-2924 |
| Hilmar Cemetery Dist. | 7911 N. Cedar | Hilmar | 95324 | 634-7655 |
| Lakewood Memorial | 900 Santa Fe Ave. | Hughson | 95326 | 883-4465 |
| Modesto Cemetery Asso. | Scenic Drive | Modesto | 95350 | 522-8659 |
| Oaklawn Memorial | 421 N. Sierra | Oakdale | 95631 | 847-1127 |
| St. Stanislaus Catholic | 1141 Scenic Drive | Modesto | 95350 | 529-3905 |
| Turlock Memorial | 575 N. Soderquist | Turlock | 95380 | 632-0128 |
| Valley Home | 30705 E. Lone Tree | Oakdale | 95631 | 847-3254 |

## CHAMBERS OF COMMERCE

| | | | |
|---|---|---|---|
| Ceres | 2503 Lawrence | Ceres | 95307 |
| Modesto | 1401 F Street | Modesto | 95354 |
| Gustine | 682 3rd Avenue | Gustine | 95322 |
| Oakdale | 351 East F | Oakdale | 95631 |
| Riverbank | 3237 Santa Fe | Riverbank | 95367 |
| Turlock | 115 S. Golden State | Turlock | 95380 |

## COLLEGES & UNIVERSITIES

California State College
800 Monte Vista
Turlock, CA 95380

Modesto Junior College
Modesto, CA 95350

## HOSPITALS

| | | | |
|---|---|---|---|
| Doctors | 1441 Florida Ave. | Modesto | 95350 |
| Emanuel | 825 Delbon Avenue | Turlock | 95380 |
| Memorial | 1700 Coffee Road | Modesto | 95350 |
| Modesto City | 730 17th Street | Modesto | 95354 |
| Oak Valley | 350 S. Oak Street | Oakdale | 95361 |
| Scenic | 830 Scenic Drive | Modesto | 95350 |
| West Side | | Newman | 95360 |

## LIBRARIES

| | | | | |
|---|---|---|---|---|
| Central Modesto | 1500 Modesto | Modesto | 95354 | 209/526-6823 |
| Ceres | 2220 Magnolia | Ceres | 95307 | 537-8938 |
| Denair | 4801 Kersey | Denair | 95316 | 634-1283 |
| Empire | 22 G Street | Empire | 95319 | 524-5505 |
| Hughson | 6935 Hughson | Hughson | 95326 | 883-2293 |
| Keyes | 5467 7th | Keyes | 95328 | 634-2931 |
| Newman | 1305 Kern | Newman | 95360 | 862-2010 |
| *Modesto LDS | 731 El Vista | Modesto | 95354 | 522-9751 |
| Oakdale | 151 S. 1st Ave. | Oakdale | 95361 | 847-4204 |
| Patterson | 46 N. Salado | Patterson | 95363 | 892-6473 |
| Riverbank | 3442 Santa Fe | Riverbank | 95367 | 869-1001 |
| Salida | 4554 Broadway | Salida | 95368 | 545-0319 |
| Turlock | 550 Minaret | Turlock | 95380 | 667-1666 |
| Valley Home | 4636 Lone Tree | Valley Home | 95384 | 847-1120 |
| Waterford | 324 E Street | Waterford | 95386 | 874-2191 |

## PROFESSIONAL ASSOCIATIONS

Stanislaus County Medical Society
2030 Coffee Road, Room A 6
Modesto, CA 95355

SUTTER COUNTY #51

County Seat: Yuba City

5103   Yuba City
5197   Rest of County

SUTTER COUNTY OFFICES

| COUNTY OFFICE | ADDRESS | PHONE |
|---|---|---|
| Assessor | 463 Second Street<br>Yuba City, CA 95991 | 916/673-6000 |
| Clerk-Recorder<br>  div from 1850<br>  pro from 1850<br>  civ from 1850 | 446 Second Street<br>Yuba City, CA 95991 | 916/673-6746 |
| Courts<br>  Juvenile<br><br>  Superior | Courthouse<br>Yuba City, CA 95991<br><br>Courthouse<br>Yuba City, CA 95991 | |
| Registrar of Voters | 463 Second Street<br>Yuba City, CA 95991 | 916/673-5140 |

ADOPTION AGENCIES

Children's Home Society
1216 Sheridan Avenue
Chico, CA 95926
916/342-2464

State Dept. of Social Services
California Adoption Service
500 Cohasset Rd., Suite 34
Chico, CA 95926
916/891-1986

CEMETERIES

| | | | | |
|---|---|---|---|---|
| Fairview Cemetery Dist. | Pacific Avenue | Trowbridge | 95687 | 916/656-2386 |
| Live Oak Cemetery | 3545 Pennington | Live Oak | 95953 | 695-3343 |
| Sutter Cemetery Dist. | 7200 Butte Ave. | Sutter | 95982 | 755-0346 |

HOSPITALS

Fremont Medical Center
970 Plumas Street
Yuba City, CA 95991

Sutter County General Hospital
1965 Live Oak Boulevard
Yuba City, CA 95991

LIBRARIES

| | | | | |
|---|---|---|---|---|
| Barber | 10321 Live Oak | Live Oak | 95953 | 916/695-3343 |
| Browns | 1248 Pacific Ave. | Rio Oso | 95674 | 633-2170 |
| Sutter | 2147 California | Sutter | 95982 | 755-0485 |
| Sutter | 750 Forbes Ave. | Yuba City | 95991 | 673-5773 |

PROFESSIONAL ASSOCIATIONS

Sutter County Medical Society
2270 Forrest Lane
Yuba City, CA 95991

TEHAMA COUNTY #52

County Seat: Red Bluff

5201 Corning
5202 Red Bluff
5297 Rest of County

TEHAMA COUNTY OFFICES

| COUNTY OFFICE | ADDRESS | PHONE |
|---|---|---|
| Assessor | P. O. Box 769<br>Red Bluff, CA 96080 | 916/527-5931 |
| Clerk<br>  b   from 1889<br>  d   from 1889<br>  m   from 1856<br>  div from 1856<br>  pro from 1856<br>  civ from 1856<br>  lnd from 1856 | P. O. Box 250<br>Red Bluff, CA 96080 | 916/527-3350 |
| Courts<br>  Juvenile<br><br><br>  Superior | 1840 Walnut Street<br>P. O. Box 99<br>Red Bluff, CA 96080<br><br>Courthouse<br>P. O. Box 950<br>Red Bluff, CA 96080 | |
| Recorder | P. O. Box 250<br>Red Bluff, CA 96080 | 916/527-3350 |
| Registrar of Voters | P. O. Box 250<br>Red Bluff, CA 96080 | 916/527-3350 |

ADOPTION AGENCIES

Children's Home Society
1216 Sheridan Avenue
Chico, CA 95926
916/342-2464

State Dept. of Social Services
California Adoption Service
500 Cohasset Road, Suite 34
Chico, CA 95926
916/891-1986

CEMETERIES

Los Molinos Cemetery
Highway 99 East
Los Molinos, CA 96055
916/384-3564

CHAMBERS OF COMMERCE

Corning Chamber of Commerce
1108 Solano
Corning, CA 96021
916/824-5550

Red Bluff Chamber of Commerce
100 Main
Red Bluff, CA 96080
916/527-6220

153

## HOSPITALS

| | | | |
|---|---|---|---|
| Corning Memorial | 275 Solano Street | Corning | 96021 |
| St. Elizabeth's | Sister Mary Columba | Red Bluff | 96080 |
| Tehama General | 1850 Walnut Street | Red Bluff | 96080 |

## LIBRARIES

| | | | | |
|---|---|---|---|---|
| Corning | 740 3rd | Corning | 96021 | 916/824-3290 |
| Gerber | 102 Samson Ave. | Gerber | 96035 | 385-1220 |
| Los Molinos | 420 N. Hwy 99 E | Los Molinos | 96055 | 384-2222 |
| Tehama | 909 Jefferson | Red Bluff | 96080 | 527-0604 |

## PROFESSIONAL ASSOCIATIONS

Tehama County Medical Society
343 Oak Street
Red Bluff, CA 96080

County Seat: Weaverville
5397 County

## TRINITY COUNTY OFFICES

| COUNTY OFFICE | ADDRESS | PHONE |
|---|---|---|
| Assessor | Main & Court Streets<br>Weaverville, CA 96093 | 916/623-6109 |
| Clerk & Recorder<br>  b   from 1890<br>  d   from 1890<br>  m   from 1890<br>  div from 1890<br>  pro from 1890<br>  bur from 1890<br>  civ from 1890 | P. O. Drawer AK<br>Weaverville, CA 96093 | 916/623-2271 |
| Courts<br>  Juvenile<br><br>  Superior | Courthouse<br>Weaverville, CA 96093<br><br>Courthouse<br>Weaverville, CA 96093 | |

## ADOPTION AGENCIES

Children's Home Society
1216 Sheridan Avenue
Chico, CA 95926
916/342-2464

State Dept. of Social Services
California Adoption Service
500 Cohasset Road, Suite 34
Chico, CA 95926
916/891-1986

## HOSPITALS

Trinity General Hospital
North Taylor Street
Weaverville, CA 96093

## PROFESSIONAL ASSOCIATIONS

Shasta-Trinity County Medical Society
P. O. Box 959
Redding, CA 96001

TULARE COUNTY #54

County Seat: Visalia
   5403  Dinuba          5415  Tulare
   5405  Exeter          5416  Visalia
   5409  Lindsay         5417  Woodlake
   5413  Porterville     5497  Rest of County


## TULARE COUNTY OFFICES

| COUNTY OFFICE | ADDRESS | PHONE |
|---|---|---|
| Assessor<br>1nd | Room 102 E<br>Civic Center<br>Visalia, CA 93277 | 209/733-6361 |
| Clerk<br>div<br>pro<br>civ | Room 201<br>Civic Center<br>Visalia, CA 93277 | 209/733-6419 |
| Courts<br>Juvenile<br><br>Superior | Room 206<br>Courthouse<br>Visalia, CA 93277<br>Courthouse<br>Visalia, CA 93277 | |
| Elections Clerk | Room 201<br>Civic Center<br>Visalia, CA 93277 | 209/733-6279 |
| Recorder<br>b<br>d<br>m<br>bur | Room 201<br>Visalia, CA 93277 | 209/733-6419 |


## ADOPTION AGENCIES

Children's Home Society
703 Truxtun Avenue
Bakersfield, CA 93301
805/324-4091

Public Social Services
Tulare County
100 E. Center Street
Visalia, CA 93277
209/733-7111


## CEMETERIES

| | | | | |
|---|---|---|---|---|
| Alta Cemetery Dist. | Road 100 | Dinuba | 93618 | 209/591-3348 |
| Cemetery Tulare | 900 E. Kern Ave. | Tulare | 93274 | 686-5544 |
| Tipton & Pixley | Avenue 144 & Road 104 | Tipton | 93272 | 752-4270 |
| Visalia Cemetery | W. Goshen & N. Giddings | Visalia | 93277 | 734-6181 |


## COLLEGES & UNIVERSITIES

College of the Sequoias
Mooney Boulevard
Visalia, CA 93277

Porterville College
900 S. Main
Porterville, CA 93257

## HOSPITALS

| | | | |
|---|---|---|---|
| Alta Hospital Dist. | 500 Adelaide Way | Dinuba | 93618 |
| Kaweah Delta | 400 W. Mineral King | Visalia | 93277 |
| Lindsay District | City Park, Box 1297 | Lindsay | 93247 |
| Memorial at Exeter | 215 Crespi Avenue | Exeter | 93221 |
| Porterville State | Box 2000 | Porterville | 93257 |
| Sierra View District | 465 W. Putnam Ave. | Porterville | 93257 |
| Tulare County | 1062 South K Street | Tulare | 93274 |
| Tulare District | 869 Cherry Avenue | Tulare | 93274 |
| Visalia Community | 1633 S. Court St. | Visalia | 93277 |

## LIBRARIES

| | | | | |
|---|---|---|---|---|
| Central Branch | 200 W. Oak | Visalia | 93277 | 209/733-8440 |
| Dinuba | 150 S. 1st | Dinuba | 93618 | 591-0778 |
| Earlimart | 950 E. Washington | Earlimart | 93219 | 849-2525 |
| Farmersville | 103 W. Visalia | Farmersville | 93223 | 747-0869 |
| Goshen | 6465 Avenue 308 | Goshen | 93227 | 625-3955 |
| Ivanhoe | 15964 Heather Ave. | Ivanhoe | 93235 | 798-1264 |
| Orosi | 12662 Avenue 416 | Orosi | 93647 | 528-4981 |
| Pixley | 151 North Pine | Pixley | 93256 | 757-3880 |
| Poplar | 14815 Road 192 | Poplar | 93257 | 784-3054 |
| Springville | 35800 Highway 190 | Springville | 93265 | 539-2624 |
| Terra Bella | 23656 Avenue 95 | Terra Bella | 93270 | 535-4621 |
| Three Rivers | 42052 Eggers Dr. | Three Rivers | 93271 | 561-4564 |
| Tipton | 221 N. Evans Rd. | Tipton | 93272 | 752-4236 |
| *Tulare Public | 113 N. F Street | Tulare | 93274 | 688-2001 |
| Woodlake | 400 W. Whitney | Woodlake | 93286 | 564-8424 |

## PROFESSIONAL ASSOCIATIONS

Tulare County Medical Society
1821 W. Meadow Lane
Visalia, CA 93277

TUOLUMNE COUNTY  #55

County Seat:  Sonora
5597  County

TUOLUMNE COUNTY OFFICES

| COUNTY OFFICE | ADDRESS | PHONE |
|---|---|---|
| Assessor | 41 W. Yaney Avenue<br>Sonora, CA 95370 | 209/532-7119 |
| Clerk<br>  b    from 1850<br>  m    from 1850<br>  d    from 1859<br>  bur from 1916<br>  div from 1850<br>  pro from 1850<br>  civ from 1850<br>  lnd from 1850 | 41 W. Yaney Avenue<br>Sonora, CA 95370 | 209/532-7111 |
| Courts<br>  Juvenile<br><br><br><br>  Superior | Courthouse<br>48 W. Yaney Avenue<br>Sonora, CA 95370<br><br>Courthouse<br>Sonora, CA 95370 | |
| Recorder | No. 2, South Green<br>Sonora, CA 95370 | 209/533-5531 |
| Voter Registration | 41 W. Yaney Avenue<br>Sonora, CA 95370 | 209/532-7111 |

ADOPTION AGENCIES

Children's Home Society
121 E. Orangeburg, Suite 11
Modesto, CA 95350
209/521-5237

State Dept. of Social Services
California Adoption Service
2400 Glendale Lane, Suite B
Sacramento, CA 95825
916/920-6897

CHAMBERS OF COMMERCE

Tuolumne County Chamber of Commerce
158 W. Bradford Avenue
Sonora, CA 95370

Twain Harte Chamber of Commerce
21162 Longeway Road
Twain Harte, CA 95383

HOSPITALS

Sierra Hospital    1/9 S. Fairview   Sonora   95370
Sonora Community   1 South Forest    Sonora   95370
Tuolumne General   101 E. Hospital   Sonora   95370

LIBRARIES

Tuolumne County Library
Joaquin Gulley Road
Twain Harte, CA 95383
209/586-4501


PROFESSIONAL ASSOCIATIONS

Tuolumne County Medical Society
1 South Forest Road
Sonora, CA 95370

County Seat: Ventura

| | |
|---|---|
| 5603 Fillmore | |
| 5608 Ojai | 5612 San Buenventura (Ventura) |
| 5609 Oxnard | 5613 Santa Paula |
| 5610 Port Hueneme | 5697 Rest of County |

## VENTURA COUNTY OFFICES

| COUNTY OFFICE | ADDRESS | PHONE |
|---|---|---|
| Assessor | 800 S. Victoria Avenue<br>Ventura, CA 93009 | 805/654-2181 |
| Clerk & Recorder<br>b from 1873<br>d from 1873<br>m from 1873<br>div from 1873<br>pro from 1873<br>civ from 1873<br>lnd from 1871 | 800 S. Victoria Avenue<br>Ventura, CA 93009 | 805/654-2295<br>654-2268 |
| Courts<br>Juvenile<br><br>Superior | 380 Hillmont Avenue<br>Ventura, CA 93003<br><br>501 Poli Street<br>Ventura, CA 93001 | |
| Registrar of Voters | Administration Bldg.<br>800 S. Victoria Avenue<br>Ventura, CA 93009 | 805/654-2740 |

## ADOPTION AGENCIES

Children's Home Society
141 S. "A" Street, Suite 204
Oxnard, CA 93030
805/486-0090

Ventura County Social Services
90 Loma Vista Road
Ventura, CA 93003
805/654-3259

Children's Home Society
234 W. Vince Street
Ventura, CA 93301
805/643-4784

## CEMETERIES

Conejo Mountain Memorial
2052 Howard Road
Camarillo, CA 93010
805/482-1959

Ivy Lawn Cemetery
P. O. Box 5188
Ventura, CA 93003
805/642-1055

## CHAMBERS OF COMMERCE

| | | | |
|---|---|---|---|
| Fillmore | 447 Main | Fillmore | 93015 |
| Oxnard | P. O. Box 867 | Oxnard | 93032 |
| Simi Valley | 1200 Los Angeles | Simi Valley | 93065 |
| Ventura | 785 S. Seaward | Ventura | 93003 |

## COLLEGES & UNIVERSITIES

| | | | |
|---|---|---|---|
| California Lutheran | 60 Olsen Road | Thousand Oaks | 91360 |
| Moorpark College | 7075 Campus | Moorpark | 93021 |
| Oxnard College | 4000 Rose Ave. | Oxnard | 93030 |
| Ventura College | 4667 Telegraph | Ventura | 93003 |

## HOSPITALS

| | | | |
|---|---|---|---|
| Camarillo State | P. O. Box A | Camarillo | 93010 |
| Community | Loma Linda at Brent | Ventura | 93003 |
| General of Ventura | 3291 Loma Vista | Ventura | 93003 |
| Ojai Valley | 1306 Maricopa Hwy | Ojai | 93023 |
| Oxnard Community | 540 S. "H" Street | Oxnard | 93030 |
| Naval Hospital | | Port Hueneme | 93043 |
| Port Hueneme Adventist | 307 E. Clara St. | Port Hueneme | 93041 |
| Santa Paula Memorial | 825 N. 10th Street | Santa Paula | 93060 |
| St. John's | 333 N. "F" Street | Oxnard | 93030 |

## LIBRARIES

| | | | | |
|---|---|---|---|---|
| Fillmore | 502 2nd | Fillmore | 93015 | 805/524-3355 |
| Meiners Oaks | 114 N. Padre Juan | Meiners Oaks | 93023 | 646-4804 |
| Oak View | 473 N. Ventura | Oak View | 93022 | 649-1523 |
| Ojai | 111 E. Ojai Ave. | Ojai | 93023 | 646-1639 |
| Oxnard | 214 S. "C" Street | Oxnard | 93030 | 486-4311 |
| Saticoy | 11158 Violeta | Ventura | 93004 | 647-1623 |
| *Simi Valley LDS | 5028 E. Cochran | Simi Valley | 93063 | |
| *Ventura LDS | 3501 Loma Vista | Ventura | 93003 | 643-5607 |

## PROFESSIONAL ASSOCIATIONS

Ventura County Bar  
141 W. Second Street  
Oxnard, CA 93030

Ventura County Medical Society  
2977 Loma Vista Road  
Ventura, CA 93003

YOLO COUNTY #57

County Seat: Woodland
5704 Davis
5706 Woodland
5797 Rest of County

YOLO COUNTY OFFICES

| COUNTY OFFICE | ADDRESS | PHONE |
|---|---|---|
| Assessor | 725 Court Street<br>P. O. Box 1327<br>Woodland, CA 95695 | 916/666-8245 |
| Clerk<br>  b    from 1850<br>  d    from 1850<br>  m    from 1850<br>  div from 1850<br>  pro from 1850<br>  civ from 1850<br>  lnd from 1850 | 725 Court Street<br>P. O. Box 1098<br>Woodland, CA 95695 | 916/666-8204 |
| Courts<br>  Juvenile<br><br>  Superior | P. O. Box 176<br>Woodland, CA 95695<br><br>Courthouse<br>P. O. Box 490<br>Woodland, CA 95695 | |
| Recorder | P. O. Box 1820<br>Woodland, CA 95695 | 916/666-8516 |
| Voter Registration | 470 Kentucky Avenue<br>P. O. Box 1098<br>Woodland, CA 95695 | 916/666-8505 |

ADOPTION AGENCIES

Children's Home Society
121 E. Orangeburg, Suite 11
Modesto, CA 95350
209/521-5237

State Dept. of Social Services
California Adoption Service
2400 Glendale Lane, Suite B
Sacramento, CA 95825
916/920-6897

CHAMBERS OF COMMERCE

Davis Area Chamber of Commerce
620 4th
Davis, CA 95616

Woodland Chamber of Commerce
520 Main Street
Woodland, CA 95695

COLLEGES & UNIVERSITIES

D-Q University
P. O. Box 409
Davis, CA 95616

University of California
Davis, CA 95616

162

## HOSPITALS

Davis Community Hospital
Road 99
Route 1, Box S
Davis, CA 95616

Woodland Memorial Hospital
1325 Cottonwood Street
Woodland, CA 95695

## LIBRARIES

| | | | | |
|---|---|---|---|---|
| Capay | Cutting Avenue | Capay | 95607 | 916/865-2046 |
| Davis | 315 E. 14th | Davis | 95616 | 756-2332 |
| Esparto | | Esparto | 95627 | 787-3426 |
| *Shields | U. of California | Davis | 95616 | |
| Winters | 1st and Russell | Winters | 95694 | 795-4955 |
| Woodland | 250 1st | Woodland | 95695 | 662-6616 |
| Yolo | | Yolo | 95697 | 662-2363 |

## PROFESSIONAL ASSOCIATIONS

Yolo County Medical Society
P. O. Box 426
Davis, CA 95616

YUBA COUNTY #58

County Seat: Marysville

5801  Marysville
5897  Rest of County

YUBA COUNTY OFFICES

| COUNTY OFFICE | ADDRESS | PHONE |
|---|---|---|
| Assessor | 215 5th Street<br>Marysville, CA 95901 | 916/674-6221 |
| Clerk & Recorder<br>m    from 1865<br>div from 1850<br>pro from 1850<br>civ from 1850<br>voter records | 215 5th Street<br>Marysville, CA 95901 | 916/674-6341 |
| Courts<br>    Juvenile<br><br>    Superior | Courthouse<br>Marysville, CA 95901<br><br>Courthouse<br>Marysville, CA 95901 | |
| Health Department<br>Vital Statistics | 370 Del Norte Avenue<br>Yuba City, CA | 916/674-6341 |

ADOPTION AGENCIES

Children's Home Society
1128 "F" Street
Marysville, CA 95901
916/742-8821

State Dept. of Social Services
California Adoption Service
500 Cohasset Road, Suite 34
Chico, CA 95926
916/891-1986

CHAMBERS OF COMMERCE

Greater Yuba City Chamber of Commerce
10th and "E" Streets
Marysville, CA 95901
916/743-6501

CEMETERIES

Sierra View Memorial Park
4900 Olive Avenue
Marysville, CA 95901
916/742-6957

COLLEGES & UNIVERSITIES

Yuba College
2088 N. Beale Road
Marysville, CA 95901

HOSPITALS

Rideout Memorial Hospital
726 Fourth Street
Marysville, CA 95901

# SECTION III

## People Who Help

## GROUPS AND INDIVIDUALS WHO HELP

It is always a good idea to touch base with any and all groups in the area of a search. They are the experts in their localities and in the state. Groups can offer invaluable information which may shorten the search time considerably. Some will offer to help without your official membership, while others require that you join before they can help. If you live near or can write to a search or support group, do become a part of it. In return, you will receive unique assistance and will establish contact with others who share your reasons for searching. In adoption related searches especially, emotional support can make all the difference in the outcome and success of your endeavors.

The following organizations were functioning in the state of California at the time of this printing. Be aware that they are only as constant as their membership and leadership. When contacting a group or individual, always send a self-addressed, stamped envelope (SASE).

ADOPTION SEARCH & SUPPORT GROUPS

Adoptee Identity Discovery
P. O. Box 2159
Sunnyvale, CA 94087

Adoptees Movement
Rt. 2, Box 265-Z
Red Bluff, CA 96080

Adoptees Research Association
Box 304
Montrose, CA 91020

Adoption Search Classes
11514 Ventura #A
Studio City, CA 91604

Adoption Search Institute
P. O. Box 11749
Costa Mesa, CA 92627

Adoptsearch
P. O. Box 572
Berkeley, CA 94701

Adoptees Liberty Movement Asso.
Western Regional Office
P. O. Box 9333
North Hollywood, CA 91609

Central Coast Adoption Support
P. O. Box 1937
Santa Maria, CA 93456

Concerned United Birthparents
7571 Westminster Avenue
Westminster, CA 92683

Genesis Society
P. O. Box 1071
Los Gatos, CA 95030

INDEPENDENT SEARCH CONSULTANTS
P. O. Box 10192
Costa Mesa, CA 92627

PACER
Palo Alto Medical Clinic
860 Bryant Street
Palo Alto, CA 94301

Reaching Out
Box 42749
Los Angeles, CA 90042

Search Finders of California
P. O. Box 2374
Santa Clara, CA 95005

Tennessee Adoptees in Search
4598 Rosewood
Montclair, CA 91763

Triad Research
300 Golden West
Shafter, CA 93263

Triadoption Library
7571 Westminster Avenue
Westminster, CA 92683

United Adoptees & Birthparents
2456 16th Street
Clovis, CA 93631
Kingsburg, CA 93631

United Adoptees & Parents
9303 E. Bullard
Clovis, CA 93612


# GENEALOGICAL & HISTORICAL SOCIETIES

| | | | |
|---|---|---|---|
| Amador County Genealogical Society | P. O. Box 1115 | Sutter Creek | 95685 |
| Antelope Valley Genealogical Society | P. O. Box 1049 | Lancaster | 93534 |
| Cahuilla Chapter NSDAR | 117 Beckley Circle | Palm Springs | 92262 |
| California Central Coast Genealogical | P. O. Box 832 | Morro Bay | 93442 |
| California Historical Society | 2090 Jackson St. | San Francisco | 94109 |
| California Society, Sons of the Revolution | 1525 Eighth Street | Alameda | 94501 |
| Contra Costa County Genealogical Society | P. O. Box 910 | Concord | 94522 |
| Covina, California Chapter DAR | 2441 N. Cameron | Covina | 91724 |
| East Bay Genealogical Society | 918 Willow Street | Alameda | 94501 |
| El Dorado Research Society | P. O. Box 56 | El Dorado | 95623 |
| Escondido Genealogical Society | 1508 Encino Drive | Escondido | 92025 |
| Fresno California Genealogical Society | P. O. Box 2042 | Fresno | 93718 |
| Genealogical Association of Sacramento | P. O. Box 28301 | Sacramento | 95828 |
| Genealogical Friends of Pasadena Library | 285 E. Walnut | Pasadena | 91101 |
| Genealogical Society of Riverside | P. O. Box 2664 | Riverside | 92506 |
| Genealogical Society of Santa Cruz County | P. O. Box 72 | Santa Cruz | 95060 |
| Genealogical Society of Siskiyou County | P. O. Box 225 | Yreka | 96097 |
| Hayward Area Genealogical Society | P. O. Box 754 | Hayward | 94543 |
| Hi Desert Genealogical Society | P. O. Box 616 | Victorville | 92392 |
| Historical Society of Southern California | 200 E. Avenue 43 | Los Angeles | 90031 |
| Humboldt County Genealogical Society | P. O. Box 868 | Arcata | 95527 |
| Imperial County Genealogical Society | P. O. Box 2643 | El Centro | 92244 |

|  |  |  |  |
|---|---|---|---|
| Indian Wells Valley Genealogical Society | 2020 South Gate | Ridgecrest | 93555 |
| Kern County Genealogical Society | P. O. Box 2214 | Bakersfield | 93303 |
| Lake County Genealogical Society | P. O. Box 1323 | Lakeport | 95453 |
| Lake County Historical Society | Box 1011 | Lakeport | 95454 |
| Los Banos, California Genealogical Society | P. O. Box 1106 | Los Banos | 93635 |
| Los Californianos | P. O. Box 5155 | San Francisco | 94101 |
| Marin County Genealogical Society | P. O. Box 1511 | Novato | 94947 |
| Mariposa County Historical Society | Box 606 | Mariposa | 95338 |
| Mendocino Coast Genealogical Society | P. O. Box 762 | Fort Bragg | 95437 |
| Mojave Desert Genealogical Society | P. O. Box 1320 | Barstow | 92311 |
| Morango Basin Genealogical Society | 55912 Desert Gold | Yucca Valley | 92284 |
| Napa Valley Genealogical & Biographical | P. O. Box 385 | Napa | 94550 |
| Native Daughters of the Golden West | 703 Market St. | San Francisco | 94102 |
| Native Sons of the Golden West | 414 Mason Street | San Francisco | 94102 |
| Nevada County Historical Society | Box 1300 | Nevada City | 95959 |
| North San Diego County Genealogical Society | P. O. Box 581 | Carlsbad | 92008 |
| Orange County Genealogical Society | P. O. Box 1587 | Orange | 92668 |
| Paradise Genealogical Society | P. O. Box 335 | Paradise | 95969 |
| Placer County Historical Society | Box 643 | Auburn | 95603 |
| Plumas County Historical Society | P. O. Box 695 | Quincy | 95971 |
| Pomona Valley Genealogical Society | P. O. Box 286 | Pomona | 91766 |
| Prospector Genealogical Society | Box 127 | Pine Grove | 95665 |
| Questing Heirs Genealogical Society | P. O. Box 15102 | Long Beach | 90813 |
| Redwood Genealogical Society | Box 645 | Fortuna | 95540 |
| Sacramento Genealogical Society | 5240 Tyosa St. | Fair Oaks | 95628 |
| San Benito County Historical Society | | Hollister | 95023 |
| San Bernardino Valley Genealogical Society | P. O. Box 2505 | San Bernardino | 92406 |
| San Diego Genealogical Society | 30 Spanish Village | San Diego | 92101 |
| San Fernando Valley Genealogical Society | 8009 Lena Avenue | Canoga Park | 91304 |
| San Joaquin Genealogical Society | P. O. Box 4817 | Stockton | 95104 |
| San Mateo County Historical Association | San Mateo Jr. Coll. | San Mateo | 94402 |
| Santa Barbara County Genealogical Society | P. O. Box 1174 | Goleta | 93017 |
| Santa Clara Historical & Genealogical | 2635 Homestead | Santa Clara | 95051 |
| Santa Maria Valley Genealogical Society | P. O. Box 1215 | Santa Maria | 93453 |
| Seal Beach Leisure World Genealogy Club | 1440 Skokie #89L | Seal Beach | 90740 |
| Sequoia Genealogical Society | P. O. Box 3473 | Visalia | 90807 |
| Shasta Historical Society | P. O. Box 277 | Redding | 96001 |
| Shasta Genealogical Society | Box 793 | Anderson | 96007 |
| Society of California Pioneers | 456 McAllister | San Francisco | 94102 |
| Society of Mayflower Desc., California | 681 Market St. | San Francisco | 94105 |
| Solano County Genealogical Society | P. O. Box 2494 | Fairfield | 94533 |
| Sonoma County Genealogical Society | P. O. Box 2273 | Santa Rosa | 95405 |
| South Bay Genealogical Society | 1121 8th Street | Manhattan Bch | 90206 |
| South Bay Cities Genealogical Society | P. O. Box 5341 | Torrance | 90510 |
| So. County, Calif. Central Coast Genealogy | 421 Cornwall | Arroyo Grande | 93420 |
| Southern California Genealogical Society | 103 S. Golden Mall | Burbank | 91502 |
| Spanishtown Historical Society | Box 62 | Half Moon Bay | 94019 |
| Stanislaus County Genealogical Society | 2307 Oakdale Road | Modesto | 95355 |
| Sutter-Yuba Genealogical Society | P. O. Box 1274 | Yuba City | 95991 |
| TRW Genealogical Society | 1 Space Park S-1435 | Redondo Beach | 90278 |
| Tuolumne County Genealogical Society | P. O. Box 3956 | Sonora | 95370 |
| Tuolumne County Historical Society | Box 695 | Sonora | 95370 |
| Ukiah Tree Tracers Genealogical Society | P. O. Box 72 | Ukiah | 95482 |
| Ventura County Genealogical Society | 2221 Lavanda Dr. | Oxnard | 93030 |
| Yorba Linda Genealogical Society | 18262 Lemon Drive | Yorba Linda | 92686 |

PROFESSIONAL SEARCH HELP

Each local genealogical or historical society is a
potential source of professional genealogists. In
general these researchers are very conscientious
and their fees are reasonable. A genealogist may
be invaluable to a searcher living out of the area.

A search for living persons is often a different
matter entirely, and may require the assistance of
a special group of individuals. INDEPENDENT SEARCH
CONSULTANTS is a national association of professional consultants and record searchers who offer
very special services, including "how to" techniques
and emotional support. ISC Consultants are highly
trained and their expertise in adoption related
searches is unequalled. At the time of this printing, the following ISC Certified Search Consultants
resided in the state of California:

Gayle Beckstead
2180 Clover Street
Simi Valley, CA 93065
ISC National Search Consultant
Specialty--Illinois

Patricia Burlingame
118 London Court
Anaheim, CA 92806
ISC National Search Consultant
Specialty--Minnesota, California

Mary Lou Kozub
2027 Finch Court
Simi Valley, CA 93063
ISC National Search Consultant
Specialty--Illinois

Nancy O'Neill
1430 Henry Street
Berkeley, CA 94709
ISC State Search Consultant
Specialty--Bay Area Counties

Mary Jo Rillera
P. O. Box 5218
Huntington Beach, CA 92646
ISC National Search Consultant
Specialty--Minnesota, California

Patricia Sanders
20111 Riverside Drive
Santa Ana, CA 92707
ISC National Search Consultant
Specialty--California, Texas, Arizona

Vikki Schummer
11514 Ventura #A
Studio City, CA 91604
ISC National Search Consultant
Specialty--California

Alberta Sorensen
1114 N. Modesto Avenue
Camarillo, CA 93010
ISC National Search Consultant
Specialty--New York, California, Immigration

(Order blank may be photocopied)


ORDER BLANK


Please send me _____ copies of SEARCHING IN

CALIFORNIA at $11.95 each, postpaid.



Name _____

Address _____

City _____ State _____ Zip _____


Total amount enclosed $_____.___ (California

residents add 72¢ state sales tax). Please

mail book order with check or money order to:


        ISC PUBLICATIONS
        P. O. Box 10857
        Costa Mesa, CA 92627